The BHPA Pilot Handbook

The British Hang Gliding and Paragliding Association

The BHPA Pilot Handbook

Written by Mark Dale, with assistance from Dave Thompson. Due acknowledgement is given to the authors of the previous editions and various articles which have formed the basis for parts of this work. These include Tom Hardie, Bob Harrison, Peter Ronfell, Joe Schofield, Steve Senior, Dennis Trott, Steve Uzochukwu and Tim Williams.

First published in the UK in 2000 by the British Hang Gliding and Paragliding Association

Revised second edition published in 2002

Revised third edition published in 2008

Published by the British Hang Gliding and Paragliding Association,
The Old Schoolroom, Loughborough Road, Leicester LE4 5PJ
E-mail: office@bhpa.co.uk
Web site: www.bhpa.co.uk

British Library Cataloguing-in-Publication Data

A catalogue record for this book is available from the British Library.

ISBN 978-0-9538468-2-5

Edited by Asgard Publishing Services

Production Editor: Joe Schofield

Illustrations by Dave Barber and Colin Fargher

Cover art by Colin Fargher, Fargher Design

Printed at Eye Press Ltd,
1 Blood Hall Farm, Debenham, Suffolk IP14 6JX, UK

CONTENTS

Introduction

The aim of this handbook is not to teach anyone to fly: that is the job of a qualified instructor. Prospective pilots who have not yet flown should attend a BHPA-registered training school and complete the appropriate courses.

The BHPA publication *Skywings Training Issue* is the introduction for pilots who are beginning their training. This handbook provides the more advanced information needed to progress to 'Pilot' rating and beyond.

During the Club Pilot course (see 'The BHPA Pilot Rating Scheme' on page 271), you will find this handbook to be a useful supplement to the instructor's words of wisdom, and once you have gained that qualification it will continue to provide authoritative information. This should be supplemented with practical help and advice from coaches and experienced local pilots. Do not be afraid to ask questions – coaches and most pilots are only too willing to help new pilots to learn.

The contents of this book are grouped in sections for ease of reference, and are not necessarily given in the order in which new pilots will progress. Use it as a reference book: dip in and out of it to find particular information as you need it. But do try to cover all of it sooner or later!

Units

In this book metric units of measurement are used throughout, with the suitably rounded imperial equivalent provided in brackets.

The only exception to this is in Section 6 – Air Law, Airspace and other Legalities. Here the units used in the legislation are given. (These are sometimes a mix of metric and imperial.)

SECTION 1
PICKING UP WHERE YOU LEFT OFF

Chapter 1: Building on the foundations

Gradual steps

Keeping clear of accidents

Keep practising your PLFs!

Flight planning with respect to other air users

Chapter 2: Launch assistants

The hang-glider nose person

The paraglider anchor person

Chapter 3: Daily Inspections and pre-flight checks

The Daily Inspection

The pre-flight check

Chapter 4: Joining a club

Chapter 1: Building on the foundations

Gradual steps

Before you can attain any of the advanced pilot skills (soaring, duration, distance or landing accuracy), you must be competent at routine flying. With many hours of practice, the qualified pilot has mastered the fundamental skills such as preparation, launch, airspeed control, turns, approaches and landings until they are executed instinctively. With total confidence in this basic proficiency he or she can then concentrate mind and actions on the demands of the more difficult tasks ahead.

The best way to progress is by following a series of gradual, structured steps. The BHPA Pilot Rating Scheme (see Chapter 30) sets out just such a series of exercises and tasks, which your instructor will have been following to structure your basic training. You should now use them yourself to guide your progress towards your 'Pilot' rating and beyond!

- Make every effort to fly regularly. If you do not get airborne for several weeks you will forget some of what you have learned.
- Before every take-off you should decide the purpose of the flight: after take-off is not the time to start thinking about what to do. As you improve your handling skills, start to look for and recognise landmarks; learn to assess visibility, cloudbase height, wind strength and direction, and weather changes; and generally become familiar with and aware of the environment in which you are operating.
- Teach yourself to analyse your own flying: by setting yourself specific tasks and evaluating how well you did them, your flying will improve. To begin with, the task should be a simple one, such as an accurately judged approach, or a landing at a precise spot. If you undershoot the spot, don't fool yourself that this was where you really meant to land. Work out **why** you undershot – then go and have another try.
- Closely examine any mistakes you make. When unexpectedly overtaken, good car drivers feel guilty that they had not seen the other car in the mirror. Good pilots should feel the same prick of conscience if they realise that they have not done their checks properly, or failed to look round before turning, or failed to check the wind direction on the approach, or suddenly noticed a glider

nearby which they had not seen before. More importantly, they should take steps to ensure that the mistake is never repeated.

- Learn how to see other aircraft in the air, and how to fly without getting in their way. Make sure you know the Rules of the Air (see page 224). Practise continually looking round and observing where other craft are; the more you do this the quicker you will build the all-important 'spatial awareness' which is essential for safe flying. Never remain looking in one direction for more than a few seconds. Don't watch your instruments – use the audio! Hang-glider pilots especially should avoid any tendency to spend time looking downwards – conflicting traffic is much more likely to be more or less at your level, so scan above and below the horizon.
- Don't forget that your club has coaches eager to help you – ask one of them to watch your flights and help you evaluate your performance.

Keeping clear of accidents

Many pilots have an accident within their first fifty hours of flying. The underlying cause of these mishaps is usually over-confidence, which makes you inadvertently put yourself into a situation that is beyond your experience and capabilities. Confidence in yourself is necessary, but the divide between self-confidence and disastrous over-confidence is very fine. Over-confidence is likely to trip you up after you have made a few successful ridge-soaring flights, when you've landed close to the 'spot', or **at any time** when you feel flying is becoming easy.

You must think for yourself and use your imagination, as well as heeding advice and remembering what you were taught in the school. There are many traps out there for the careless or unwary pilot! One golden rule well worth remembering is **'never try more than one new thing at a time'**. Too many incident reports start with 'I was trying out a new glider at a site I hadn't been to before...'.

Remember – a good pilot is a thinking pilot is a safe pilot.

Keep practising your PLFs!

Paraglider pilots should practise parachute landing falls (PLFs) regularly; they really are a lifesaver when things go wrong. Get into the habit of preparing for a PLF every time you come into land – at the last minute (if you get it right) you can simply open your feet to keep your balance. It isn't necessary to stick rigidly to the standard 'whole body' approach, but the basics of a PLF are essential:

- Get your feet down early!
- Clamp your feet and legs together firmly, and bend your knees slightly.
- Turn your feet so that the side of the leading boot will hit the ground first (never the toes or heels).

Then – if you have time:

- If you can turn your upper body as well, then do it.
- Tuck your head well down onto your chest.
- Try to keep your arms close in to your body. Once safely on the ground, be prepared to use the standard drag-back technique of pulling in one of the control lines or rear risers until the canopy is under control. The method is foolproof, especially if you are on your back at the time!

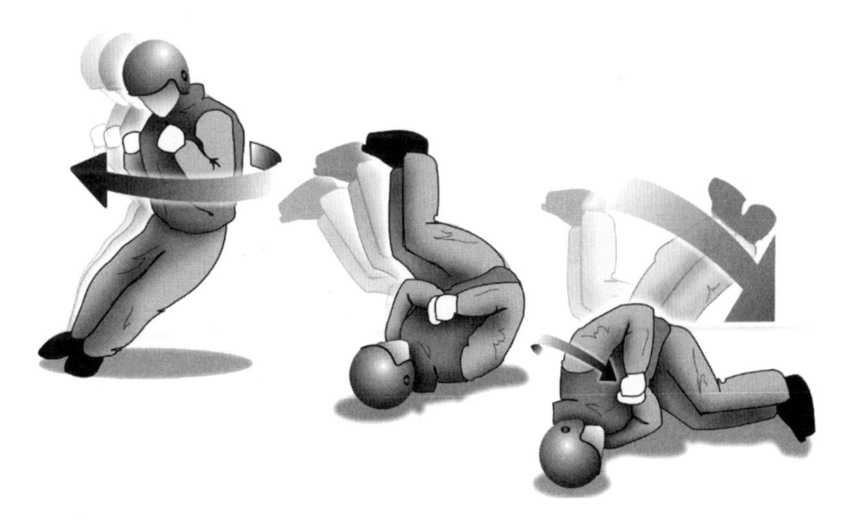

Figure 1.1 *The Parachute Landing Fall*

Flight planning with respect to other air users

As explained in Section 6, you have a legal and moral duty to ensure that your flight can be made safely. Even if you only plan some ridge-soaring at your local site, you should be aware of any local airspace restrictions and you should take the steps outlined below. If you plan to fly cross-country then you should be familiar with the whole of Section 6, and should take all the additional steps outlined there.

Whenever you fly you should call Freefone 0500 354802 to check on Royal flights, Red Arrows displays and other Temporary Restricted Airspace (RA[T]).

You should also check the NOTAMs (see Chapter 24) for any other activities that may affect your flight. You can subscribe to a NOTAM service or to a twice-weekly Temporary Navigational Warning information bulletins (TNWs) postal service; or you can use the Web to access all the NOTAMs for that day at www.ais.org.uk (there's no need to register, just enter the username: 'BHPAuser' and password 'password'). If you use the postal service, you should be aware that details may have changed after the bulletins were printed and posted.

Additionally, if you are flying midweek (non English Bank Holiday) you should let the military pilots know. There are two linked systems for this.

Five hundred of the busiest flying sites have allocated Site Codes. (The codes for your club's sites will be in your club site guide.) On these sites it is possible to activate a temporary avoidance zone around the notified site (1nm diameter/1000ft agl) by contacting the Low Flying Booking Cell by 20:00 the day before (16:00 on Sun). (Later submissions will still be passed on to military pilots, but as a warning rather than creating a temporary avoidance zone.)

For all other sites the standard CANP (Civil Aircraft Notification Procedure) should be used if five or more gliders are likely to be operating. This does not establish an avoidance area but it does ensure that military pilots will be alerted to your presence. Because it can take up to four hours to get the information out to all the military pilots before they take off, the notification procedure should be started as soon as possible – ideally the evening before. **In both cases take the following steps:**

Use Freephone 0800 515544 (or Fax 0800 3892225 or E-mail witlfos-lbfc@wittering.raf.mod.uk).

Provide the following details:

(a) Activity. Hang/paragliding (If the site is one of those with a site code then state 'Hang/paragliding Avoidance Area' here.)

(b) Location: Site grid reference (2 letter 6 figure) and name. (If the site is one of those with a site code then state that first.)

(c) Area of operation. (With the notification system this is a maximum of 2NM radius. With the avoidance area system it is always 1nm diameter.)

(d) Date and time flying will start / finish.

(e) Expected number of gliders

(f) Contact telephone number (ideally a mobile that will work on the site).

(g) Normal contact details (if different to (f)).

You will be given a unique Reference Number to note.

The Low Flying Booking Cell is manned Monday to Thursday 07:00 - 23:00 and Fri to Sun 07:00 -17:00. If you use the fax or E-mail contact out-of-hours you will be called back by phone with the Reference Number when the office is next manned and the associated notification has been passed to military pilots. You can only assume that you have avoidance/notification status once you have received this.

If at any stage it becomes clear that the site won't be used after all you should cancel by calling 0800 515544, quoting the Reference Number and amending the details.

The personnel manning the Low Flying Booking Cell are a helpful bunch whose sole aim is keeping us all safe. If your flying situation doesn't exactly match the criteria above it is still worth giving them a call for advice – they might still be able to do something to help.

Chapter 2: Launch assistants

The hang-glider nose person

Hang-glider pilots sometimes forget to clip in before attempting to launch. It is also possible to clip in to the wrong place, to have the harness incorrectly fitted, straps twisted, legs not through leg loops, or hang height not properly adjusted. Any of these failings could easily result in a serious accident.

To help prevent these unnecessary accidents, the hang-glider nose person's duties extend beyond simply assisting with controlling the hang glider before launch. If you are acting as nose person, you must insist that the pilot carries out a full hang-check as part of the pre-flight checks, and you must provide the thorough check that is required. All pilots should become proficient at doing this.

The nose-person protocol works on the principle that 'two heads are better than one'. What one person might miss, the second person should pick up.

Insist that the pilot you are assisting performs a full hang-check. (If he[1] refuses, then refuse to help him take off.) Take your time checking him. Have a look at his hang glider – does it look OK? When he does the hang-check, examine his hang-loops and karabiners. Is he hanging on the correct loop? Are there a few centimetres of slack in the backup? Are the 'crabs' (karabiners) locked? Have a look at his base-bar clearance, check that his helmet is on and fastened, and ask him to physically check that his legs are through the leg loops. In this way a good nose person greatly contributes to a pilot's safety.

When the pilot is ready to launch, watch for other gliders in the air so that you can advise the pilot of their position and movements (you will have the better viewpoint at the hang glider's nose). Then tell the pilot if either wing is trying to lift. You should not be supporting the hang glider in any way when you let go. Don't let go until the pilot shouts **'release'**. When he does, quickly move out of the way in a pre-arranged direction. The pilot has enough on his hands without having to avoid you as well!

Ensure that your willingness to act as a nose person is never abused. If it is windy and turbulent, make sure that the pilot has really thought

[1]Here, and in other places where necessary, 'he' has been used to mean 'he or she' to aid readability.

about the flight: a nose person can be misused to enable a pilot to take off into conditions that are too strong for sensible flying, and where the turbulence on a landing approach could be severe.

Cliff launches

Here your personal safety is dependent on the siting of the take-off point, so you must have a say in its position. Make sure of a safe place to stand and to retreat to; it may be necessary to anchor yourself. Check that curlover in the wind is not going to push you both towards the edge. If you cannot find a safe point, the correct and safe option is to abandon attempts to fly from that site. No flight is worth risking the nose person's life!

The paraglider anchor person

The term 'anchor person' refers to a helper who steadies the paraglider pilot (by holding on to the harness) during ground-handling and launching. In general the use of an anchor person is not recommended, although it has some value during basic training. You will sometimes find an anchor person used on soaring hilltops when pilots, having inflated their paragliders, are finding it difficult to penetrate forward to the hill face to launch. A fellow pilot will try to assist by pushing or dragging the pilot forward. This usually creates at least as many problems as it solves, and can actually be the cause of accidents.

Before calling for an anchor person to help you, consider just what problem you are trying to overcome:

- Is it that your inflation technique is inadequate? (In which case go and practise it.)
- Is it that you inflated in the wrong part of the hill? (Move, and try again – but bear in mind that if the wind is too strong to push forward on the hill top it may well be too strong for safe flying...)
- Is it that the wind is too strong to launch safely on your own? (In which case why are you launching?)

You should also bear in mind that at least one anchor person has been killed when a canopy was unexpectedly gusted up and he was too slow letting go.

Chapter 3: Daily Inspections and pre-flight checks

As gliders and equipment become more complicated, the importance of a learned sequence of careful checks before flight becomes progressively greater. These checks are broken down into two key stages:

1 the Daily Inspection (DI), which is a thorough check of your equipment carried out at the start of each flying day

2 the pre-flight checks that ensure that the critical points are checked before you launch.

The Daily Inspection

During training you learned how to do a Daily Inspection on a glider to check that it was:

- properly rigged
- in good condition
- safe to fly.

Carry out your Daily Inspection carefully, either in the way that you have been taught, or according to the manufacturer's instructions. Make yourself a checklist if you find this helpful. If you have any doubts about anything from a dented tube to a frayed suspension line, ask a coach or a more knowledgeable pilot to give you a second opinion.

Carry out a full Daily Inspection check **every** time you rig your glider and after any drag-back, ground loop, heavy landing, or similar uncontrolled terrain-interface event!

Hang-glider pilots should use the mnemonic 'SWANK' to remind them what to check as they work their way around the glider. It stands for:

Sail
Wires
Airframe
Nuts and bolts
Kingpost

Ensure that you develop a routine method that takes in every detail. And do it the same way every time.

Don't forget to DI your harness

Make sure that the connectors (e.g. karabiners) are of a type that have been proved to be satisfactory – you should double-check that tension is only applied in the approved direction; avoid any sideways or twisting strain. Paraglider pilots, in particular, should make sure that accessories and their connectors cannot foul or catch on anything – it has been known for suspension lines to get caught in speed-bar snap-hook connectors. Check the security of all buckles: several reports have been received of buckles becoming unfastened during the launch or take-off run. **Make sure your emergency parachute is correctly stowed and is secure.**

- Never just hope the glider will be OK – one day it won't be!
- Don't allow yourself to be distracted from what you are doing: if your Daily Inspection is interrupted, start again from the beginning.

The pre-flight check

Before every flight it is essential that you carry out a pre-flight check. You do not want to be halfway through your take-off when you notice your helmet still on the ground, or find you have doubts about some connection that you cannot see...

Various attempts have been made over the years to produce a complete, easy-to-remember list of the vital actions you must cover before every launch. The one detailed here should be used by paraglider pilots and hang-glider pilots alike. The memory aid is the phrase '**W**ill **G**eordie **H**ave **H**is **C**at **A**board?', with the first letter of each word being the prompt. (Draw a mental picture of a paraglider pilot flying with a cat on his knees or a hang-glider pilot flying with a cat on his shoulder!)

Paragliding:

Will **G**eordie **H**ave **H**is **C**at **A**board (**T**oday)?

W = Wind and weather

Check:

- wind direction – is it shifting around?
- wind strength – is it varying much? Is it satisfactory for your level of experience? Will it remain satisfactory?
- visibility – will it remain satisfactory?
- weather – is any rain approaching? Are there any signs indicating likely turbulence?

G = Glider

Give your glider a quick 'once-over' to confirm that nothing has altered since your DI. Check:

- laid out properly?
- cells clear?
- lines untangled?

H = Helmet

Check:

- that you are wearing one.
- that it fits snugly and will not drop over your eyes.
- that it is fastened – and won't fall off.

H = Harness

Check the five main points:

- left leg-strap fastened?
- right leg-strap fastened?
- chest strap fastened and adjusted so that the distance between the risers is as specified for the glider?
- left maillon/karabiner locked?
- right maillon/karabiner locked?

Check that any cross-bracing straps are secure and adjusted, and that the speed system (if fitted) is correctly connected.

Check that the emergency parachute is stowed correctly and that the handle is within reach.

C = Controls

Check:

- control handles in the correct hands?
- correct risers held appropriately?
- control lines free-running?

A = All clear

Check:

- that your take-off path is clear – nothing to trip you or wrench your ankles
- that you are well clear (in every direction) from bushes, posts or other fixed obstructions, and from roving people or livestock. (A mishandled launch can use up a lot of space in any direction.)
- that no gliders or people are about to appear suddenly from below the brow, on their way up
- that the airspace above, in front and below you is clear from other air users and will remain so during your take-off sequence
- that no one is about to overshoot their top landing and need the airspace you are about to occupy.

(T = Turn direction)

If you are using the 'traditional' reverse launch, check which riser is on top: that shoulder must go back when you turn to face into wind.

You are now ready to launch.

Hang gliding:

For hang-glider pilots the memory aid and checklist order is identical. Just the detail of what you are checking for changes in a few respects.

Will **G**eordie **H**ave **H**is **C**at **A**board?

W = Wind and weather

Check:

- wind direction – is it shifting around?
- wind strength – is it varying much? Is it satisfactory for your level of experience? Will it remain satisfactory?
- visibility – will it remain satisfactory?
- weather – is any rain approaching? Are there any signs indicating likely turbulence?

G = Glider

Give your glider a quick 'once-over' to confirm that nothing has altered since your DI.

Check:

- quick-release points (nose, base-bar corners, pull-back bridle)
- batten elastics engaged
- tip sticks correctly fitted
- under-surface zips and inspection points closed
- luff-lines not caught under battens
- nose-cone fitted.

H = Helmet

Check:

- that you are wearing one
- that it fits snugly and will not drop over your eyes
- that it is fastened – and won't fall off.

H = Harness

Carry out the hang-check. This is accomplished in one of two ways:

a) Lying down (preferred way)

With assistance from the nose person, lie down and check:

- that you are clipped in properly (to both the main and the backup hang-loops) and that the karabiners are locked
- that your clearance above the base-bar is sufficient (about 5-8cm/ 2-3in): swing back and forth to check this
- that your harness is worn properly and is comfortable
- that your harness straps are untwisted
- that your legs are through the leg loops
- that the emergency parachute is stowed correctly and that the handle is within reach.

b) Stand-up method

Stand up and, holding on to the front wires, lean forward to tighten the straps. Turn your head and check:

- that you are clipped in properly (to both the main and the backup hang-loops) and that the karabiners are locked
- that your harness is worn properly and is comfortable
- that your harness straps are untwisted
- that your legs are through the leg loops
- that the emergency parachute is stowed correctly and that the handle is within reach.

Note: This method does not allow you to check that you are clear of the base-bar.

C = Controls

Check:

- trimmer tension set for take-off?

A = All clear

Check:

- that your take-off path is clear – nothing to trip you or wrench your ankles
- that no bushes, posts or other fixed obstructions, or roving people or livestock, are within leading-edge range
- that no gliders or people are about to appear suddenly from below the brow, on their way up
- that the airspace above, in front and below you is clear from other air users and will remain so during your take-off sequence
- that no one is about to overshoot their top landing and need the airspace you are about to occupy.

Still clear? – Yes. Then off you go and enjoy yourself.

All the above checking may seem very complicated or long-winded. Be assured that it isn't. If you have been thoroughly taught, doing all this should be automatic for you. If it isn't, then get practising. After all, it's your personal safety that is at stake. Memorise this phrase:

Will **G**eordie **H**ave **H**is **C**at **A**board?

Chapter 4: Joining a club

The most difficult stage of any pilot's career is that between leaving the school and becoming a fully integrated member of a BHPA club. In school you will have had an instructor to choose the site for the day, help with the weather assessment, check conditions and so on. Once you have your Club Pilot rating you are deemed to be qualified to do all this for yourself. But let's be realistic: you will have now bought your own glider (which you may not yet be familiar with), you will possibly have a new harness and helmet, you will be flying new club sites, and you won't have your trusted, dependable instructor with you. So how many new things is that?

At this stage all too often pilots fail to judge the forecast correctly, and make numerous wasted trips to the wrong hills in unsuitable weather, before becoming disillusioned with the sport and giving up. Or they get to more or less the right hill in not quite the right weather, get airborne and give themselves a serious fright (or worse). Or they go to a site and seriously upset the landowner by breaking site rules that they didn't know of.

The way to avoid many of these problems is to join your local club, and to take full advantage of the coaches who are there to offer free guidance, help and encouragement to new pilots such as yourself. (In fact you should join your local club even before gaining your Club Pilot rating, so that when you are ready to 'swap over' from the school the transition is seamless.)

While each club will have its own way of working, you will be encouraged to attend club meetings. Here you will meet fellow pilots and coaches, and hopefully be given means of contacting them on possible flying days. You will probably find that there are several other new pilots in the club; it is especially beneficial to team up together. Finding that there are other pilots with the same problems can be a great help, as can seeing others overcome a hurdle that you are still struggling with. You will also meet the pilots who volunteer to take on the tasks of negotiating and securing the use of sites, liaising with local authorities and other air users, producing regular newsletters, and organising social and informative meetings – i.e. the club committee. Buy them a drink!

Your school should be able to inform you about local clubs. A list is available from the BHPA office – the address is on page 2. Contact numbers for many of the popular clubs are also carried each month in *Skywings*.

SECTION 2
KNOW YOUR EQUIPMENT

Chapter 5: Hang gliders

Maintenance

Tuning and trimming

Certification

Storage

Buying your first hang glider

Trimmers and compensators

Chapter 6: Paragliders

Maintenance

Tuning and trimming

Certification

Storage

Buying a paraglider

Speed systems and trimmers

Chapter 7: Safety equipment

Emergency parachutes

Helmets

Paraglider back pads (back 'protectors')

Hang-glider wheels

Emergency pack

Chapter 8: Harnesses, connectors, hang-loops, clothing

Harnesses

Connectors

Hang-loops (hang glider)

Clothing

Chapter 9: Instruments, navigation tools & related equipment

Instruments

Navigation tools and related equipment

Chapter 10: Tow equipment

Hang-glider winch and aerotow tow releases

Paraglider tow releases

Chapter 5: Hang gliders

Maintenance

In general you should refer to the appropriate section of the user manual for your glider, and you must contact the manufacturer for advice if you have any doubt about acceptable limits of wear and tear.

The airframe

The airframe can take a beating during the flying season. Aluminium tube is very strong, but it is easily damaged by scratching and denting. Most gliders have enclosed tubes and mylar leading edges, so it may be very difficult to inspect the airframe properly, but it must be done somehow. An annual strip-down is a good idea irrespective of how careful you've been.

Should you be unlucky enough to have an accident, then have the glider stripped down prior to repair, to check for hidden damage. It often happens that a pilot will catch the right wing-tip, and so check it for damage; only later will it be discovered that the transferred loads had bent the left inboard leading edge, or some other unsuspected part of the airframe.

Do not attempt to repair or straighten tubes: replacement with genuine manufacturer's parts is the only safe course of action.

The control frame

This is probably the most misused part of the whole glider. Inspect it not only for dents and scratches, but also for bends and wear on all pivot holes. Straightening a bent control frame weakens it. Don't do it! If you bend an upright, you will almost certainly have bent the heart-bolt that links the upright tops to the keel. Be sure to inspect it.

Rigging wires

Check that tangs and thimbles are not twisted when you rig; most damage occurs this way. Distortion can force a thimble out of the eye, and put strain on the wire next to the ferrule where it is least flexible. This quickly leads to broken strands.

Check your wires for kinks and damage, especially close to the swages. Kinks significantly weaken wires. Examine each swaged joint for corrosion. This shows as rust or as a fine white powder. Wires do not last for ever: most manufacturers stipulate that the lower (flying) wires should be replaced annually, or after 100 hours' use (whichever happens first). Make sure you do this: there are many recorded instances of older wires failing... And bear in mind that stainless-steel wires will look like new even on the day they fail!

The sail

When parking your glider, do not leave it standing up if there is any wind. The load on the sail stretches the cloth unevenly and accelerates wear. Any hang-glider sail, no matter how perfect it was to start with, deteriorates with time and use.

Roll a sail, rather than folding or crumpling it. Each time a new fold is made, a faint line appears in the sailcloth. Even new sails have such marks. They are caused by the resin or filler in the sailcloth breaking up. After rolling the sail neatly, secure it with ties at least 25mm (1in) wide, and always transport your glider in a tight-fitting bag that won't flap.

Sail repairs and cleaning

Small holes and tears up to 25mm (1in) long in non-stressed areas – i.e. well away from the trailing edge, sail fixing points or other highly stressed areas – can be dealt with by gluing a small repair patch onto one or both surfaces. The glider manufacturer will be able to sell you self-adhesive patches. Any other sail damage should be referred to the manufacturer.

Dirt is a real problem, and no amount of washing or sponging with mild, soapy water (the popular recipe) seems to make any real improvement unless done very soon after getting the sail dirty. Even then it only works for mud rather than general grime. If you do use even the mildest soap, hose off the sail with clean water to avoid the soap chemicals continuing to attack the stitching.

Reflex

At least once a year you should check the reflex settings on your glider. Precise details will be in the user manual. The procedure usually involves running a line from the corresponding batten ends on both wings and measuring their height relative to the keel. It is a fact that hang gliders lose reflex over time, and your nominally safe, certified glider will become unsafe if you do not keep these settings adjusted to the manufacturer's figures. Take time, do it carefully, and get it right. If you have any doubts or questions that the manual does not answer, seek advice from the manufacturer or manufacturer's agent.

Tuning and trimming

With most modern hang gliders there are only two basic tuning operations. You may wish to adjust the trim speed, or you may need to tune out any tendency for the glider to turn one way or the other. If you have some other problem with your glider, contact the manufacturer for advice. **Never fiddle about yourself!**

The following general notes are for guidance only. You should consult your glider's manual for the precise details applicable to that particular type of machine.

Trim speed

The flexing of the leading edges, and therefore the amount of washout in the wing, is to some extent governed by the load the glider is supporting. So with a heavyweight pilot the wing will tend to washout more, and with a lightweight pilot less. This will result in slight changes to the location of the wing's centre of pressure. To compensate for this, on most hang gliders it is possible to move the hang-point forward or backward over a small range.

To check the pitch trim of your glider, choose a smooth soaring day, gain 60-90m (200-300ft) and head out into wind. Relax your grip of the bar. If you feel the glider nosing up and slowing, let it slow. If it begins to feel mushy, approaching the stall, then your hang point needs a small forward shift. If the opposite occurs and you feel that you have to maintain a slight push-out on the bar to achieve your best minimum-sink speed (just above the stall), then your hang point needs shifting aft. Land, move your hang point – only one hole at a time (or a couple of centimetres maximum) – and test-fly it again. When you have finished, get a helper to check that your backup loop has a few centimetres of slack in it as you move over the full pitch range.

Tuning out turns

Some gliders exhibit a tendency to turn in a particular direction when flown hands-off. The most common reason for this is that the glider has sustained slight damage at some time, so the starting-point in curing this tendency is to check that both leading-edge tubes are straight and undamaged.

The next thing to check is the battens: do they accurately match the batten plan? Are they in matching pairs, or has one obviously been distorted? At this stage just note what you find (unless it is obvious that you stood on a batten and kinked it while rigging last time – in which case carefully correct it to the shape shown on the plan and test-fly the glider to check the repair).

Next compare the tensions in the batten elastics: are they equal at corresponding stations on each wing? – i.e. is number six elastic on the left wing at the same tension as number six elastic on the right wing?

Finally, check the wing-tips: there are many ways of securing the sail at the wing-tip, and most allow some form of adjustment. Irrespective of the method, check and see whether both sides are equal and whether they correspond with any datum marks.

Now consider your best course of action. If the glider has a tendency to turn when flown hands-off, the wing on the side that was lifting is producing more lift than the other wing. To cure the turn you must either decrease the lift in the lifting wing or increase the lift in the dropping wing. There are several ways of 'adding lift' to a wing, but you must only use the methods recommended in the user manual. These may include slightly increasing the batten-elastic tensions, or slightly increasing the camber in the battens, or increasing the sail tension ('shimming the tip'), or setting an adjustable tip in a more trailing-edge-down position. Decreasing lift is accomplished by doing the opposite in each case.

Whatever you do (and be guided by the user manual), use only one method, and make one small adjustment at a time, test-flying the glider in between. (Use your logbook to keep a record of what you have done, and your comments about the results.) In general your choice of method should be directed towards whichever factor seems to be most different from the standard setting. If small adjustments of the type specified in the user manual are not restoring normal operation, contact the glider manufacturer (or the UK importer) for advice.

Certification

In the early days of hang gliding, structural failures and 'luffing dives' were common causes of accidents. In the early 1980s, vehicle-based methods of testing for these sorts of problems were developed, and these form the basis of the BHPA Hang Glider Airworthiness Certificate of Type Compliance scheme. Very similar schemes are run in the USA by the Hang Glider Manufacturers Association and in Germany by the DHV.

To gain an Airworthiness Certificate of Type Compliance, a manufacturer has to prove that a particular glider type meets all the various requirements laid down in the BHPA Airworthiness Manual.

There are five key areas:

A. Drawings and specifications

All materials, processes and dimensions must be fully documented and acceptable.

B. User manual

The owner must be supplied with sufficient information to operate the aircraft safely.

C. Structural strength

The machine must be strong enough for flight in all likely conditions. The BHPA requires that a normal hang glider must be capable of supporting a load of four times the maximum specified pilot weight when loaded positively (e.g. normal manoeuvring) and twice the weight if it is loaded negatively (e.g. in turbulence). To ensure that regular production gliders meet these targets, the test example has to sustain 1.5 times these loadings.

D. Stability and handling

These must meet certain minimum standards. Here dynamic rig-testing of pitch characteristics is combined with flight tests.

E. Manufacture

The quality control of the manufacturing process must be satisfactory. In the case of gliders of foreign manufacture, the responsibility for this is normally lodged with the UK importer, who must inspect each machine against the specification and ensure that it conforms.

Issuing the Certificate

The precise requirements are revised and updated from time to time as necessary. If the glider type successfully meets these requirements, the manufacturer is issued with an 'Airworthiness Certificate of Type Compliance' (colloquially referred to as a 'C of A').

The Verification Placard

The next thing you need to know (as a glider purchaser or owner) is whether the particular glider you are concerned with is identical to the one that was tested. That is the role of the Verification Placard (also colloquially referred to variously as the C of A sticker, keel sticker, data label etc.). This placard (which must be attached to the glider's keel) is your guarantee that the glider in front of you conforms to type in every respect, and is so covered by the 'type approval'.

Registration

Some gliders do not have a Verification Placard issued by the BHPA, HGMA or DHV, usually because they differ in some way from the certified type. It is sometimes possible for pilots to operate such gliders under the registration scheme, if certain criteria are met (and fees paid!). Registered gliders carry a placard to this effect.

This scheme allows the BHPA to ensure that its members do not unwittingly fly suspect gliders, and that prototypes are treated with due care. It also provides a mechanism whereby owners can be contacted directly if a problem comes to light with their particular glider type. (The BHPA Office has further details of this scheme.)

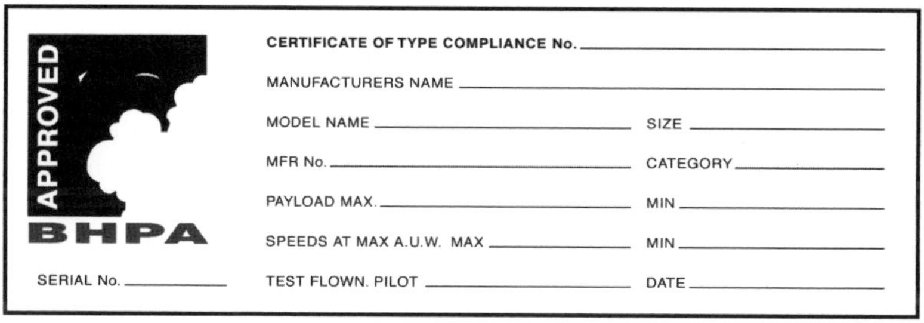

APPROVED
BHPA
SERIAL No.
CERTIFICATE OF TYPE COMPLIANCE No.
MANUFACTURERS NAME
MODEL NAME SIZE
MFR No. CATEGORY
PAYLOAD MAX. MIN
SPEEDS AT MAX A.U.W. MAX MIN
TEST FLOWN. PILOT DATE

Figure 5.1 *BHPA Verification Placard*

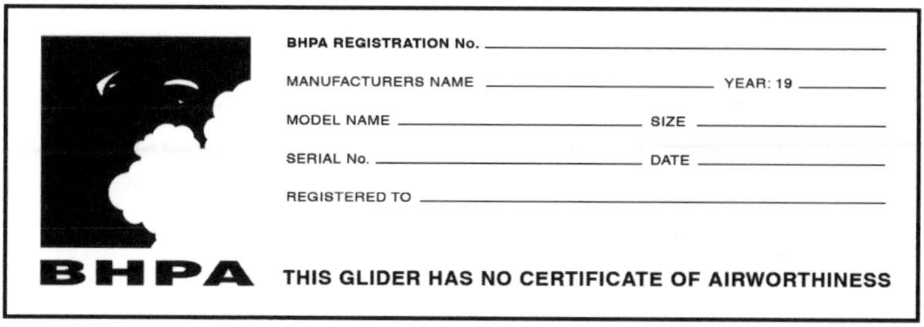

BHPA
BHPA REGISTRATION No.
MANUFACTURERS NAME YEAR: 19
MODEL NAME SIZE
SERIAL No. DATE
REGISTERED TO
THIS GLIDER HAS NO CERTIFICATE OF AIRWORTHINESS

Figure 5.2 *BHPA Registration Placard*

Storage

Hang gliders should be stored completely dry, properly packed, in a cool, dry place. The glider should be supported clear of the ground on at least three well-padded supports. Fresh air should be free to circulate around the glider. If the glider gets wet, then the bag should be left open (or off) and the glider should be opened out to dry as soon as possible. Damp storage will result in unsightly mildew on the sail (virtually impossible to remove) and potentially catastrophic airframe corrosion.

If the glider is flown on or near the coast it will also be susceptible to corrosion from the salt in the air. Hose the glider down with running fresh water and allow it to dry before storing it.

Buying your first hang glider

Nowadays there is a wide choice of intermediate gliders available from the manufacturers, developed especially for the new Club Pilot. Choosing one of these is a straightforward operation: discuss your choice with your instructor, check that the model is produced in your size, and check that it is certified and carries the Verification Placard. Then select your colours, pay your money, and go flying!

Buying second-hand is rather less easy. You may be lucky and find one of the newer intermediate types available second-hand (check the adverts in *Skywings*). Or you may be offered a less suitable alternative glider at a much more favourable price... But there are many pitfalls for the unwary:

Airworthiness

Many gliders can be considered unsuitable, simply because they are not of a certificated type and thus there is no proof of the soundness of their design.

Handling

Some gliders have very poor handling. Usually such gliders were never meant to be suitable for inexperienced pilots and were hardly suitable for experienced fliers. Only consider purpose-built intermediate gliders.

Performance

You may find yourself offered a second-hand high-performance glider. Beware! These can fly very fast, accelerate very quickly and require a large amount of skill to land accurately, especially if space is at all limited and if the wind is light. Leave high-performance gliders well alone until you have at least 50 hours soaring on an intermediate glider. Leave extra-high-performance gliders well alone until you have well over 100 hours.

Former World Champion Rob Whittall, perhaps one of the most naturally gifted pilots ever born, didn't move on from an intermediate glider until he had over 100 hours experience. Nevertheless he managed to go from training school to World Champion in just over three years – it obviously didn't hold him back!

Condition

You should bear in mind that intermediate gliders often lead a hard life – a five-year-old glider that has had a couple of intermediate pilot owners could well be nearly worn out.

Get experienced independent help

Given the factors listed above, you will appreciate why it is vital that any second-hand glider is inspected and test-flown by an instructor or coach before you part with any money.

Even if you buy a brand-new hang glider you should ask an instructor or coach to fly your glider before you do, to check that it is set up correctly. When allowed to fly hands-off, it should automatically fly straight and at the correct trim-speed. Usually your instructor or coach will be able to make the tuning adjustments required to fix any small problems.

Trimmers and compensators

Trimmer (VB/VG)

Many hang gliders are fitted with a device that allows the pilot to alter the sail-tension in flight. The pilot pulls a cord on the base-bar which, through a pulley system in the keel pocket, in turn pulls the cross-tube centre junction back a little along the keel. This forces out the leading edges, thus tightening and flattening the wing. These devices have various names, such as 'VB' (variable billow), 'VG' (variable geometry) or 'Magic Trimmer'.

Tightening the wing usually gives a performance increase, but at the expense of stiffer handling. For this reason you should usually take off with the trimmer either completely slack or only on a little, and you should release the trimmer fully well before landing. (Check the user manual for detailed recommendations.)

The range of cross-tube movement available with the trimmer is carefully set at manufacture and is listed in the user manual. Do not adjust this, as pitch stability can be adversely affected.

Compensator

As you operate the trimmer, the nose angle is increased, as is the sail tension, particularly in the trailing edge. On gliders with kingposts and luff-lines, if the reflex is adequate when the trimmer is off then it can be excessive when the trimmer is on. (Excessive reflex degrades performance and can spoil the handling.)

A compensator is a simple device that automatically adjusts the luff-lines as the trimmer is operated. In practice the compensator is usually a cord attached halfway along the front top wire at one end and attached (via a pulley at the kingpost base) to the cross-tube junction at the other. As the cross-tube junction moves backward and forward according to the trimmer setting, so the compensator pivots the kingpost top backward and forward, varying the luff-line tension.

The danger with compensators is that the necessarily precise adjustment of the luff-lines is now at the mercy of the adjustment of a single cord. If the cord fails, the luff-lines return to their lowest position, which means that the glider is probably unsafe unless it is flown with the trimmer on. If your glider is fitted with a compensator, make sure that a visual inspection of the condition of this cord is part of your Daily Inspection, and make sure that you check the reflex settings regularly (at least once a year).

Chapter 6: Paragliders

Maintenance

A paraglider can be easily damaged. Has it been nose-dived into the ground? (This can easily burst cell walls.) Has it been dragged over rough ground? Has someone trampled over it in heavy boots? The bad news is that, even if you can answer 'No' to these questions, and even if you do look after your equipment carefully, degradation will still occur. Lines will shrink and fabric will deteriorate. Because of this, regular and detailed checks are essential. There are many locations around the UK where such checks can be carried out and advice given – ask your dealer.

Care of the glider

One of the main problem areas is degradation of the wing caused by ultraviolet light due to repeated exposure to the sun. This can lead to a breakdown of the fabric coating, resulting in an increase in the porosity of the fabric and massive detrimental changes in the paraglider's flight characteristics. The effects of UV can be lessened by not leaving the canopy spread out in the sun for any longer than is necessary. The use of a large 'stuff sack' will help with this.

Avoid getting the paraglider wet. If this does happen, dry it as soon as possible to prevent the build-up of mildew. Dry the paraglider naturally, avoiding direct contact with sources of heat.

The paraglider must never be allowed to come into contact with chemicals or fuels such as can often be found in car boots. These substances will damage the whole paraglider – and the damage may not be immediately visible.

For cleaning the paraglider, follow the manufacturer's instructions; gentle sponging with fresh water is usually the best option.

Fabric repairs

Repairs to minor tears in the canopy fabric can be carried out using self-adhesive rip-stop repair tape. The tear must be patched on both sides, and the patches must be 'rounded off' so that there are no corners that might peel. The patches should be large enough to cover the damaged area completely, and positioned so that the weave on one side is at 90 degrees to that on the other. The secret is to avoid any sharp edges or a 'hinge' effect with the surrounding fabric. Tears are considered to be minor if they are no more than 10cm (4in) in length and are not near a seam or load-bearing area. If in doubt, seek professional help.

Suspension lines

Lines are typically constructed from either sheathed Kevlar or sheathed Dyneema. Kevlar deteriorates with repeated bending and ageing, resulting in the lines weakening significantly over time. Your dealer should check for this when you take your paraglider for its annual service. Dyneema tends to shrink over time, with 10cm (4in) shrinkage on a typical paraglider line being not uncommon. This shrinkage can have a major effect on the paraglider's flight characteristics. It is a relatively simple job for your dealer to check the lines and re-stretch them to the factory settings if necessary.

Check all your lines regularly. You can easily spot frayed or broken outer sheathing, but internal damage takes a little more time. It isn't difficult; simply run your finger and thumb down each line in turn while applying light tension. You will then easily detect even slight kinks and broken or damaged inner cores. Most line breaks occur within 1cm (0.4in) of the end of a stitched line.

If you have a damaged line, take it to your dealer and get a matched factory replacement. That way you can be sure that the length and material will be correct and the vital geometry of your glider unaltered. While you are at it, check your risers for wear and damage, and check your maillons (see page 69). Damage to lines, risers and fabric damage other than that mentioned above should only be repaired by the manufacturer or his appointed agent.

Paragliders should always be returned to the dealer or manufacturer for an annual inspection!
A BHPA Annual Canopy Inspection form (available at www.bhpa.co.uk/members/forms/index.php) should be used so that the appropriate extent of the service is clearly agreed and understood.

Tuning and trimming

A paraglider should be fit for flight from new, requiring no tuning or trimming. But unfortunately it is not unknown for new gliders to have lines rigged incorrectly at assembly, or to have some other manufacturing or assembly defect. It is therefore extremely important to have any new glider thoroughly inspected and test-flown by the dealer before you fly it. The control-line lengths should already be at the certified settings on new canopies, but this needs checking on second-hand ones. Minor alterations to these lengths may be permissible (check the user manual) to allow for the individual pilot's preferences, but in general you should not fiddle about or you may discover painfully that your paraglider now has nothing like the certified flight and stability characteristics.

Certification

All paragliders flown by BHPA members must carry proof of acceptable certification. 'Acceptable certification' means that the paraglider must carry a wing-tip Verification Placard confirming that it has AFNOR, SHV or LTF (formerly DHV) certification. For parascending canopies, BHPA 'Ascending Parachute' certification is also acceptable.

In the absence of proof of acceptable certification in the form of a Verification Placard, BHPA rules require the paraglider to be individually registered. Acceptance is not automatic, being dependent upon certain criteria being met and fees paid. (The BHPA Office has further details.)

Understanding the systems

Paragliders can be certified to the CEN standard (EN926-1 and EN926-2) or to the virtually identical German LTF (formerly DHV) standard. A French paraglider test organisation, called 'Aerotests', issues certification to the French issue of EN926, whilst in Switzerland a test organisation called 'Air Turquoise' issues certification to the identical Swiss issue of EN926. The completely separate but virtually identical German LTF standard is used by the German DHV test department.

Both the CEN and LTF systems are in two parts. Part one deals with testing the structural strength of the type. In part two the flight characteristics are explored – which means evaluating how easy it is to get out of control, and how difficult it is to recover from such situations.

With the CEN standard, the manufacturer submits a paraglider for testing in one of four classes: A, B, C or D. The paraglider is then evaluated against the specific programme of tests for that class, and must meet measured criteria. Any glider that passes the 'A' class tests will have extremely good flight/stability characteristics suitable for beginner pilots at a school; the criteria for the 'D' class allows gliders with extremely dubious flight/stability characteristics to pass.

In the LTF system the glider is either failed or awarded a grade of 1 to 3 for its behaviour in each test. The paraglider is then given an overall grade: 1, 1/2, 2, 2/3 or 3. Grade 1 is for paragliders with safe and easy flight/stability characteristics and grade 3 denotes gliders with distinctly difficult and 'unfriendly' flight/stability characteristics.

The key point with both systems it that you **must** assess your own piloting ability accurately. If you are a new Club Pilot (Novice) you must only consider buying an 'A' or 'B' class glider (or LTF grade 1 or 1/2). Anything else will give you a lot of nasty surprises – which may put you off the sport for good, and which may be extremely painful.

NB. You may find some second-hand gliders that were certified to an earlier version of the CEN standard. These were graded Standard, Performance or Competition.

When you have at least 50 hours logged, are 'Pilot'-rated, are practised and familiar with the standard recovery techniques, fly 'actively', fly regularly and often, and are happy to accept an increased level of risk, then you might consider a 'C' class (or LTF 2) paraglider – but you would probably still have more fun on the 'B' class glider!

'D' class (or LTF 3) paragliders are for 'Advanced Pilot'-rated pilots who run SIV courses, have their hours measured in hundreds, and accept that sooner or later they will have a serious accident.

Evaluate your abilities accurately, buy a glider of the appropriate class, and have many happy hours of fun.

The table opposite sets out the current EN 926 and LTF classification systems, and the older CEN classes, and provides a rough guide to the relationship between them. (This table is provided for guidance only: the classes or grades under the different systems do not correspond precisely.)

'Serial class'

You may hear the phrase 'serial class' mentioned. This term has various definitions, but is generally used in the competition world to refer to higher-performance gliders certified below the level of LTF grade 3 or CEN 'D' class. Many competitions run separate scoring classes for pilots flying such gliders, in an effort to improve competition safety.

The 'Grandfather' clause

Many of the low-performance round and wing canopies used for towed paragliding (parascending) were out of production long before the modern certification schemes emerged. Those canopies of a type with a proven history of safety and reliability established over many years are dealt with individually under the registration scheme. Such registered

Rough guide to paraglider classifications

EN 926 classification, description and BHPA recommendations

A: Paragliders with maximum passive safety and extremely forgiving flying characteristics. Gliders with good resistance to departures from normal flight.

For all pilots including pilots under all levels of training.

B: Paragliders with good passive safety and forgiving flying characteristics. Gliders with some resistance to departures from normal flight.

For all pilots including pilots under all levels of training.

C: Paragliders with moderate passive safety and with potentially dynamic reactions to turbulence and pilot errors. Recovery to normal flight may require precise pilot input.

For pilots familiar with recovery techniques, who fly "actively" and regularly, and understand the implications of flying a glider with reduced passive safety. *(Recommended minimum: BHPA Pilot rating)*

D: Paragliders with demanding flying characteristics and potentially violent reactions to turbulence and pilot errors. Recovery to normal flight requires precise pilot input.

For pilots well practised in recovery techniques, who fly very actively, have significant experience of flying in turbulent conditions, and who accept the implications of flying such a wing. *(Recommended minimum: BHPA Advanced Pilot rating)*

New EN926 classification	Latest DHV classification (03)	Old AFNOR/CEN classification
A	1	STD.
B	1-2	
C	2	PERF.
D	2-3	
FAIL	3	COMP.

gliders can be identified by their wing-tip registration placard. The BHPA also has an airworthiness testing and certification scheme for new parascending canopies.

Storage

Your paraglider should be stored in a cool, dry place away from direct sunlight or heat sources. Always pack your glider as loose as possible, to prevent fabric strain that can deform the wing. If it is to be stored for long periods of time (e.g. over winter) then pack the canopy separate from the harness to ensure that it is packed as loose as possible. This should enable some air to circulate and so prevent mildew problems arising from any residual dampness. When packing your glider, vary the methods of folding the canopy to prevent the same panels being folded each time.

Buying a paraglider

As a newly qualified Club Pilot, the prospect of buying a new glider can be daunting, given the vast choice of intermediate gliders available. Discuss the matter with your instructor and others whose judgement you trust, making sure the shortlisted gliders have CEN/AFNOR 'A' or 'B' and/or LTF 1 (or 1/2) certification. Make sure that the gliders are available in the correct size for your weight. Most designs are produced in three or more sizes to suit different pilot weights; you should examine the handbook (make certain that you get one with the particular canopy you buy) and other literature to ensure that you fall within the published weight range. Weights are normally quoted as 'Total weight in flight' but check carefully. Total weight in flight means the weight of the pilot (fully dressed and booted for flying), the harness, helmet, instruments, emergency parachute equipment and the paraglider. Also make sure that there are no harness restrictions that will be difficult or expensive to comply with (e.g. can the glider only be flown with a fully cross-braced harness?)

Then fly the shortlisted gliders and select the one that you feel happiest on. Bear in mind that nearly all paragliders feel good in smooth ridge lift, but they can feel very different in thermic conditions: the wonderfully responsive 'lively' handling you found on the ridge could feel frighteningly unmanageable in rougher air. Make sure you talk to someone who has owned that type of glider and flown it in a range of conditions. If everything checks out, choose your colour scheme, pay your money and go flying!

Buying second-hand is more complicated, though again the advice of your instructor will be invaluable. The second-hand market is large, and there are some good canopies out there, but there are also many pitfalls for the unwary.

Airworthiness

Make sure your prospective purchase has its airworthiness Verification Placard stuck or stitched onto one of the cells. They are usually found at the wing tips or on the centre cell. The Verification Placard will contain, among other things, the make and model of glider, date of manufacture, certification category, weight range, and the type of harness the glider was tested with. Avoid gliders with no Verification Placard!

The glider should also come with its user manual. This gives details of weight ranges, replacement line lengths, handling characteristics, do's and don'ts, and other useful information.

The working life of a paraglider is not infinite: you might get three or four hundred hours if it is looked after very carefully. It can be difficult to determine the condition of a second-hand wing; again the advice of your instructor or another experienced pilot will be helpful. In general, a wing that has been well cared for and looks (and feels) in good condition, probably is, and vice versa. Lines can be more difficult to check than the canopy fabric. Unless the age and strength of the lines can be verified, budget for replacements (these can be anything from £50 to £200, so check the cost before buying!). If in any doubt, don't buy. There are plenty of good second-hand paragliders to be had.

Handling

All modern gliders in the CEN 'A' and 'B' classes (or LTF 1 and 1/2 grades) will have acceptable handling characteristics, but you need to check that the handling suits you. Seek your instructor's advice on the canopy's suitability – and again, try before you buy.

Performance

There are many older high-performance gliders for sale second-hand at what appear to be very reasonable prices. Beware: their performance invariably came at the expense of safety and stability. Unfortunately, many of these older high-performance gliders have very good handling, and so feel deceptively pleasant to fly. Only when they depart from normal flight is their true nature revealed! It is far safer, and more fun, to gain a couple of years' experience on a suitable glider in the knowledge that it has no handling or stability quirks. The resale value of old high-performance gliders is also limited whereas reselling a modern intermediate glider is much easier.

Speed systems and trimmers

Most modern paragliders now come with a speed system as standard, and some also have trim tabs.

Speed system

The speed system is simply a means of altering the geometry of the risers, usually by means of a foot stirrup, enabling the canopy to fly faster. When the pilot pushes on the foot stirrup (or speed-bar as it is more commonly known), this pulls on the risers via a series of pulleys and results in a reduced angle of attack. The more the pilot pushes on the speed-bar, the faster the canopy will fly, up to the point where the bar can be pushed no further. On releasing the pressure on the speed bar, the canopy will resume its normal flying trim.

A speed system gives a greater range of flying speeds. This allows the pilot to fly quickly through sink, or more efficiently into wind, or to race towards a goal field. They are not designed to aid flying in conditions that would normally prove to be too windy! If the speed system has to be used as a way to prevent being 'blown back' when ridge-soaring, you should consider this an emergency situation, and should land as soon as safely

Figure 6.1
A typical paraglider speed system

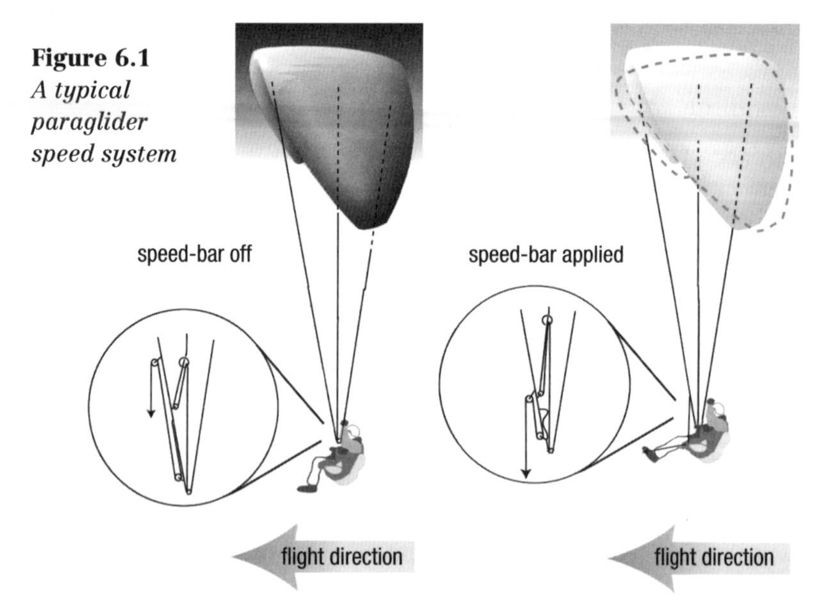

practicable – usually at the bottom of the hill, where the wind is less strong. You should ensure that you identify the conditions that caused this, and make sure you are never caught out in the same way again.

The danger with speed systems is that in reducing the wing's angle of attack they make tucks and collapses much more likely, so flying in turbulent air with the speed-bar on is almost certain to lead to problems. (If your wing has been certified with a speed system, then this tendency will have been checked for, and at least some margin of stability will be present when the speed system is in use.)

Though speed systems all follow the same principles, they can be quite different in their setup. Follow the manufacturer's instructions carefully when setting one up.

Trim tabs

Trim tabs (trimmers) are another way of altering the angle of attack of the canopy and thus affecting the speed. They are usually attached to the rear risers, and are operated by pulling the tabs through a locking cam device that holds them at the required position. This will lengthen or shorten the riser depending on how the tab was set, increasing or decreasing the trim speed accordingly. A claimed advantage of tabs over a speed-bar is they stay where you put them, but this must be balanced by the fact that you cannot revert to normal (safe) trim just by relaxing your feet. If the canopy has collapsed while trimmed fast, the recovery will be more difficult.

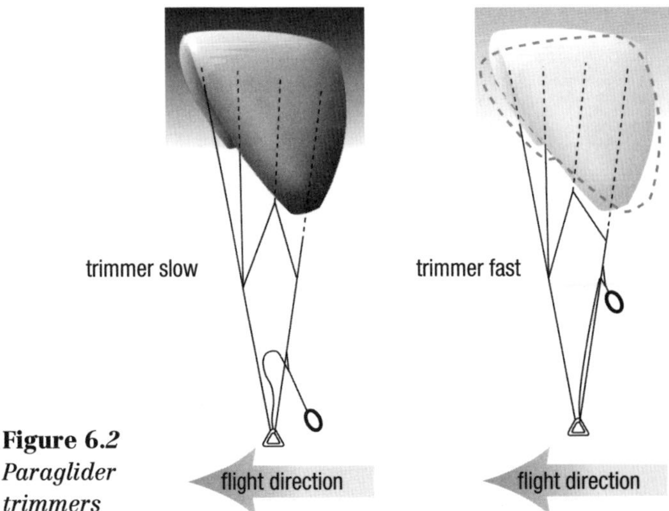

Figure 6.2 *Paraglider trimmers*

Chapter 7: Safety equipment

Emergency parachutes

An emergency parachute gives you a second chance, perhaps a final chance, when some catastrophe occurs. This section details the important points about buying, installing, maintaining and using a parachute. Hopefully this will increase the chances of the emergency-parachute system working successfully if it is ever needed.

The basic parachute system comprises the canopy and its lines, its bridle and the attachment to the harness. The system is completed by the deployment bag, which holds the packed canopy and lines, all stowed in a container which is fitted securely to the pilot's harness.

The early emergency parachutes produced for hang gliding used round or 'conical' shaped canopies. Since the late 1980s virtually all emergency parachutes produced for hang gliding and paragliding are of the pulled-down-apex design (or variations on it). A central line holds the middle of the open canopy more or less level with the skirt, so that air pressure forces the skirt out and the canopy presents the maximum drag area for the smallest amount of material. Such designs are also very rapid opening. The downside of these types is that some designs can be very unstable and can produce massive opening shocks: both of these can be catastrophic, so it is important that you buy a properly independently tested and approved product.

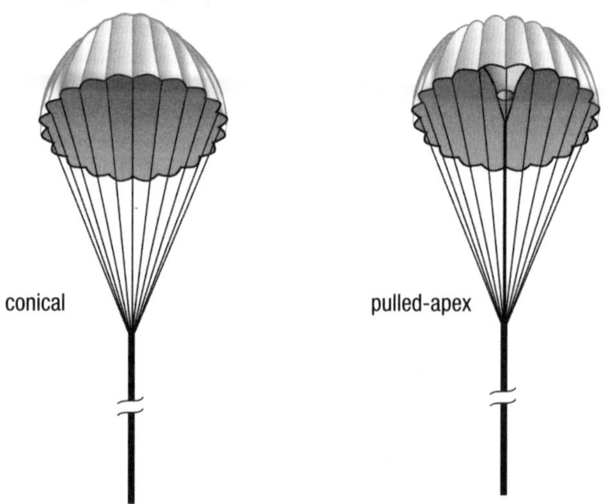

Figure 7.1 *Conical and pulled-apex emergency parachutes*

Choosing a parachute

Buying a parachute that is clearly marked as conforming to the CEN standard EN12491 is strongly recommended. Such parachutes will have passed rigorous speed of opening tests, descent rate tests (max. 5.5m/s), stability tests and strength tests. In the strength test the manufacturer has the choice of two test speeds, and the successfully certified parachutes therefore carry on the certification label the warning: 'not suitable for speeds in excess of 32m/s (115km/h)' OR 'not suitable for speeds in excess of 49m/s (176km/h)'. Other than checking the certification label and deciding whether you will be happy with the lower speed certification or whether you want the added strength of the higher speed tested alternatives, the final very important thing you need to do is check that it is available in a size suitable for your total weight in flight (this figure includes the weight of your glider).

If you buy a parachute not certified to EN12491 then the earlier DHV and AFNOR standards give some measure of quality assurance, but you must be careful to ensure that the parachute you select will give an acceptable descent rate at your total weight in flight. Look for one with documented rates of descent at different loads, and choose one that will give a descent rate of less than 7.5m/sec (ideally around 5.5m/sec) at your total weight in flight.

Descent rates / equivalent fall height: As the expected descent rate increases, so does the likelihood of injury and its severity. A descent rate of approximately 5.5m/s (18ft/s) is recommended as this keeps the likelihood of injury low while keeping all the other design factors (parachute bulk, weight) manageable. Slightly higher descent rates are acceptable, but a descent rate of 7.5m/s (24.5ft/s) should be regarded as being the maximum limit: any existing parachute system that will, at your all-up weight, give you a sea-level descent rate greater than 7.5m/s should be replaced.

It is sometimes easier to visualise vertical descent rates by equating them to stepping off a wall of a certain height. 5.5m/s (18ft/s or 12.3mph) is your velocity when you hit the ground after stepping off a wall 1.5m (5ft) high. A descent rate of 7.5m/s is equivalent to a drop of 2.5m (8.2ft).

When you have imagined falling from this height onto your feet and doing a PLF, try imagining falling from this height onto your back, or your side, or your head...

You should also bear in mind that in an actual emergency, factors such as lift, sink, altitude, a semi-inflated paraglider or a damaged hang glider may all conspire to increase or decrease your descent rate.

Buying second-hand

There is nothing intrinsically wrong with buying a second-hand parachute, but you are strongly advised to have it inspected by a BHPA-licensed 'Parachute Systems Checker and Packer'. Many parachutes sold to hang glider pilots in the 1990s were far too small and could produce fearsome descent rates if ever used at typical hang glider payloads, assuming the opening shock did not burst them or break the pilot's harness. These should be avoided. The licensed packer will check that the parachute is the right size for you, has been well looked after, is not too old (ten years should be considered as the total life of a canopy – those without dates of manufacture, the manufacturer's name and serial numbers should be avoided) and that it is in good serviceable condition.

Checking parachute area

There are many ways of measuring parachutes. To avoid confusion, BHPA-licensed packers all take the following simple steps:

1. Measure from the peripheral hem in the centre of a gore up to the very apex of the parachute (including the lines). This gives the y dimension.
2. Measure the width of the gore at the peripheral hem, and halve this figure. This gives the x dimension.
3. Multiply x by y to give the surface area of the individual gore.
4. Multiply the result by the number of gores to get the total surface area of the parachute.

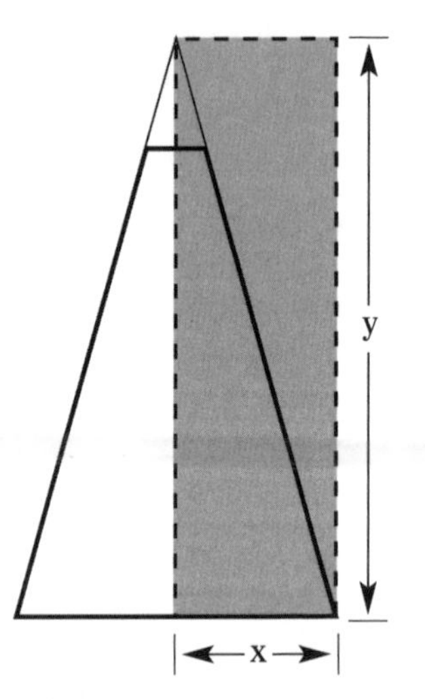

Figure 7.2 *Measuring the surface area of a gore*

Estimating descent rates where no data is available

The graph below can be used to indicate the likely descent rate of a typical PDA canopy given your total weight in flight and the canopy area. (Check that your parachute area is measured using the BHPA method.)

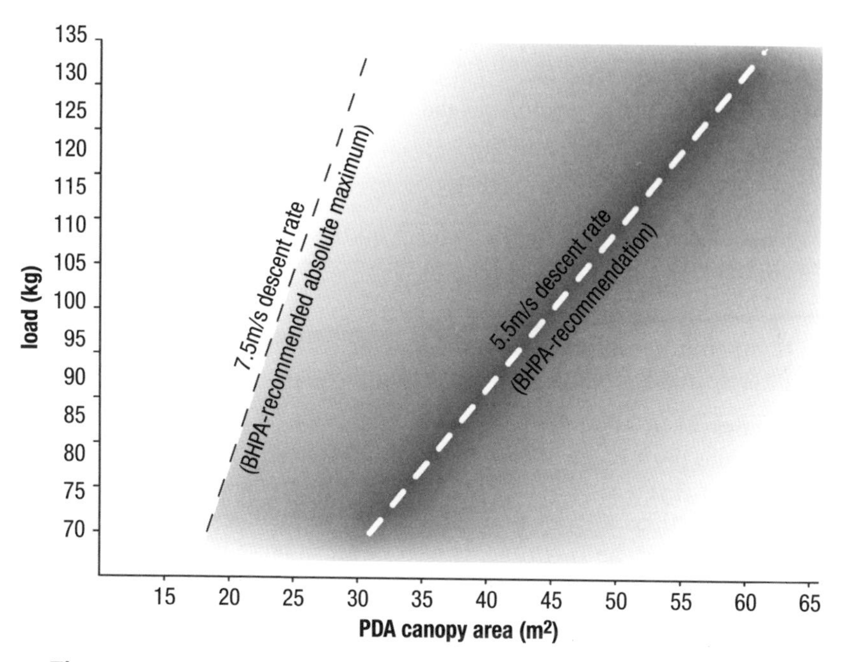

Figure 7.3 *Graph of canopy area against load for typical pulled-down-apex parachutes*

This graph is based on a Cd (Coefficient of drag) of 1.2, typical of many simple pulled-down-apex designs, although the actual Cd of a particular canopy will depend on a number of factors, including canopy shape, fabric permeability, line lengths and drive. ('Drive' means that the PDA canopy glides – usually contrary to the designer's intent and expectation – and so creates lift, which helps reduce the descent rate: the downside is that your ground impact energy may be increased because of the lateral velocity, which may be significant.) The real descent rate is further complicated by stability. Live drop tests have shown that there can be a huge disparity in the way parachutes descend: whilst some are stable, many oscillate or 'cone' (a swirling sycamore-like action) which can greatly affect the descent rate. So this graph can only provide a 'ball-park' indication.

The graph should not be used when actual data is available, nor for anything other than conventional (non-slotted, non-steerable) PDA canopy types.

User manual

Ensure you receive a user manual with your parachute: this should contain instructions for installing it, using it and re-packing it, as well as data on performance, size and recommended load.

Make sure that the parachute has the correct bridle for your glider type:

- Hang-glider parachutes require a six-metre bridle to keep the parachute clear of the wreckage.
- Single-riser paraglider parachutes require a short bridle with an additional Y-bridle to connect it to the two harness-attachment points.
- Multi-riser paraglider parachutes connect the appropriate risers directly to the left and right harness-attachment points.

The complete system

Having the perfect parachute is not much use if it won't fit in your harness, or if you can't get it out of your harness when you need to, or if the connections to your harness are not strong enough. Emergency parachutes must be regarded as part of a complete system. For this reason you are strongly advised to buy a system from a BHPA-licensed packer, who will have the knowledge required to sort out the whole package, rather than just selling you an expensive component which may actually be of little or no use to you.

Installing

Always unpack and inspect a parachute before fitting it to your harness: it is not unusual to find faults in brand-new equipment, so check carefully. Be aware that many parachutes are shipped 'packed for transit' and look ready for use but are not!

The parachute's outer container must be mounted in a suitable place on the harness (although in many cases it is built into the harness). It may be on the front or on either side; with paraglider harnesses it could also be on the back or even under the seat. All of these positions have advantages and disadvantages:

- Does the pack get in the way during take-off, flight or landing?
- Does the pack location involve extra connections when putting the harness on for flight (which might be forgotten)?

- Is the mounting secure, so that the deployment bag can be extracted easily?
- Can you see the handle?
- Can you easily reach the handle with either hand? If you can only reach it with one hand, you have only half the chance of a successful deployment!
- Is the handle likely to get accidentally caught and cause inadvertent deployment?

Make sure that the parachute fits properly in the harness: quite a few harnesses have been manufactured with parachute containers which are far too small, and you may need to have such a container enlarged so that you can fit a parachute of suitable size.

Make sure your emergency-parachute riser is correctly attached to your harness. Modern certified paraglider harnesses are supplied with tested loops on the shoulders: you must attach the parachute to both of these so the load is spread equally. With hang-glider harnesses the emergency parachute is connected to the main harness suspension point, using a separate steel maillon connector. The bridle(s) must be carefully routed to ensure that no twists will occur as your emergency parachute deploys and that the bridle(s) will not get tangled with your paraglider risers/hang glider hang-strap – or with you, the pilot – you do not want the bridle around your neck! (See the section on connectors in Chapter 8.)

Check the whole system when it is put together, with you suspended in the harness in full flying kit:

- Is the strop on the deployment handle strong enough to withstand the force of the pull?
- Is the strop on the deployment handle the right length? It must pull the outer-cover closure pins completely clear before starting to drag the deployment bag out. If not, it will be impossible to extract the parachute no matter how hard you pull!
- Can you easily deploy with either hand?

If you are not 100% confident that you fully understand the whole list of items that must be matched and checked to create an effective emergency parachute system, then get a BHPA-licensed packer to install it properly for you and explain the system to you. In fact, even if you have put the system together yourself and feel confident that you have done a good job, why not invest in your future by having an independent pair of eyes give it a check-over? Pilots of all abilities have been responsible for the many packing and installation errors discovered over the years.

Maintenance and repacking

Ideally every pilot should learn how to repack his or her own parachute, and so become completely familiar with the system. You can learn how to do this at a parachute-repacking evening organised by your local club (make sure that a BHPA-licensed packer will be supervising the evening). Alternatively, take your equipment to a BHPA-licensed packer and get the packer to show you how to repack it. (If you really don't want to understand your emergency system, simply get the packer to do a full inspection and repack.)

Repacking should be carried out at the intervals recommended in the parachute's user manual. In the absence of such recommendations, check and repack your parachute every six months. (If it has become damp it should be aired immediately and repacked when completely dry.) Repacking provides an opportunity for a close examination of the entire parachute system for general viability and wear and tear. It also allows replacement of the rubber bands, which perish, with new bands of exactly the correct specification.

By fitting a parachute your chances of surviving an in-flight catastrophe have been increased, but you are now exposed to the danger of experiencing an in-flight emergency in the form of an unintentional deployment. Approximately one in three deployments are unintentional! – this is mainly because pilots fail to check and maintain their equipment adequately.

Pre-flight checks

As part of your pre-flight actions:

- Check that your parachute container is properly closed and that any closure pins are secure and free to release.
- Check that the deployment handle is accessible.
- Check that no slack loops of riser have slipped out of your parachute container.
- Check that you have easy access to your hook knife.

Be particularly careful with Velcro closure systems. As Velcro gets old, it can get clogged. It can also lock together over time, so a pull that is easy when the parachute is first assembled can become almost impossible after six months. Pin closures are generally much better, but still need constant vigilance.

Don't be the next pilot to end up dangling beneath your 'chute when you least expect it!

Using your emergency parachute

Practising

Once you've got your system sorted out, the next job is to learn how to use it. Your emergency parachute's user manual should advise you how to deploy for real, and how to practise (on the ground). Some clubs and schools have built suspended systems that you can strap into for practising deployment. Make full use of any simulator to which you have access: practise looking, grabbing and activating your parachute handle with first your right hand and then your left hand. Make sure you know whether the container requires you to pull in a certain direction. The slowest elements in deploying the emergency parachute are invariably:

- making the decision
- getting the parachute out of the harness and thrown.

Time and effort spent in practising these actions and improving these parts of the system will pay the biggest dividends.

When to deploy

With situations such as a structural failure of your hang glider or paraglider, the appropriate action is clear: deploy the parachute!

With paragliders there is a range of less clear situations where control of the canopy has been lost but may be regained. The decision whether or not to deploy will depend on the height that will be lost during your attempts at recovery and your initial proximity to the ground. Several pilots have been killed (and many injured) impacting the ground while still trying to recover control of their paragliders, when their parachutes would almost certainly have saved them. The crucial point is that **any efforts to regain control of the paraglider must be secondary to the key concern of monitoring your height.** Recovering from a complete mess is very satisfying if you have plenty of height to play with; however, descent rates can be extremely fast when a canopy is spinning out of control. Don't leave deployment to the last minute.

If in doubt, throw it out!

Cumulonimbus

Do not deploy your parachute as a method of escaping from a cumulonimbus (not that you should ever allow yourself to get anywhere near one!). You will in all probability be swept up into the thundercloud while dangling powerlessly underneath your parachute.

In such an emergency situation hang-glider pilots are probably best advised to try to fly away from the danger, while a paraglider pilot's best option is probably to use the spiral dive rapid-descent technique. This will give a much higher descent rate than a parachute – perhaps 15m/s (50ft/s). Of course, if you have suffered catastrophic structural failure in the cloud your outlook is rather bleaker – you can throw the parachute and risk being swept up, or delay the throw and risk your parachute and/or harness being shredded by the opening shock. Whilst the latest CEN certified parachutes will survive an opening after a very few seconds of free-fall, most will not. And few, if any, current paraglider and hang-glider harnesses are designed to take free-fall parachuting shock loads. So keep clear of cu-nimbs.

Deploying your parachute

1 **LOOK** for the deployment-bag handle. Harnesses (especially paraglider harnesses) can have a number of adjustment straps that may easily be confused with the parachute deployment handle in an emergency. Be sure to look for the correct handle so you don't waste precious time tugging on the wrong strap – many parachutists have died through pulling a strap instead of the correct handle.

2 **Reach and grab** the handle securely. If your right hand is not available, use your left!

3 **Get the parachute out.** Some container systems require you to pull the handle in a certain direction to release the curved pins (safety locks) before you can extract your parachute. Some Velcro configurations require you to peel the opening flap downward to extract the parachute. It may even be that you need to use both hands to get the parachute out! Make sure that you know your equipment.

4 **Look for clear air and throw the parachute out towards it.** Throw hard. If it is possible, throw the parachute towards the sky, or upwards and out.

   - You can throw better if you grab the whole parachute deployment bag using both hands.

- Your riser(s) should come to full extension followed by your lines and canopy. If you get a good throw away from you, your system will open with less loss of height. If you drop your emergency parachute below you, you risk entanglement. You will also fall a greater distance before the parachute inflates and takes your body weight.
- You may want to avoid throwing the parachute down between your legs.
- Hang glider pilots may wish to avoid throwing the parachute through the control frame as this could result in the glider inverting, which usually limits the pilot's ability to adopt a sensible landing position.

5 **Look to make sure your parachute has opened.** The deployment bag should release and the canopy start to deploy as soon as the bridle is at full stretch. If it does not, try yanking the bridle several times very hard. Hopefully, the parachute will inflate and the bridle will be yanked out of your hand. If this does not release the deployment bag, pull the parachute back in, hand over hand. Throw the parachute again.
   - If the deployment bag has released but your canopy has not yet inflated, yank vigorously on the bridle. This will help to spread the suspension lines and open an air channel.
   - If you are pulling on a parachute bridle, never wrap the line around your hand and let it go immediately the parachute starts inflating. The parachute will inflate with tremendous energy.

6 **Prepare for impact.** Paraglider pilots should assume the PLF position (see 'Keep practising your PLFs!' on page 11). Hang-glider pilots should unzip their harness and climb into the control frame, keeping their weight distributed towards both corners of the base-bar. If this is not possible, concentrate on getting into a foot-down/head-up position with your feet together and your knees slightly bent. Keep your arms and head tucked in. Try to use your legs as shock-absorbers by allowing them to flex as you impact. Allow your body to roll in the direction of the impact.

After you impact, disconnect from the glider immediately (getting injured by being dragged across the countryside after a successful emergency-parachute descent would be a shame). Do whatever you need to do to get away from the glider and parachute, even if it means cutting the bridle or cutting your harness (use your hook knife). Deflate the parachute by grabbing the hem at one side and taking it forward into the wind.

Radio your friends to let them know your position and condition. You should also contact the local police, who may be launching a full-scale search if a member of the public has seen your descent and reported it.

Preventing paraglider re-inflation

With paraglider emergency-parachute systems it is possible for the paraglider to re-inflate after the emergency parachute has been deployed, and then for the two to 'fight' during the descent, sometimes with disastrous results. Various methods of disabling your paraglider to prevent this happening have been suggested, but the most important point here is that this problem is far less likely to occur if your parachute is the correct size for you. The lower your rate of descent under parachute, the less likely your paraglider will want to continue 'flying'.

If you do find yourself under your emergency parachute, and needing to disable a re-inflated paraglider, you must avoid any asymmetric action which could result in a free wing-tip thrashing around uncontrollably. Pulling both 'C'-risers (to create a 'C'-line stall) has been recommended by European test pilots, and may give additional drag, further slowing your descent.

Steerable/gliding emergency parachutes

Any steerable/gliding emergency parachute will have twin risers, or possibly four risers. As with most parachute design alternatives, the steerable emergency parachute concept has a trade-off. The main reason for having a steerable emergency parachute is so you can steer yourself away from any danger during the descent. The disadvantages are:

- Because these parachutes rely on forward glide for them to create lift, they require the paraglider to be disabled or released, otherwise it will re-inflate
- They tend to be complicated to re-pack, with more chance of difficulties when opening
- If you do not have the space to manoeuvre for a landing into wind, an uncontrolled landing is likely to be downwind, at wind speed plus glide speed.

Because of the hang-gliding requirement for a long single bridle, a steerable emergency parachute is not an option for hang-glider pilots.

Paraswivels

Some hang-glider emergency parachutes are supplied with a swivel fitted into the bridle. It is not unusual for a broken hang glider to spin like a sycamore seed as it descends under an emergency parachute, and the swivel is intended to prevent the parachute suspension lines being twisted together if this happens. Such twisting could ultimately result in the canopy mouth being closed, with obvious dangers. Paraswivels are more common in countries where high-altitude flights are made regularly, and where a parachute descent is likely to take tens of minutes rather than the tens of seconds likely in the UK.

Summary

- An emergency parachute should be part of your flying equipment.
- Choose one that will give you a true (non-gliding) descent rate of around 5.5m/sec (never more than 7.5m/sec) at your total weight in flight - including the weight of your glider.
- Preferably choose a certified emergency parachute
- Make sure that it is correctly connected to your harness and correctly installed (so that it can be deployed when you want, and won't deploy unintentionally.)
- Maintain it properly (which includes having it repacked regularly).
- Make sure you know how to use it, and use it when you need to!

Helmets

Over the past forty years there has been a great deal of research into helmet technology, and the recent European CE standard 'Helmets for Airborne Sports' (EN 966) has benefited enormously from this accumulated knowledge.

A helmet's effectiveness can only be measured by expensive controlled testing of transmitted 'g' loads and other parameters, so you should place your trust in the CE standard and should only consider buying a helmet that conforms and is marked accordingly.

The helmet's function

We wear helmets to try to prevent head injury, especially brain damage. The major cause of brain injury in an accident is through acceleration or deceleration of the brain. Think of the brain as a jelly in a jar: if a person falls over and bangs their head on a kerbstone, then the head is brought to a very sudden stop, but the brain inside tends to continue moving, before impacting the side of the skull and ricocheting back. This can cause bruising, bleeding or even tearing of the brain. Minor brain 'shake' can result in concussion and amnesia, while greater accelerations can cause permanent brain damage and even death.

The helmet's primary role is therefore as a shock-absorber, to help minimise such injury. The principal factor in providing the necessary shock-absorption is the helmet's impact liner, which is usually constructed from very precisely constituted expanded polystyrene foam that crushes progressively on impact.

The other protective functions of airsports helmets are to minimise local deformation of the skull (and consequent skull fractures) by spreading any impact point loads (the shell and liner both play a part in this), and to minimise the chance of any object penetrating the skull. For this reason the outer shell is designed to have some resistance to penetration.

Of course, none of these protective functions can be achieved if the helmet falls off your head during an accident, so an efficient retention system is a key requirement with any type of helmet.

Buying a helmet

The CE standard 'Helmets for Airborne Sports' details shock absorbency, penetration resistance and retention system requirements that a helmet must meet if it is to be legally sold for airsports use. Besides this, the helmet type has to comply with certain design requirements (ensuring adequate field of vision and head mobility) and it must be clearly marked and supplied with certain user information.

How can you be sure that the helmet you are buying meets this standard? This is easy: first check that the helmet carries a CE mark, then check the label on the helmet: it will give the number of the standard, which is EN 966. (There may be national prefixes such as BSEN 966 or DINEN 966 but the number will always contain the EN 966 element.) It will also give a set of code letters identifying the helmet category: helmets for hang gliding and paragliding are coded HPG. So if you buy a CE-marked helmet with a label showing it complies with EN 966 in the HPG category, then you are buying a helmet built specifically for our sport which is certain to provide a high level of protection while still remaining compatible with our activities.

Once you have identified a selection of helmets meeting this standard you should then decide whether you want full-face or open-face style. Both styles have their good and bad points; in airsports usage there is no clear evidence that one is always better than the other, so choose according to your personal preferences. Now try several helmets on and select the one that gives you the most comfortable close fit. With it unfastened, check that there is no side-to-side movement. Then, with the helmet fastened securely, attempt to pull or roll the helmet from your head. Be fairly brutal in this, especially when attempting to roll it forward off your head by lifting it at the back of your neck. (If it comes off you may find that you can adjust the retention straps. If, despite careful strap adjustment, you can still get the fastened helmet off your head, reject it.) Finally you should check that your vision is unimpeded and that you can swivel your head freely to look over both shoulders.

Caring for the helmet

Once you have bought your helmet, do not paint it or cover it with stickers unless you are sure that these will not attack the shell. As part of EN 966, a warning will be carried on the helmet if the shell is made from a material known to be adversely affected by contact with hydrocarbons, cleaning fluids, paints, transfers or other extraneous additions, so be guided by this.

Look after your helmet, and be careful not to drop it, as its ability to protect you may be diminished. Change your helmet after a bump – once the cell walls of the expanded polystyrene 'bubbles' have been buckled, they lose a large proportion of their strength, even though they appear to have sprung back to the original shape.

Helmets do not last for ever. Sweat, ultraviolet light, temperature changes, damp and general wear and tear will all take their toll. Five years is about the limit that a helmet should be expected to last, so any helmet older than that should be replaced.

Finally, and at the risk of stating the obvious, you should remain aware that even the very best helmets can only provide a strictly finite amount of protection – so don't buy a new helmet and start thinking that you are Captain Invincible!

Paraglider back pads (back 'protectors')

The current situation

Work has been carried out in Europe to study the effectiveness of various impact pads or back-protection systems. This work has shown that the 'back protectors' previously on sale (around the year 2000) included some that were literally worse than useless. On the brighter side, this work has also shown that it is possible to produce some sort of back-protection system for a paraglider harness that has some protective benefit – although this is limited and a PLF will always be much more effective! However, at the moment you have virtually no way of knowing whether the back pad you are considering buying represents the ultimate in 21st-century protective technology or a significant danger to your health which would be better left well alone.

The ideal back pad

First, what is this 'protector' supposed to protect you from? Let's look at the list for helmets: impact shock (from hitting the ground hard), point impact (from landing on a small rock) and penetrative injury (from being skewered by a spike).

Impact shock

A back pad should be able to absorb and reduce the forces produced when you hit the ground. The damage done to your body will be a function of the force with which you hit the ground, and that will be (as always) mass × acceleration. In this case the acceleration is negative, and therefore referred to as deceleration. If you can do something to reduce the deceleration you will reduce the force in direct proportion – and could reasonably expect a corresponding reduction in your injuries.

The best way of reducing deceleration is to increase the stopping distance, and this can be achieved by placing a layer of material between the ground and the pilot. The difficult part is to find a material that will progressively deform during the impact and so provide smooth deceleration. (A PLF massively increases the stopping distance, and sheds the load progressively. That is why they are so effective.)

Special energy-absorbing foam can be effective, as can expanded polystyrene, progressively deforming structures, and controlled-leak airbags. But the science is very involved: the wrong grade of foam can actually increase the risk of injury, as can an airbag that bursts. Unfortunately the only way of evaluating the shock-absorption qualities of any such device is to test it in the laboratory. The experts can't judge the shock-absorbing qualities of a particular design or material by look or feel – so there is no chance that the layman will be able to.

You should also bear in mind that the research mentioned earlier shows that the **best** 'protector' current science could provide (and money could buy!) would struggle to save a pilot from back injury in a drop from only 2 metres (6.5ft).

Point impact

If you fall on a rock, your back protector should spread the impact over as large an area as possible, thus minimising injury. To do this it would probably need to have a shell, perhaps made from some sort of plastic, polycarbonate, fibreglass or Kevlar. But there are serious drawbacks to shells, especially rigid ones, in that they will only support those areas of the body in contact with them. If you sit in a rigid shell which hits the ground, those parts of the body within the shell will come to a rapid halt, while the unsupported parts carry on moving. The force is therefore focused on these areas. This is not just theory: many pilots using rigid shell 'protectors' have suffered severe back injury to the upper back in backside-first impacts. The point of injury was where their rigid 'protector' finished – and had concentrated the loads. **Avoid any 'protector' that has a rigid shell.**

Penetrative injury

Such injuries are virtually unheard of. If you feel that you must protect against this risk, you will need a very heavy-duty shell, possibly made from some sort of plastic, polycarbonate, fibreglass, Kevlar, titanium, or similar material, with some complex articulation to avoid the dangers of rigid shells.

Other requirements

The ideal back protector should also be rugged and lightweight, and should present no restriction to movement (so you can still do a PLF).

Conclusions

In an uncontrolled backward or backside-first impact, a good back pad should lessen the impact force by a small percentage – and it may also prove useful if the ground is rough. But there is presently no easy way of identifying the good back pads. If you are buying a back pad, avoid any with a one-piece rigid shell, demand written evidence of any scientific testing carried out on the product, and try to find out what qualifications the designer has.

Even if you do find a back pad which you believe to be the best, you should treat it like a parachute and make every effort to ensure that you never have to use it. Fly in less turbulent conditions and places. Fly a 'safe' canopy. Fly in a fairly upright flying position: this will help ensure that if disaster strikes you will arrive 'crumple zone' (i.e. legs) first. An upright flying position should also help you perform an effective PLF. A PLF will always be far more effective than a back pad at absorbing energy!

Hang-glider wheels

All low-airtime hang-glider pilots should fly with a set of wheels fitted to the glider base-bar. These can dramatically reduce the chance of injury (to the pilot or glider) during a failed take-off or landing. In this case size does matter, and you should be looking for wheels of around 23cm (9in) diameter. (Smaller wheels have little chance of rolling on unprepared ground.) Wheels are mandatory for pilots learning to tow or aerotow, and for dual flying. They are strongly recommended passive-safety aids for pilots of all abilities.

The only time when wheels may cause problems is when launching from ramps on alpine sites. Here the ability to steady the glider by standing it securely on its base-bar can be very useful, especially if the wind or thermals are making 'choosing the moment' rather demanding.

If your glider is fitted with a trimmer that involves operating a cord cleated on the base-bar you will need one wheel to have a specially adapted non-rotating hub. These are available from a number of hang-gliding equipment retailers.

Emergency pack

Emergency packs for paragliding or hang gliding are available from many schools and dealers. These typically include a bridle knife, a whistle, dental floss (useful if you're in a tree for passing down to your rescuers so they can attach a proper rope), pencil and paper.

Chapter 8: Harnesses, connectors, hang-loops, clothing

Harnesses

Paragliding and hang-gliding harnesses come in a bewildering variety of types, sizes, and colours, with an equally bewildering number of special straps, pockets, pulleys and so on. This chapter should help guide you through this maze.

Irrespective of whether you fly hang gliders or paragliders, or whether you intend to buy a new glider or a used one, the priorities when choosing a harness are to ensure that it is strong enough, holds you securely, and is suitable for the task. Beyond that you should choose one that is easy to use and comfortable, as you will hopefully be spending a considerable amount of time in it. (Flying with an uncomfortable and ill-fitting harness is a guaranteed way to make your flights short!) Make sure that at least you have a hang in the harness before you buy, but ideally 'fly before you buy' as this will give the most accurate impression of the harness. And bear in mind that your harness will almost certainly be kept longer than your glider, so it makes good economic sense to buy a good one to start with.

Paragliding harnesses

Certification

The first thing to check is that the harness has either CEN or DHV certification. This tells you that the type has passed load tests, and so is unlikely to fall apart on you! Next check that the harness will be compatible with your wing: paragliders are certified with a given harness and the geometry of the harness is noted. To remain within certification, the glider must only be flown with that harness or one with the same geometry (see 'Stability' on page 65).

Condition and build quality

Look at the stitching – particularly around stress points such as leg-loops, shoulder-straps, hang-points and buckles. Examine the buckles and clasps – they should ideally be made from stainless metals rather than being chrome-plated, and they should certainly not be made from cheap plastic materials.

Comfort

The seat should be long enough to support your thighs fully, yet not so long that it digs into the back of your knees. The seat should also be wide enough to accommodate your backside, yet not so big that it allows you to slip about. The back of the harness should give support to your back, and the arrangement of the straps should allow you to attain a comfortable flying position. Make sure that the straps fit comfortably across your shoulders and chest (particularly important for female pilots) and make sure there are no straps digging into your back.

Adjustment

Paraglider harnesses are very unusual in aviation in that they are worn quite loose. If you tighten the harness too much you will find it impossible to stand upright for taking off and landing. Get your dealer or instructor to help adjust it so that it is just snug when you stand upright. Then check that it is still easy to get into the seat just by sitting back.

Check that the harness allows an easy transition between a sitting-back flying position and an upright flying position without the need to pull on risers or adjust straps in flight. This is particularly important when preparing to land or when flying in turbulent air. (Avoid very supine flying positions – these can make it very difficult to get upright for landing, especially in an emergency, so making an impact onto your back much more likely. They also increase the chances of getting the risers twisted in a spin or aggravated collapse.)

Emergency-parachute system

Check that the harness has the facility to mount an emergency-parachute system, either internally or externally (depending on your preference) – and be sure that it will accept the size of parachute system that you require. Check the location of the deployment handle – for example, if you are a left-handed pilot are you happy to have the deployment handle on the right?

Storage space

The harness should have plenty of space for tucking away glider bags, back pad, camera, and food and drink.

Harness geometry

There are three main geometry types for paraglider harnesses: the classic, the cross-braced and the semi-cross-braced. These different layouts significantly affect the way that pilot weightshift is transmitted into the risers (and hence to the canopy) and, with the mechanism running in reverse, the way that the pilot is supported during canopy disturbances and collapses. Unsurprisingly, the 'feel' of the glider is also altered. (See Chapter 12 for information on weightshift technique.)

The **classic harness** is a descendant of the parascending/parachuting 'leg-loop' harnesses, but with the addition of a seat board. They have a single strap across the chest, and can also have all the usual comfort padding and fittings.

These harnesses allow very easy weightshifting, and give you enormous feedback from the wing. This can be valuable for knowing what the canopy is doing, and in getting early warning of conditions getting turbulent, but it can make for a very alarming ride in any turbulence. This alarm is not misplaced: in a collapse you will fall to the collapsed side, which will almost certainly aggravate the situation and complicate re-inflation.

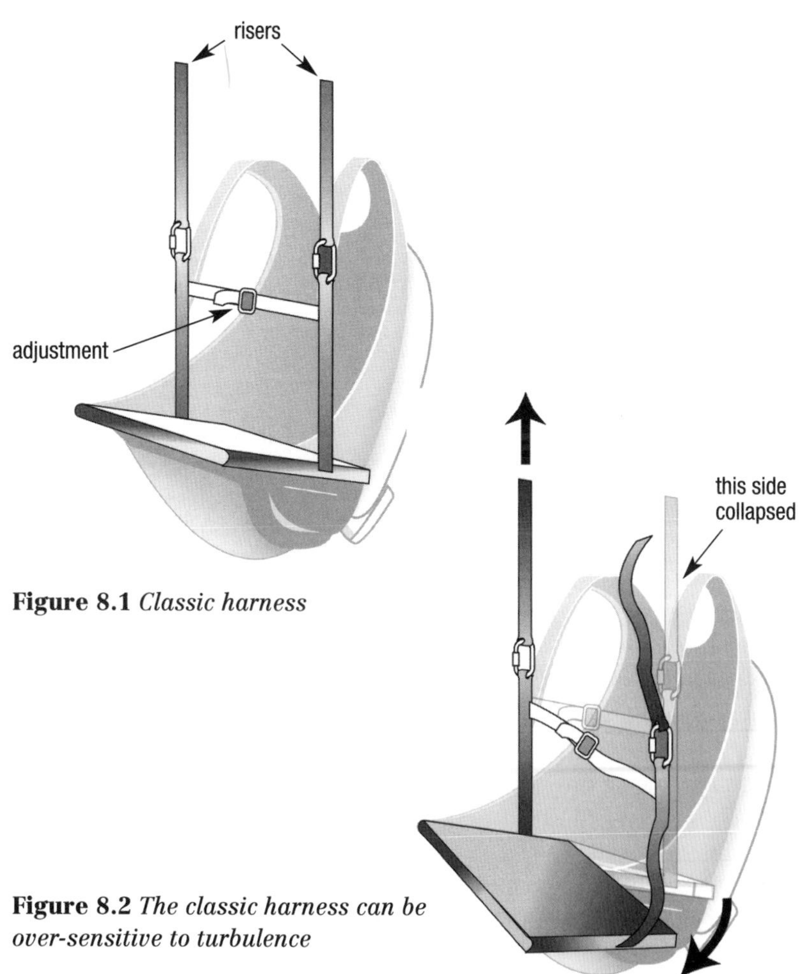

Figure 8.1 *Classic harness*

Figure 8.2 *The classic harness can be over-sensitive to turbulence*

The **cross-braced harness** replaces the single chest strap with two separate diagonal straps which cross, forming an X in front of the pilot. On some designs the cross-bracing straps are of fixed length, but more often they are adjustable.

The cross-bracing makes the harness very stable, but inhibits weightshift; if it is done up tight then no weightshift is possible at all. Feedback from the canopy is also reduced, and this can make the wing feel very dead. With the cross-bracing loose, the glider will feel very responsive when flown in smooth conditions, but alarmingly twitchy when flown in turbulence.

In a collapse you won't fall to one side – which is much less disconcerting than the classic harness. Instead the cross-bracing transfers the pilot's weight to the inflated side, which can actually aid recovery by helping to straighten the course, and by increasing the internal pressure.

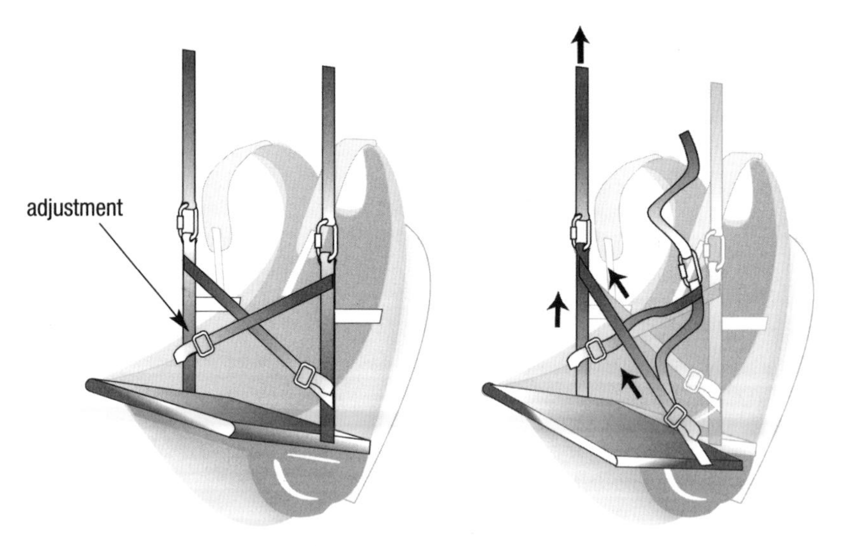

Figure 8.3 *The transfer of load in a cross-braced harness can make it feel reassuringly stable*

The **semi-cross-braced harness** is effectively a combination of the classic and cross-braced types. Effectively the X of a cross-braced harness has a short chest strap inserted in the middle. With the chest strap loose, the harness behaves very much like a classic harness: with the chest strap drawn tight, the harness behaves like a cross-braced harness. Most modern harnesses are of this type. The drawbacks are that they are difficult to adjust in the air (without totally releasing the controls – which you should never do), and that adjusting the cross-bracing also alters the distance between the risers, which can increase the likelihood of twisting the risers if the canopy spins.

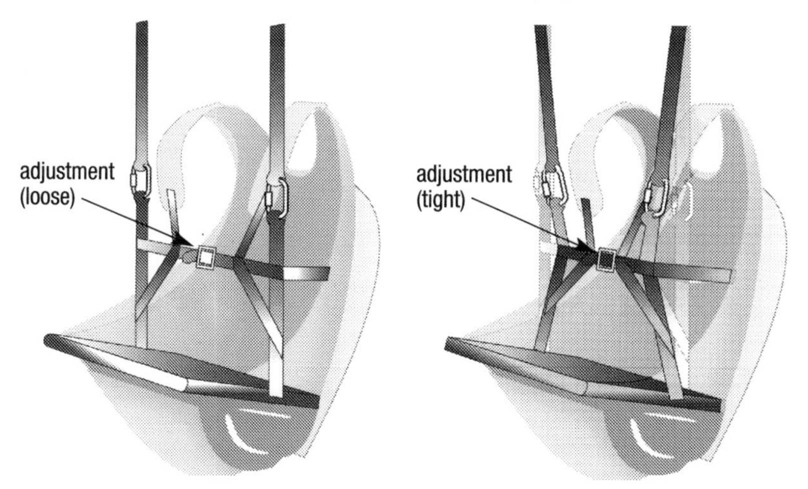

Figure 8.4 *The semi-cross-braced harness offers a good compromise*

Stability

As will be apparent from the previous section, the type of harness and the way it is set up can have a massive bearing on the stability and recovery characteristics of a paraglider. It is for this reason that the CEN paraglider certification wing-tip Verification Placard includes details of the type of harness and the key dimensions. When you buy a new canopy you can see the label, note which harness should be fitted and what the measurements should be, and make sure that you use the same setup. However, most of the current harnesses conform to a standard geometry in that the hang points are a set distance from the seat and a set distance apart. This standard distance is usually about 40cm (15-16in) for both dimensions. The DHV records a harness classification on the paraglider's Verification Placard: GH or GX. This refers to their harness certification categories – see the table below.

GH	The canopy may be flown with any harness other than fully cross-braced types. (If a semi-cross-braced harness has adjustable cross-bracing, this must not be tight.)
GX	The canopy must only be flown with fully cross-braced harnesses (those harnesses which the DHV have classified as belonging in group GX).
GHGX or blank	There are no harness restrictions.

Hang-gliding harnesses

The first harness you encountered will almost certainly have been the **training harness** at school – a fabric apron with suspension webbing and ropes. You may have progressed to a **stirrup harness** for your first flights in prone position – this is similar to the training harness, but with a bar attached by ropes on each side against which you push your feet.

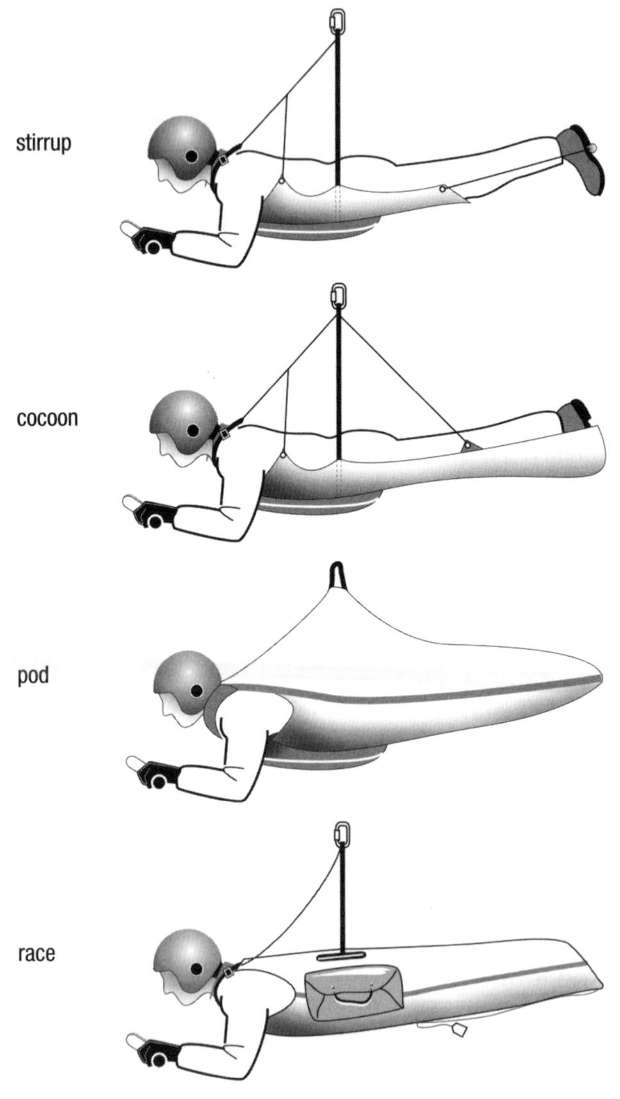

Figure 8.5 *Hang-gliding harness types*

Cocoon harnesses were popular for a few years in the early 1980s but are rarely seen now. Once you are in the prone position the cocoon harness is like a hammock, so you can relax into it at full length, but the back is open. They can be comfortable, though they are not as warm as a pod, and they are troublesome to run with – to the extent of being a hazard in a nil-wind take-off unless some special technique is used.

Next we come to the **pod**. This used to be the most successful harness type, combining ease of use (once you've got it on!) with high comfort levels. Generally these harnesses have a 'hump-back' appearance, a fully enclosed top half (which the pilot has to step into and pull up like a tight-fitting pair of one-legged trousers) and a zip-up 'boot' for your legs and feet. This gives little mobility with the zip done up (so don't forget to unzip before you land!), but in flight you should be warm and comfortable. Most of these harnesses were made of a stiff fabric which means that the boot of the harness is easy to locate with your feet without having to look for it after take-off.

Finally we get to the **'race'** harness. This is a variation on the pod theme, where generally ease of use has been sacrificed for a 'go-faster' low-drag appearance. They are invariably 'front loaders', consisting of a top which is put on like a waistcoat and then zipped and buckled up, and a zip-up 'undercarriage bay' for your legs and feet. Usually the suspension point attaches to a solid back plate or a system of rods, with a sliding arrangement that is supposed to allow you to get upright for take-off and landing.

Certification

Only the DHV has a certification scheme for hang-glider harnesses. It is well worth choosing a type that has passed these tests. With non-certified types you are taking it on trust that the manufacturer knows what he is doing!

Condition and build quality

Look at the stitching – particularly around stress points such as leg loops, shoulder straps, hang points and buckles. Examine the buckles and clasps – they should ideally be made from stainless metals rather than being chrome-plated, and they should certainly not be made from cheap plastic materials.

Comfort and adjustment

New harnesses can be bought 'off the shelf' or made-to-measure. Usually the ready-made harnesses come in a variety of sizes. There should be no such thing as an uncomfortable harness if you buy new. Women may like to note that a woman's centre of gravity is generally 5-8cm (2-3in) lower than that of a man of similar height, so the made-to-measure service should take account of this in positioning the hang point correspondingly further down the back of the harness.

Some of the pod-style harnesses have an adjustable foot stirrup that can be moved to accommodate small differences in leg length. Other than that, there is effectively no adjustment possible with modern harnesses. If it isn't comfortable when you buy it, it won't get any better.

Ease of use

The other important factor to look for is ease of getting out of the prone position. You should be able to swing from prone to upright in one fluid, unimpeded movement, and stay there. Unfortunately, many of the current close-fitting competition harnesses make this movement very difficult. For this reason such harnesses are to be avoided until either you have the experience to cope with this level of difficulty (say 50 hours) or – preferably – until the manufacturers improve their designs. The 'hump-back' pods do not suffer from this defect and so are much easier to use.

Check the operation of the zip. Some seem to involve a complicated system of tabs and strings, and at least one make has these located right next to the parachute-deployment handle. Pulling the wrong one could spoil your day! (See Chapter 19 for advice on what to do if the zip gets stuck.)

Emergency-parachute system mounting

Check that the harness has the facility to mount an emergency-parachute system, and that it is in the position where you want it. Make sure that the container will accept the size of parachute system that you require. Check the location of the deployment handle – for example, if you are a left-handed pilot are you happy to have the deployment handle on the right? Do not compromise on these points!

Storage space

The harness should have plenty of space for tucking away a lightweight glider bag (cross-country bag), food and drink, and your camera.

Special harness considerations if towing

Check that the harness has purpose-designed tow attachment points: some harnesses have apparently ideally placed loops that are not designed for towing from (and are not strong enough)! Towing with a chest-mounted release applies abnormal loads to the harness, by trying to pull the front of the harness away from the pilot. Guard against this by either using a back strap on an open-backed harness or by only using a fully enclosed harness. Cocoon harnesses must not be used (other than for wheeled launches), as it is far too easy to trip over the bottom of the apron. Pod harnesses are ideal.

All harnesses must be checked regularly to ensure that the tow-bridle/release mounting loops are secure, and that the tow-bridle/release remains virtually in the 'at rest' position (relative to the pilot's chest) when under towing loads, as otherwise it can jam against the base-bar.

Connectors

For both paragliders and hang gliders the main connection points are the harness-to-glider connections and the emergency-parachute connections. Karabiners and maillons (connectors developed for climbing and available from most good outdoor shops) are invariably used in these locations. Generally karabiners are quickest and easiest to use, so these are preferable where the parts will frequently be connected and disconnected (as with the hang-glider harness-to-glider connections). Maillons are most often used where the connection is rarely disturbed (e.g. the emergency-parachute bridle attachment).

Karabiners and maillons

Karabiners

Generally karabiners have a hinged gate to allow the attachment of ropes and webbing. While this may be a simple 'snaplink' spring-loaded gate, most gates have some form of positive locking mechanism to prevent them from being opened inadvertently. The main forms are the screw gate (a simple threaded sleeve screwed down over the gate) and the 'twistlock' (where a spring-return sleeve is rotated half a turn to unlock the gate, springing back to lock it). Plain gate (snaplink) karabiners should not be used for paragliding or hang gliding, as it is too easy for the gate to be opened inadvertently (trapping straps that shouldn't be in there, and releasing straps that should!). Even with twistlock gates it is possible that contact with a backup loop or similar could rotate the sleeve and open the gate, so the safest type is the screw gate.

Maillons

Maillons invariably use a long threaded sleeve-nut to bridge the short open portion. This can tend to unscrew, so it should be nipped up finger-tight and then given a further one-eighth turn with a small spanner. (A couple of drops of 'threadlock' from a car accessory shop will ensure it stays put.) Be careful not to over-tighten alloy maillons as they can be damaged.

Materials
Connectors are made of steel or aluminium alloys. Steel connectors are very hard-wearing but heavier than their alloy counterparts. Alloy connectors are as strong and much lighter, but are significantly weakened by scratches, general abrasion and salt-water corrosion. Because of this, alloy connectors need much more frequent inspection and replacement. If you tend to fly at the coast you should use steel connectors to prevent corrosion problems.

Connector size
The quoted size of a connector is the general diameter of the material from which it is made (e.g. 6mm). Larger sizes than are strictly necessary for strength are usually chosen, because a larger diameter is much kinder in applying loads to webbing.

Connector strength
Connectors are only capable of supporting their design load with the load applied end-to-end and with the gate closed (with the gate open they can lose over two-thirds of their rated strength). A connector's strength across the minor axis is a small fraction of its quoted strength, so steps should be taken to ensure that the loads are not applied in this direction.The usual method is to place rubber bands (or electrical tape) around the webbing loops so that they grip the connector tightly in the desired position.

Karabiners are primarily designed for use with rope, which slides into the corners of D-shaped designs, so correctly applying the load along the spine. Avoid using stiff, wide webbing with karabiners with these angled ends, as load spread along the end face can lead to both the webbing and the karabiner failing significantly below their rated strengths.

All good-quality connectors will have their strength stamped on the spine; they are now marked in newtons (the SI unit of force), but older ones may still be marked in kilograms. Karabiners are marked with their breaking strain, while maillons are marked with their safe working load or working load limit (SWL or WLL). The safe working load or working load limit is usually 20 percent of the breaking strain, so make sure that you understand the markings. (Beware of cheap imitation maillons that have no tensile strength marked on them. Buy only from reputable sources.)

With hang gliders, for the main suspension connection it is usual to use a 12-mm karabiner with a breaking strain of 2500kg (24.5kN). With paragliders it should be assumed that the entire load is going to be taken on one connector (this will happen in a major deflation), so again a connector with a safe working load limit of at least 500kg (5kN) is required. This will usually mean using a pair of 6-mm stainless maillons (or 12-mm karabiners).

Connector care

- Check regularly for burrs and sharp edges, surface cracks, distortion and corrosion.
- Keep them clean and free from grit by washing in warm water with a drop of washing-up liquid. Allow them to dry at room temperature in a well-ventilated room.
- Wash alloy connectors thoroughly after use in sea air.
- The gate should have a smooth action with an efficient locking system. It can be lubricated with silicon spray (or WD40), but wipe off any excess.
- Avoid any contact with acids or alkalis.

Parachute bridle attachments

A good emergency parachute of the correct size should never give you more than a 15-g opening shock, and you will only get anywhere near this sort of figure in a free-fall deployment. So a connector that can withstand a load of at least fifteen times your all-up weight in flight **without exceeding 50 percent of its breaking strain (or no more than 2.5 x the SWL)** will be more than adequate. This means that a hang glider pilot will typically need to use an 8-mm standard oval stainless maillon rapide (1,100kg/11kN SWL). With paragliding there are usually two connections to the harness, but each of these needs to be individually capable of taking the entire maximum load. (Don't assume load sharing.) 7-mm standard oval stainless maillons should be suitable (900kg/9kN SWL).

With normal soft 25-mm tubular webbing emergency parachute bridles, you should use standard oval stainless maillons, as these tend to self-align under load. If you are connecting wider, stiffer webbing then some form of quadrilateral-shaped maillon may be better suited, but make sure that the loads are applied along the major axis by preventing the maillon from rotating.

Hang gliding: the parachute will use a single long bridle that should be connected to the main suspension point of the harness. (If the parachute bridle is attached to the main clip-in karabiner then the pilot is not protected against karabiner failure, and the parachute load may be incorrectly applied to the karabiner. Indeed, there is a possibility of a three-way loading that could destroy the karabiner.)

Paragliding: the parachute may use a single short bridle or have a two-riser design.

Single-bridle parachutes need to be connected via a 'Y' bridle to the two attachment points built into the harness, one at each shoulder. (Some older harnesses may not have shoulder emergency-parachute attachment points. In these cases it is permissible to attach to the main paraglider attachment points, but pay special attention to the bridle routing and possible interference between the connectors.)

Two-riser parachutes are connected directly, one riser to each shoulder attachment point.

Fabric-to-fabric connections: These should be avoided wherever possible. Fabric junctions may fail under shock loads because of rapid temperature increase. The effect is most likely when soft and hard synthetic tapes are looped together. Join bridles, loops etc with metal maillons or karabiners. If a fabric junction is unavoidable, one of the loops should be securely sheathed in natural (non-synthetic) material such as cotton.

Hang-loops (hang glider)

Most modern hang gliders are supplied complete with hang-loops and backup loops constructed by the glider manufacturer. If you are a follower of the 'belt and braces' approach to personal safety, consider getting your backup loop from a climbing shop – complete with a sewn tab giving its guaranteed breaking strength and a UIAA stamp.

You will be looking for a 'sling' (a closed loop), made from nylon or perhaps one of the modern materials sold under various trade names (Spectra, Dyneema and Technora), with a breaking strain of around 2,000kg (20kN). 'Lark's foot' this securely around the keel (see Figure 8.6), ideally over a piece of grip tape attached to the keel.

British climbing and safety equipment manufacturers produce slings to BS 5750 quality-assurance standard. This means that all sewn joints are of a set pattern, with the thread, number of stitches, and rows of stitches quantified in great detail. Some of these manufacturers use computer-automated sewing machinery in order to guarantee consistency.

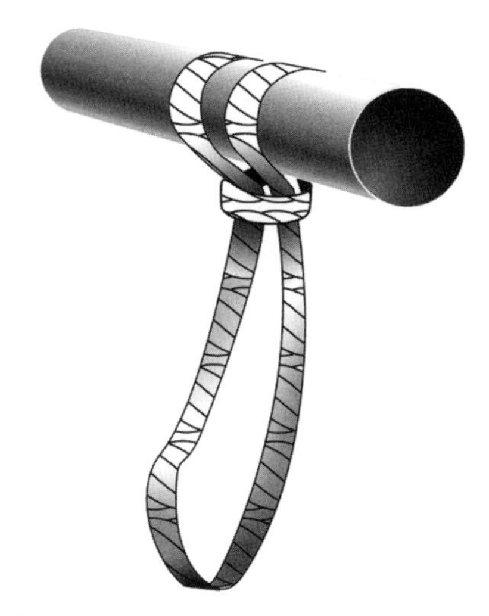

Figure 8.6 *Hang-loop 'lark's foot'*

Webbing care

Inspect all hang-loops regularly for cuts, abrasion, chafing and stitching damage. Replace them at the first sign of damage. (An otherwise pristine loop with a couple of small nicks in one edge was found to have lost one third of its strength. On other types a nick in the edge can lead to the webbing unravelling!) Be especially vigilant if your glider employs a kingpost hang-point, as in this case there are more sewn joints and two narrow-radius webbing-to-metal bearing points.

Do not put knots in a sling. These can reduce its strength by up to 50 percent, the average reduction being of the order of 30 percent. Wash out mud and grit with warm water, and dry the sling slowly in an airy place. Do not leave it exposed to direct sunlight, and do not leave it wet. Avoid all contact with solvents, acids, alkalis and similar chemicals. If the webbing surface has gone fluffy (surface fibrillation), replace the loop. Always fly with a backup loop – these have saved many pilots' lives!

Clothing

It is important to be comfortable and warm when flying, as this allows the brain to concentrate on more important things, such as flying the glider. Even on a hot summer's day it gets pretty cold up at the clouds: it also gets pretty cold hanging about on windy hilltops! The most important factor in staying warm is combating wind-chill, so you need clothing that is both windproof and insulated. Most of the flying suits currently on the market have these features, and are available in colours ranging from the subtle to the outrageous. Two or three thin layers are better than one thick one, so buy a flying suit that gives you enough room to wear a fleece underneath it on colder days.

Gloves are important, as it is usually the fingers that get cold first. Good gloves should keep the hands warm, yet still give enough feel to allow you to fly the glider properly and under full control. (For winter flying some hang-glider pilots use 'bar mitts'. These are permanently attached to the base-bar, and once airborne the pilot slides his hands into them.)

For paragliding it is essential to have a suitable pair of boots. Boots should have soles with good grip and should give support to the ankles. Again there are a number of boots on the market which are specifically designed for paragliding, most of which are good if a little expensive. A good pair of hill-walking boots will do the job just as well, provided that the lace hooks are taped up to prevent lines getting caught in them. Paragliding boots tend to be a little lighter than walking boots but are not always as robust.

You should consider wearing **sunglasses** when flying in bright conditions, to shield the eyes from wind-blast and from harmful rays. Good-quality sunglasses will eliminate nearly all ultraviolet and infrared light. Some lens types also enhance cloud definition, giving better visibility when high. Choose a pair with polycarbonate lenses (not cheap plastic or glass which could damage your eyes in an accident), and ensure that they can be worn comfortably under your helmet.

But remember – in failing light conditions, such as those encountered late in the day, sunglasses can dangerously restrict visibility. This is especially important when descending from a last-light flight where the light levels high up above the ridge are suddenly exchanged for the near-dark of the valley bottom.

Chapter 9: Instruments, navigation tools and related equipment

Instruments

Although paragliders and hang gliders can be flown without any instruments at all, they are valuable aids to soaring, navigation and extracting maximum performance.

On the debit side, instruments can go wrong. They should be used only as an aid to flying, and not relied on for safety.

Altimeter

An altimeter is used to indicate the glider's height. This information is essential if flying under or over 'no-go' airspace (see Chapter 24). Atmospheric pressure reduces as you gain height, and an altimeter is effectively a barometer that measures the air pressure and indicates this on a dial (or more commonly an LCD display) calibrated in feet or metres of height. Most paragliding and hang-gliding instrument packages allow the pilot to switch between two or three different altimeter functions. This enables the pilot to read his vertical position as **Height** (vertical distance above take-off), **Altitude** (vertical distance above mean sea level) or **Flight Level** (vertical distance above the 1013.2-millibar pressure level). (See the section on 'Using an altimeter' in Chapter 24.)

Variometer

This is another pressure-sensitive instrument that indicates your rate of ascent or descent. This information is essential for efficient thermal- and wave-soaring, and useful for ridge-soaring. A visual readout (by LCD display or meter) is usually combined with a variable audible tone (to save you having to take your eyes away from the more important task of looking where you are going!). Some varios have a range of options, with an audio tone for up, and a different tone for down, with variable thresholds to control when these tones start. (It is usually possible to turn them off altogether for some peace and quiet!)

Averager

This feature, included in many varios, gives the average rate of climb over a set period. This period can usually be altered, depending on the unit. An averager gives an overall impression of the lift and irons out short bursts that may give the impression that the lift is stronger than it really is.

Alti-vario

Many manufacturers package the altimeter and variometer together into one neat unit: the alti-vario. An alti-vario is an essential purchase for those wishing to make the best of thermic conditions. There are a large number of units to choose from, with a variety of features and covering quite a price span.

Total energy

If, while searching for rising air or thermalling, you allow your airspeed to vary, the vario will report these minor climbs and dives. This can give you a very distorted view of the air around you. (Was that a thermal? Or was that just me slowing the glider down?) An alti-vario with a 'total energy' function (and the necessary airspeed probe) prevents this confusion by ignoring height variations resulting simply from changes in the glider's airspeed and only indicating 'genuine' rates of climb (or sink).

Airmass

On an alti-vario with an 'airmass' function, the vario will compensate for the glider's sink rate at the speed it is flying, and only indicate the rate of ascent or descent of the airmass rather than the glider. This can be very useful when flying fast to escape from an area of sinking air: after a while you start to question whether the 'six down' showing on the vario is due to the fact that you are in bad sink, or whether it is just due to the fact that you are flying so fast. If you slow up and wait for the speed to stabilise, only to find that you are still in the bad sink, you will have wasted valuable height. But if you have escaped from the sink area, flying around at high speed unnecessarily will also waste valuable height. The airmass function gives you the information you need. Again this requires an airspeed probe and information on the polar curve of the glider (see page 214).

Airspeed indicator (ASI)

The ASI indicates the speed of the glider through the air (airspeed). Like the altimeter, it actually indicates pressure changes – the pressure of the airflow at the pitot head or entry point on the instrument. This means that it can only give accurate readings if it is clear of disturbed air around the wing or structure (position error) and is pointing directly towards the airstream. Alti-varios offering this ASI facility usually require the purchase of a 'speed probe' that plugs into the unit and either attaches to the glider or hangs below it on a wire.

For ordinary flying the ASI should be used only as a guide, and it should never be relied on as a stall-warning indicator.

Barograph

This instrument records altitude at set time intervals and allows a trace of the flight to be plotted. The barograph, now usually a data-logging function of a pilot's GPS, may be officially certified to give evidence of record-breaking attempts. Most allow data to be downloaded to a PC to enable the flight to be analysed further.

Navigation tools and related equipment

Global Positioning System (GPS)

GPS units were originally designed for the military, but hand-held civilian versions rapidly became popular with walkers and sailors as a cheap and accurate navigational device. The GPS unit works by locking onto a number of the 24 special satellites orbiting the earth. By timing the signals from these it is able to triangulate its position to an extraordinary degree of accuracy – usually about 10 metres (33ft) or even less. Most GPS units allow waypoints (or competition turnpoints) to be stored in a route which can then be followed, the GPS being able to give heading and distance to the various way-points. In flight the unit is also able to give groundspeed and distance covered.

A GPS unit and an alti-vario used in combination are able to give competition pilots important information concerning optimum glide speeds to reach turnpoints or goal fields. For route verification GPS is now an invaluable part of the competition pilot's equipment. Their only drawback is that you have to look at them to read them, which could divert attention away from keeping a good lookout.

Compass

A compass is an essential piece of equipment when flying cross-country, especially when flying unfamiliar sites. It can be almost impossible to follow a map accurately without one, owing to constant circling in thermals and the fact that the land appears to flatten out as you gain height.

An ordinary hand-held compass will do the job, though these only work when horizontal, which leads to obvious problems in flight. The floating-ball type as used in boats is a lot better as they are not affected by the pitching and rolling of the glider. Good-quality floating-ball compasses can be expensive, however.

When using a compass to plot an intended cross-country route it is important to remember that a compass will point to magnetic north and that the grid on the map will point to true north. This difference, called the 'magnetic variation', must be taken into account when calculating bearings. Each map will state the variation when that particular map was printed – magnetic variation is not constant. In practice, hang-glider and paraglider pilots do not fly in straight lines on compass headings for hours at a time. Rather, the compass is used to give a general direction to look for your next landmark, and small inaccuracies are not important.

Map holder

There are now a number of map holders available that allow you to read maps easily while flying. Those designed for paraglider pilots generally take the form of a large, clear-fronted pocket which clips to the harness and sits on your lap in flight. The better ones allow the map to be turned for those longer flights, and also contain space for varios, compass, camera, sandwiches and other useful odds and ends. Hang-glider pilots use a holder which folds over the centre of the base-bar. In either case, the map holder is an essential piece of cross-country kit.

Camera

A camera used to be an essential piece of equipment for the competition pilot or defined cross-country flight pilot. In competitions, databack cameras were used to record the pilot's time at start-gates and turnpoints. For defined cross-country flights (e.g. 'out and returns' and 'triangles') a camera can still be used for proving that the turn-points were correctly rounded. However for competition flying (see page 268), turn-point verification is now achieved by downloading a track-log from the pilot's GPS.

For normal flying it is often nice to get a picture of your left boot while over the local area to bore your friends with in the pub. 'Point and shoot' cameras are the best for obvious reasons, and there is a vast range costing from a few pounds to several hundred pounds. The camera should be easy to get to in flight and should be secured so it can't fall. Hang-glider pilots interested in 'wing-tip' shots of themselves should pay careful attention to counterbalancing the weight of the camera with a similar weight on the opposite wing.

Radio

There are two types of radio currently in use by UK paraglider and hang-glider pilots: those on the 'air band' AM frequencies and those on the VHF FM 2-metre (Amateur) band frequencies. The use of 2-m radios from the air is currently illegal, although the BHPA Airspace Panel is working hard to change this situation. This may take some time as discussions are held at both national and EU levels. That said, most UK and European pilots use 2-m radios and the sets are readily available, reliable, efficient and cheap.

For further details see the section on 'Radios' (page 222) in Chapter 23.

Chapter 10: Tow equipment

Hang-glider winch and aerotow tow releases

In the early days of hang gliding many serious accidents occurred when pilots tried to find ways of tow-launching, based on towing the glider, as with sailplanes. The major breakthrough was the 'centre of mass' principle, which recognised that for the pilot to retain weightshift control the tow force should be directed through the combined centre of mass of the pilot and glider. (This is a point somewhere on the hang-strap just above the pilot's back.) Since that breakthrough, further refinement and experimentation over the years have revealed that safe hang-glider tow-launching is possible as long as:

- at least half the tow force goes to the pilot. (The ideal is approximately two-thirds of the force going to the pilot, but anywhere between 50 percent and 100 percent works.)
- any remaining tow force that goes to the glider is applied close to the glider's centre of gravity.

The 'tow leg' system

In the winch-based training environment the 'tow leg' system is commonly used. This system involves a glider release (fitted to the end of a short semi-flexible 'leg' attached to the glider keel in front of the kingpost), and an 'umbilical' fitted to the pilot's harness, near the hips. The towline is fitted with a large-diameter (approx. 75mm/3in) ring, and attached to this is a 'threader'. The threader is routed from the towline ring, through a ring at the end of the pilot's umbilical, back through the towline ring, and then up to the release at the end of the tow leg. This means that the tow force is applied two-thirds to the pilot and one-third to the glider, which gives a very stable tow. To release, the pilot operates a cord (this may be held permanently in the pilot's hand) which operates the clasp at the end of the tow leg. The threader 'unthreads' itself and the pilot can then fly free.

Just in case the threader fails to clear the umbilical ring, which would mean that all the tow force was now on the pilot, there is an emergency release on the umbilical. This must never be operated if the line is still attached to the tow leg – being towed 100 percent from the pilot is not life-threatening: being towed 100 percent from the glider can result in immediate and instant catastrophe!

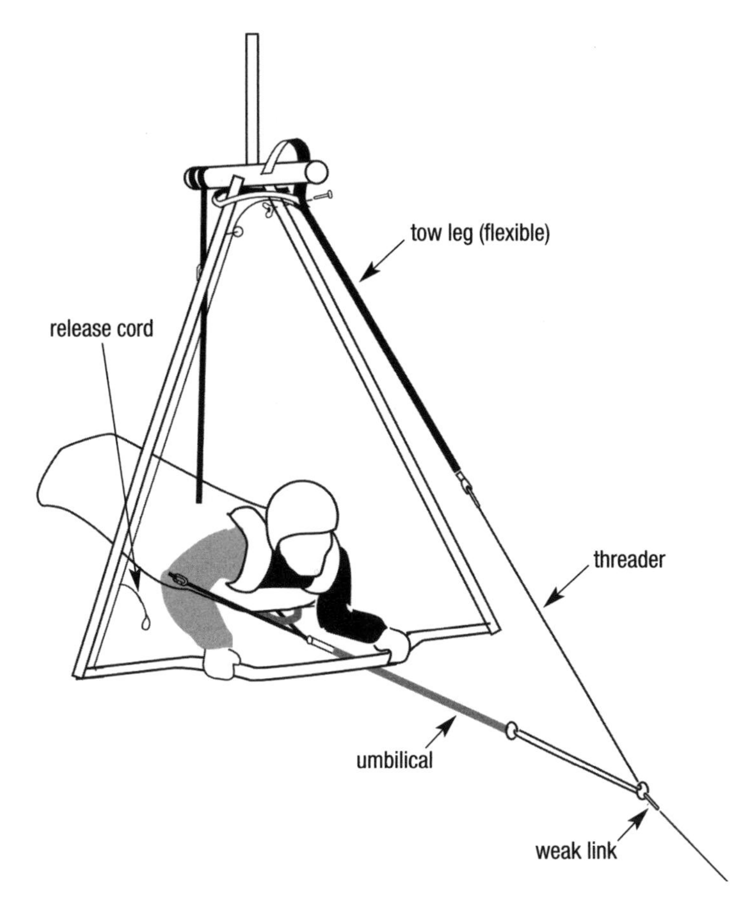

Figure 10.1 *Tow-leg bridle system (set up for winch launching*

Chest release

The chest release is used by aerotow pilots and experienced winch-launch pilots. As the name implies, this is a release mechanism built onto a spreader bar that attaches directly to the upper chest area of the pilot's harness. When using this system, the tow force is applied 100 percent to the pilot. Often these pieces of equipment incorporate two separate release mechanisms; this is for winch-launching, where the relative angle between the glider and the winch changes dramatically during the launch. To allow for this, the towline terminates with two lines, one slightly longer than the other. At take-off the shorter line coming through the control frame tows the glider. As the glider climbs, this line would eventually foul the base-bar, so the pilot releases this top line and continues the tow with the bottom line, which passes under the control frame.

Webbing-mounted release mechanisms ('spinnaker' releases) are sometimes used by aerotow pilots instead of rigid chest releases. They are light, cheap and simple, but have the down side that the cord that activates them moves around, which can make finding it very difficult in an emergency. There is also a possibility of the clasp springing back and striking the pilot's face after a high-tension release or line break.

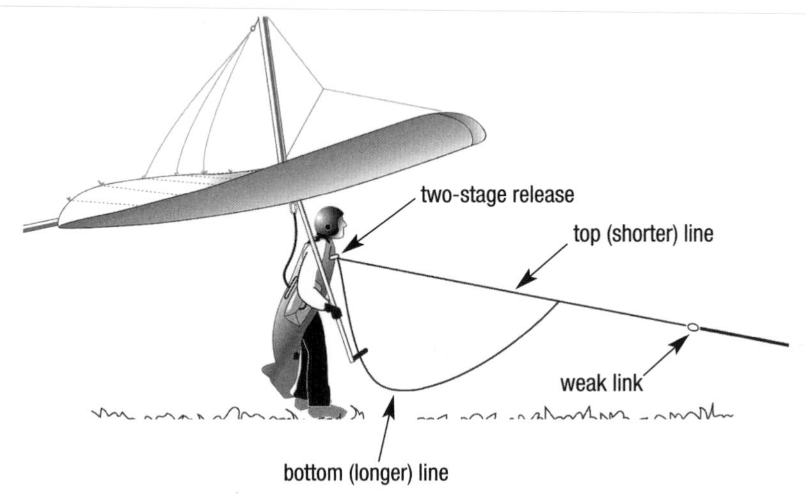

Figure 10.2 *Two-stage bridle system (set up for winch launching)*

Some points about releases:

- Ensure that the release can be operated with a one-handed single movement.
- Harness-mounted releases must be securely attached. Rigid spreader-bar chest releases should have two separate secure mountings – a single cord through the release is not sufficient.
- The release **must** operate and release the line under conditions of zero line-tension, so if for example a speed oscillation has developed the glider pilot can drop the line before the next surge.
- Pilots who already use a chest release for winch-launching are strongly recommended to use the same release for aerotowing, provided that it meets all the other requirements.
- The pilot tow load must not be asymmetrically applied as this will result in the pilot twisting.

- Be very wary of releases based on the 'three-ring circus' principle. Properly engineered, this system works beautifully, and very gentle trigger pressure operates the release even with very high towline forces. Unfortunately this isn't the case with most webbing and cord lightweight versions: on some examples the trigger pressure required at high towline forces exceeds the capabilities of the average pilot.
- Always check compatibility between the release you are using and the towline end fitting. Some clubs use a simple rope loop at the end of the towline; some use small steel rings or ovals; while others use large steel rings. Some releases that work faultlessly with a 25mm steel ring will jam solid with a rope loop. Others that work beautifully with a rope loop will lock up with a small steel oval – and so on.

Paraglider tow releases

Paragliders, like hang gliders, must also be towed from a point close to the centre of mass. This means either feeding the tow force (via a pilot-operated release mechanism) to the main risers at a position just above the maillons or karabiners, or to special built-in tow-release mounting points on the harness main risers.

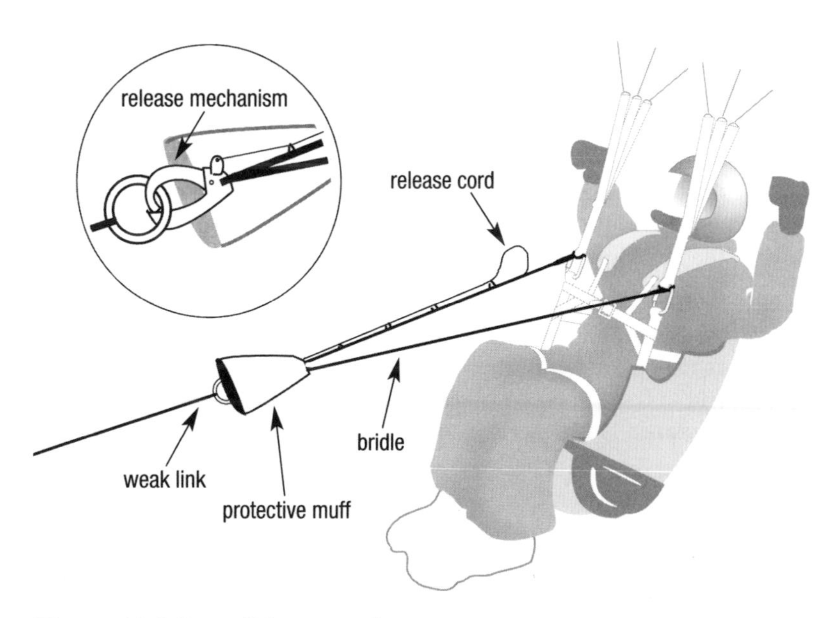

Figure 10.3 *Paraglider tow-release arrangement*

If the tow force is fed into the main risers just above the maillon or karabiner connector, then it is vital that the connector is not inadvertently wrongly loaded. A short webbing loop arranged as shown in Figure 10.4 guards against this possibility.

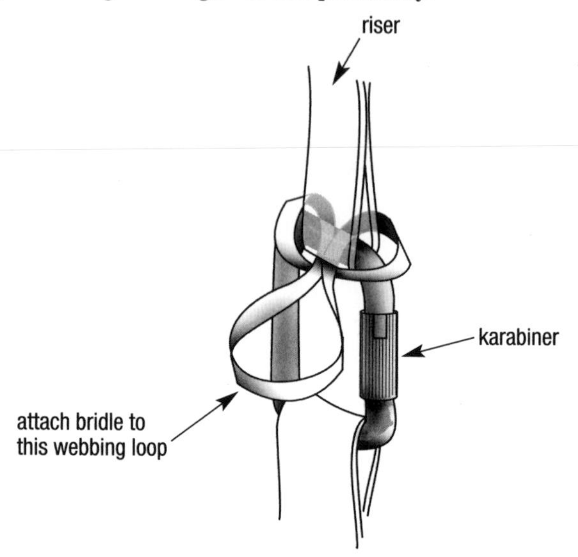

Figure 10.4 *Recommended bridle attachment*

For paraglider towing the release is usually mounted on a short 'Y'-bridle that positions the release centrally, about 30cm (12in) ahead of the attachment points. The actual release mechanism is usually either a 'three-ring circus' (adapted parachuting technology) or a spinnaker clasp (adapted sailing technology). Because of the danger of the release springing back into the pilot's face after a high-tension release or line failure, the mechanism should be encased in a protective padded muff.

Some releases sold for paraglider towing use a rigid spreader-bar mounting, much like hang-glider chest releases. These are attached to the risers using the same loops as with the other systems, but without the 'Y' bridle. Care must be taken to ensure that the ability to set the harness distance between risers correctly is not compromised.

Any springing back on release (or weak-link failure) is minimised with this system, so there is no need for the protective muff. Also the release trigger is closer to the pilot, who can operate it directly. But because the release and its mounting bar are more substantial, they could potentially pose an additional hazard in a failed landing.

SECTION 3
IMPROVING YOUR FLYING

Chapter 11: Hang-gliding techniques

Hill-launches

Flying in stronger winds

Going prone

Developed turns

Landings

Stalling

Chapter 12: Paragliding techniques

Launches

Landings

Slope-landing

Weightshift turning

Slow flight

Rapid-descent techniques

Instability and active flying

Chapter 13: 360s & approaches (hang gliders & paragliders)

360-degree turns

Approaches

Chapter 14: Tow-launching

Introduction

Training

Tow-launching in general

Signals

Winch-launching hang gliders

Tow-launching paragliders – hang gliders

Chapter 15: Soaring

Ridge-soaring

Thermal soaring

Wave

Cross-country flying

Chapter 16: Flying with others

Mixing paragliders and hang gliders

Avoiding overcrowding and conflict

Safe flying on the ridge

Safe flying in thermals

Chapter 11: Hang-gliding techniques

Hill-launches

Taking off in nil or light wind (unassisted)

There is nothing difficult about nil-wind take-offs provided that you remember that the glider has to be accelerated by running hard through stationary air until enough lift has been generated for the wing to fly. The run must be definite, enthusiastic, and long enough to obtain adequate airspeed. The acceleration should be steady and the transition from ground to air smooth, clean and free from jerks. Let's look at it stage by stage:

Flight plan and checks

- Decide your flight objectives.
- Assess the site and conditions, relating these to your hang glider and your own capabilities.
- Carry out all your normal DI and pre-flight checks.
- Plan your take-off and the flight. (In light winds there is a distinct possibility that you will be landing at the bottom of the hill – so now is the time to check the field approaches and work out a plan.)

Carefully choose your launch position. This is vitally important for an easy, safe take-off. While it may appear daunting, the ideal is to be running down a steep incline, such as the face of the hill (as long as it is not sheer!). This way gravity is aiding your efforts, and, as long as you hold the angle of attack constant, take-off is inevitable within a very few steps. (If you go to fly in continental Europe, where many take-offs are in thin air, zero-wind conditions at mountain altitudes, it is usual to find a ramp that is set at something like 45 degrees.)

Do not be tempted to 'have a run at it' from a position some way back across a flat hill-top: almost always you will arrive at the edge with insufficient airspeed. You then have the choice of lunging off semi-stalled (which usually results in a crash into the trees) or of trying to run round the edge and down the face. This change of direction means that your glider will now be meeting the relative airflow at an inappropriately nose-high angle of attack – and there is very little chance of persuading it to fly before the trees arrest your progress!

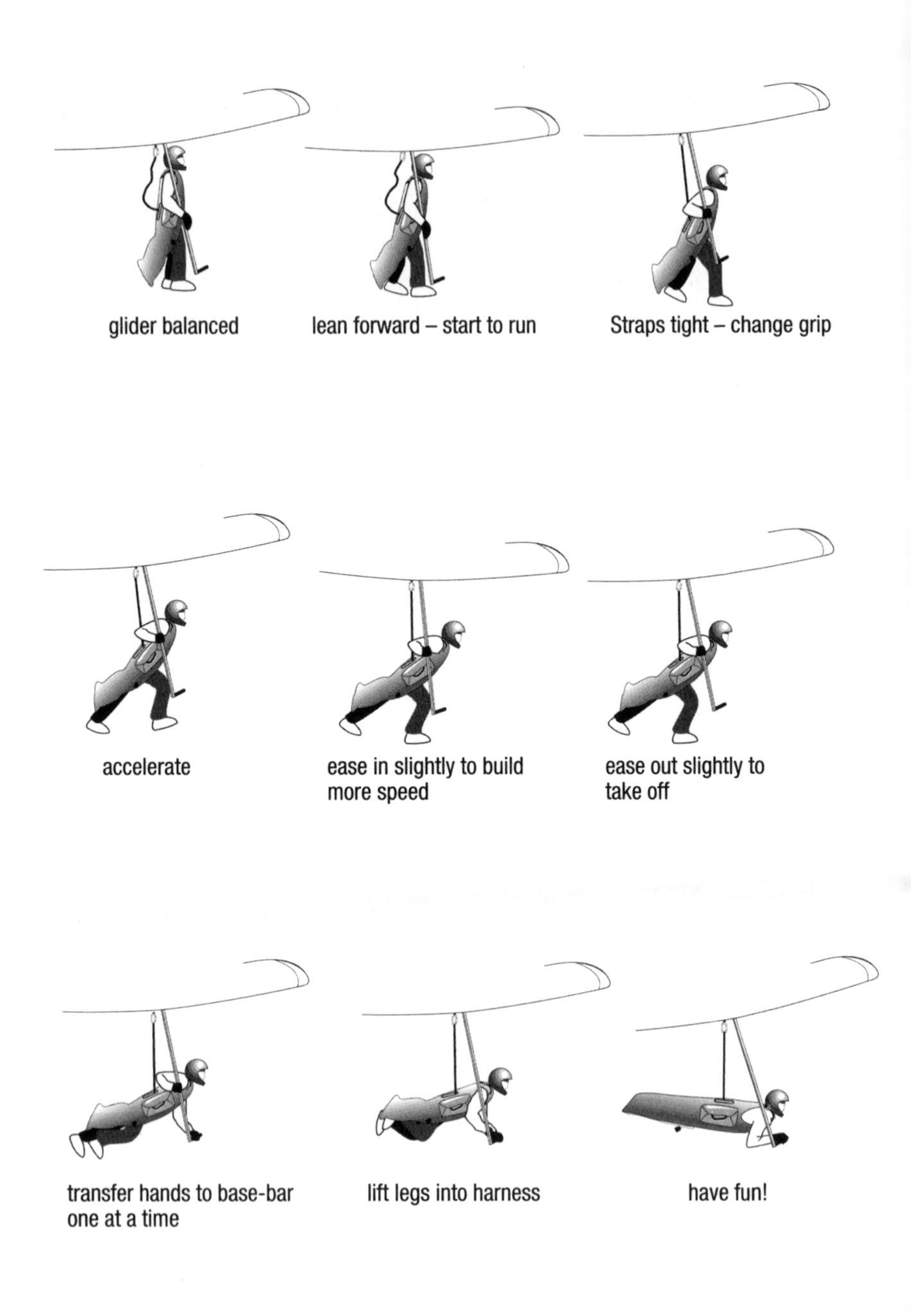

Figure 11.1 *Hang-glider launch sequence*

Glider and pilot poised

Get balanced with one foot forward, ready to run, and with wings level and at the appropriate angle of attack. If the angle of attack is held too high, the wing will remain stalled, and no matter how much effort goes into the run, you will only produce drag. After a few yards you will be wondering why so much effort does not bring the desired results. If the angle of attack is held too low, you will need to generate more speed than your legs can provide, and you will end up tripping over your own feet as the glider accelerates over your head.

Get steady. Never be rushed into starting until you are ready. Be positive and committed.

Accelerate

Lean forward. The very first motion should be you pushing the glider forward with your shoulders.

Accelerate smoothly, holding the angle of attack constant. Look ahead!

Transition

As you accelerate forward the airspeed over the wing will build up and produce more and more lift. Quite quickly, enough lift will be generated to help support the glider's weight, and you will start to feel your burden becoming increasingly light. Soon the glider itself will begin to fly. As it does it lifts up, and will continue to do so until something stops it. This, if you have remembered to clip in, will be your hang-loop! You will feel your leg straps go taut.

You will need to **change your grip** as the glider lifts. Resist any temptation to 'jump' – the glider is only producing enough lift to support its own weight at this stage.

Tow with your shoulders: Once the glider has lifted from your shoulders the energy is now being transmitted up the hang-loop – so lean forward and continue to accelerate by running hard. This will allow the airspeed to increase until the wing is capable of supporting the whole weight. At this point the glider has reached its **minimum** flying speed. However, flying on the verge of the stall isn't very safe, especially near to the ground.

Ease in slightly: By easing in just slightly on the control frame you will be able to get a couple more steps in (they will actually be giant strides), so gaining you another three or four miles per hour of airspeed.

Take-off

Now you can relax the back pressure on the uprights and you will lift cleanly from the ground. Once airborne, adjust your flying speed to suit the conditions, and adjust your heading for your desired course.

Go prone (see 'Going prone' on page 92), but remember that there is no rush to do this. The priority is flying the glider and fitting in with other traffic. So look ahead!

Taking off in stronger wind (assisted)

Flight plan and checks

Carry out all the normal pre-flight actions as described for nil- and light-wind take-offs. This will include assessing the site and conditions, your normal DI and pre-flight checks, planning your take-off and the flight. (And a plan of action in case you fail to soar.)

Carefully choose your launch position.

Ask an experienced pilot to act as your nose person, and brief him thoroughly on what he is expected to do (see 'The hang-glider nose person' on page 14).

Glider and pilot poised

Get your glider balanced, with the wings level and at the appropriate angle of attack. You may find it best to let the glider float up to the straps-tight position. (Be prepared to change your launch point if you find you are having trouble getting the glider to feel balanced. You **must** get both wings lifting equally before launching.)

Lean forward, with the bar in.

Get steady. At the instant everything is balanced, shout **'Release!'**

'Release!'

Check that your nose person has gone, and accelerate forward. Be positive and committed.

In strong winds you will take off as soon as you move forwards at all, but if the wind is lighter, 'lean into' the glider and ease the bar out using minimal rotation as you take off.

Take-off

Ensure you are penetrating forward away from the hill. If necessary ease the bar in to increase penetration. Go prone (no rush – look ahead!).

Changing your take-off technique

You will have learned at school that there are two basic methods of taking off. These are:

- **Straps-loose** For light to moderate winds
- **Straps-tight** For moderate winds and above

In practice, the 'straps-tight' method is simply the second half of the 'straps-loose' method. With more wind you will sometimes find it more convenient to let the glider float up to the 'straps-tight' position before you commence the actual take-off. Use the method most suited to the conditions, your equipment and your preference.

Taking off from a sheer cliff or crag (assisted)

These situations require a completely different technique – and can be hazardous as there is no margin for error.

The airflow up the front of the cliff can be almost completely vertical – and the glider has to be positioned in this airflow before launching. (Any attempt to run from behind the edge will result in the nose entering the vertical flow first, and the glider will literally be flipped onto its back!)

The nose of the glider must be held low by a secured, very experienced nose person, who will guide it into the airflow. Often 'wing persons' are also needed to help get the glider positioned so that both wings are lifting equally. Just behind the edge there can be severe turbulence and rotors to contend with, so just getting the glider to the launch position will require a nose person and two wing persons – and sometimes someone on the rear keel to guard against rotor surges from behind! Make sure that a coach or instructor guides you, and watch several other take-offs to get a clear picture before having a go yourself.

Do not try taking off from sheer edges in light winds. One step is not enough to gain safe flying speed.

Flying in stronger winds

After you have collected a few hours in the air you may feel confident about flying in stronger winds than you have experienced before. However, if your reason for flying is because no other pilot can be seen having difficulty, or because you have recently been frustrated by bad weather and want to get back into the air, be cautious. Never rush your progress – it isn't worth it!

If the wind speed is at or above the normal cruising speed of your hang glider (32-40kph/20-25mph), it will be necessary to fly at a faster airspeed, to avoid drifting backward. Flying at faster speeds is that bit more difficult, and the air is likely to be rougher. Your initial strong-wind flights should not be made in winds above 32kph (20mph), nor should the wind be gusty.

Some sites are known to be very unpleasant in winds of over 40kph (25mph), with especially hazardous take-offs. On other sites experienced pilots will fly in winds as strong as 48kph (30mph). Take advice from coaches and other pilots about the local conditions. Bear in mind that they will probably be flying faster gliders than yours, and that strong conditions feature in many accident reports. Work up to these stronger conditions a step at a time.

Always bear in mind that you will have to land at the end of your flight – and turbulence and rotor will be far worse in stronger winds. It is very easy to take off into conditions that are not much fun to fly in, and very dangerous to land in! Flying in stronger conditions is usually just not worth the additional risks.

Going prone

So far your training will have been carried out using a semi-prone harness. Your instructor will convert you to the fully prone position during your Club Pilot course, when he judges that you are ready.

Harness

For your first prone flights, a stiff pod-type harness (with the zip removed) is ideal. Your instructor will make sure that the one you use fits you, that it is in good condition and that it is set up properly for you.

Ground practice

A few moments spent hanging in a simulator (or in the glider on the ground) will help you to familiarise yourself with your new body position and with the action of lifting your feet into and out of the harness, and will allow you to practise the control movements fully prone.

Pitch control

In order to increase airspeed you have to move the bar down your chest from the shoulder position. At speed, the bar will be out of sight, which feels insecure at first; it is therefore important that you become thoroughly used to this new experience. Practise pulling on full speed and then returning the bar to the normal flying position.

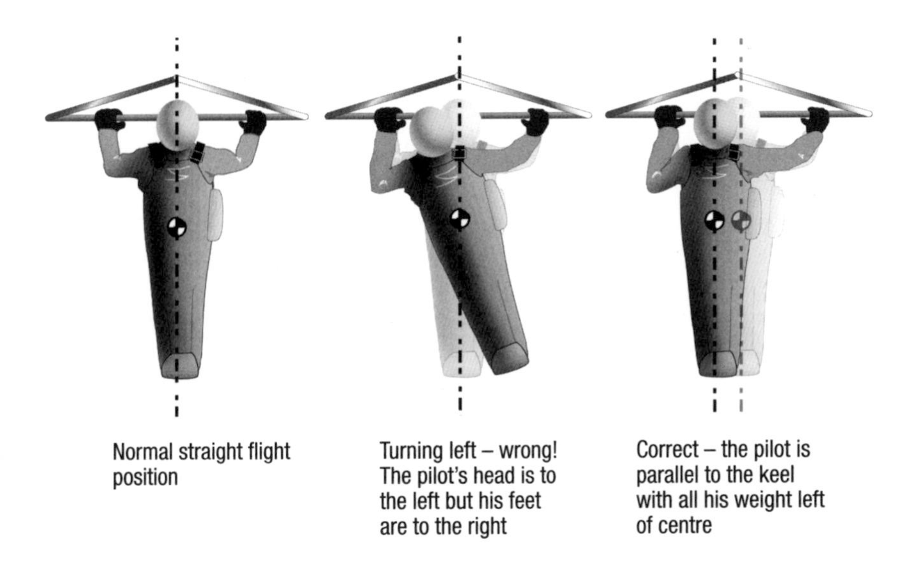

Figure 11.2 *Initiating roll: keep parallel to the keel*

Roll control

When flying fully prone for the first time, it is easy to pivot about the main harness strap, your head going one way and your feet the other. This results in no actual shift of your centre of mass relative to the glider, and hence no change of direction. As you will have been taught semi-prone you should not make this mistake, and you will be used to moving parallel to the keel without leaving your feet behind. Even so, having your legs outstretched straight behind you can leave you confused if you are not absolutely clear on what you are trying to do. Remember: 'lead with your backside!'

First time prone

Start by flying a few uncomplicated descents to the bottom landing field; a wind of 8-20kph (5-12mph) is ideal. On your first flight, stay in the take-off/landing attitude, legs dangling, until well clear of the hill. When you are good and ready – go prone. Don't look down or lose control while finding the foot entrance. If at any time you feel uncertain, scared or disorientated, then drop out of prone at once. Get back into the semi-prone position you know well. **This is your greatest safeguard.** Just being aware that you can do this makes going prone easier and safer.

Practise gentle turns. Don't rush it. Think about your flying, and try to keep your legs parallel with the keel.

When it comes to the landing, get your legs down in good time, so that you are in the familiar semi-prone position well before touch-down.

Zipping up

After a few successful flights in prone, your instructor will refit the zip to the harness so that you can 'zip up' in flight. Remember: this means that you will need a good few seconds of time flying one-handed to open the zip before landing; and that sometimes the zip may jam, or the cord may get caught. So always open the zip and check you can get your legs out while you have several hundred feet of height.

If you are ridge-soaring, free your legs before you turn in for your top-landing approach: that way, if you have a problem, you can carry on soaring while you sort it out – much better than trying to fly a landing approach one-handed in rough air.

For advice on what to do if the zip gets stuck, see Chapter 19.

Faults in going prone

Make sure you avoid the following mistakes:

- Failing to gain or maintain correct airspeed. Remember that, even though you are learning a new method of roll control, pitch must always have priority. Keep the glider flying. (Many accidents have happened because pilots look down at their feet to find the stirrup or foot entrance, and at the same time unwittingly ease out on the control bar. Using a stiff pod-style harness makes finding the entrance easy, and so will help avoid this danger.)
- Trying to tuck your undercarriage away too soon, too near the ground. Concentrate on flying until you have some height, and then tidy up.
- Failing to get the undercarriage ready for use in good time when landing. (When you start using the zip, the time to unzip is when you make the decision to land – not as you near the ground.)
- Trying to learn to fly prone with an unfamiliar glider or on a new site. This is a recipe for disaster. When making any changes of harness, or glider, fly a site with a forgiving take-off and easy landing area. Leave those cliffs with a narrow beach at the bottom well alone. **Remember: only one new thing at a time!**
- Not listening to the advice from your instructor.

Developed turns

As with all turns, the number-one priority is to look out. Check the airspace you are about to turn into; check the airspace in front of you; check that no one is flying across the back of you into the airspace you are about to turn into. And keep checking all the time you are turning.

From the normal flying position, check that you have adequate speed for the turn before banking the glider. Then roll the glider, keeping your body parallel to the keel. As the glider rolls, move your weight back to the centre to hold the bank angle constant, and ease out slightly on the control bar to keep the turn and airspeed constant. (In a more steeply banked turn, you will need more initial airspeed, more roll input, and more push-out on the control bar. Less of everything for a gentle turn.)

If the turn seems to be getting out of control, or your speed is increasing, take off the bank before attempting to reduce speed. Remember that pushing out in a turn increases the tightness of the turn.

Landings

For most of us, landings come in two types: good ones and crashes.

Even dropping the nose is a crash. If it happens more often than very rarely, it is a clear indication that your technique is faulty and requires working on before you get hurt. Anyone breaking uprights regularly should take even more heed of this warning, as it is simply a question of when and where you eventually break yourself. If necessary, go back to school and let them sort your landing technique out.

Landing technique

So what is a good landing technique?

Landing techniques can be considered as points on a scale. At one end there is the strong-wind landing, while at the other is the nil-wind landing. All other weather conditions require the use of a technique somewhere between the two extremes. Near the middle of this scale is a crossover point where the wind speed in the landing area equals the glider's stall speed. In winds above your stall speed the glider is flown onto the ground, while in winds below your stall speed the glider must be stalled onto the ground (to kill its forward speed).

All this sounds rather complicated on paper. In practice it's very easy to judge whether you are moving forward over the ground at a rate of knots (in which case a big lift-killing, speed-killing flare will be required), or at a gentle speed (in which case a gentle flare is required), or hardly at all (in which case no flare is required).

Before looking at the two extreme cases in detail, one fundamental point must be clearly understood: **good approaches lead to good landings.** In each case it is assumed that you have got yourself into an 'ideal position', about 30m (100ft) up, into wind, wings level, and the right distance back from your chosen landing area taking into account the conditions and glider type (well back in light winds, less so in stronger winds). If you can't consistently manoeuvre into this position, it is your circuit planning that requires attention – ask your coach for advice on this.

Landing in nil or light wind

These landings require very precise timing of the flare. Your ground-speed will be high, so any misjudgement can involve hitting the ground or the glider very hard. Be prepared for considerable float in 'ground effect'. From the 'ideal position' you should:

Increase speed

- Maximum glide speed provides good control response.
- Get your legs clear of the harness, but keep them back and your shoulders down.
- Move your hands to the uprights, level with your head.
- Look ahead, and maintain your airspeed.

Hold off

- Level off so that you fly parallel with the ground and about 1m (3ft) above it. This is called 'rounding out'.
- Maintain this height by allowing the bar to move out in small stages, slowly bleeding off speed.

Flare

- When it is no longer possible to maintain 1m (3ft), flare out and up in one swift, full movement.
- Land on your legs.

Finish

- Unclip.
- Move the glider out of the landing area.
- Park securely.

Common faults

- Slowing the glider down on the approach.
- Moving the body into an upright position – this results in less flare being available (important in nil wind).
- Flaring too early – the glider climbs, the pilot pulls the control bar back, the glider noses in. Never pull back!
- Flaring too gently – here the glider climbs and stalls, the nose drops through (as with most stalls) and you stuff in.
- Flaring too late – here the glider simply mushes forward, with the nose stalling and dropping, the tips still flying, and you hanging out the back wishing you were elsewhere. The correct flare rotates the nose up near the vertical, killing all lift and forward energy – the wing effectively becomes a huge drag brake. The centre of gravity of the wing will now be slightly behind you, so that as you stop, the wing will fall back and you end up with the control frame resting on your shoulders.
- Trying to 'run the glider on'. Once your feet are on the ground, the transfer of your weight to the ground effectively removes your weightshift pitch control and so removes your ability to flare positively. Pushing out on the control frame no longer works – the glider is just pushed forward without the nose rotating up.
- Not looking ahead – your judgement of height depends on your peripheral vision.

If it all goes wrong

If the landing really does turn to worms and you are about to nose in a big way, let go of the uprights in the last split-second, and try to cross your arms on your chest before impact. This prevents broken arms and wrists and frequently allows the uprights to survive too!

If nil-wind landings are giving you trouble, why not put some wheels on your glider and go back to the training slope or to the winch field next time there are light winds, and spend an afternoon practising. If you can, get your coach or an instructor to watch you to see if they can identify the problem area – once that's correctly diagnosed, doing something about it becomes easier.

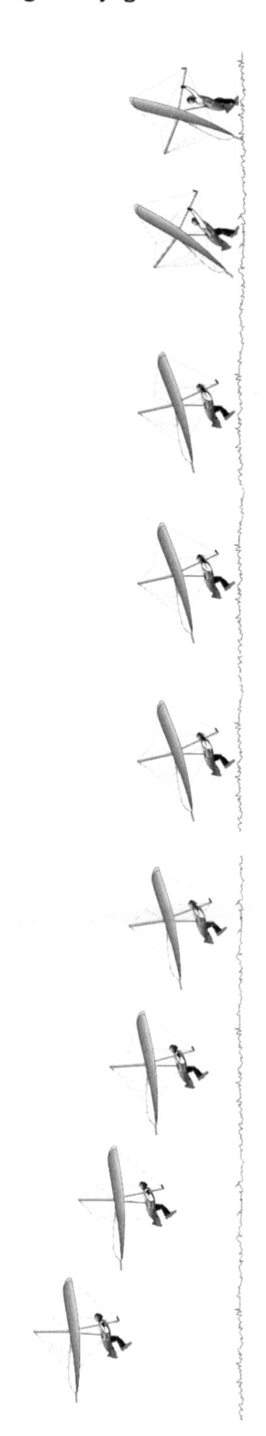

Figure 11.3 *Light-wind landing sequence*

Landing in strong wind

This is usually a top-landing. It is easier to judge than a nil-wind landing as the relative speeds are low, but if you get it wrong the penalties can be very high. Getting blown over, or landing out of wind in strong-wind conditions can be very expensive and very painful.

When landing in strong winds you will almost always encounter turbulence of some degree, and you will always encounter wind gradient. So, from the 'ideal position' you should:

Increase speed

- Come out of prone, and get your body upright. With your hands at shoulder height on the uprights increase speed to at least 8kph (5mph) above max. glide speed (50-75mm/2-3in of pull).
- Ride the bumps – don't tense up.
- Look ahead. Adjust your speed as necessary – don't let it drop off as you descend through the wind gradient.
- Keep the glider straight into wind.

Touchdown

- Alter your speed to give you a firm touchdown with slight forward speed. Do not flare!
- Get the base-bar onto the ground promptly.
- Step through the A-frame and grab the front wires.

Finish

- If the wind is very strong, wait for help.
- Unclip, and move out of the landing area.
- Park the glider flat and well secured.

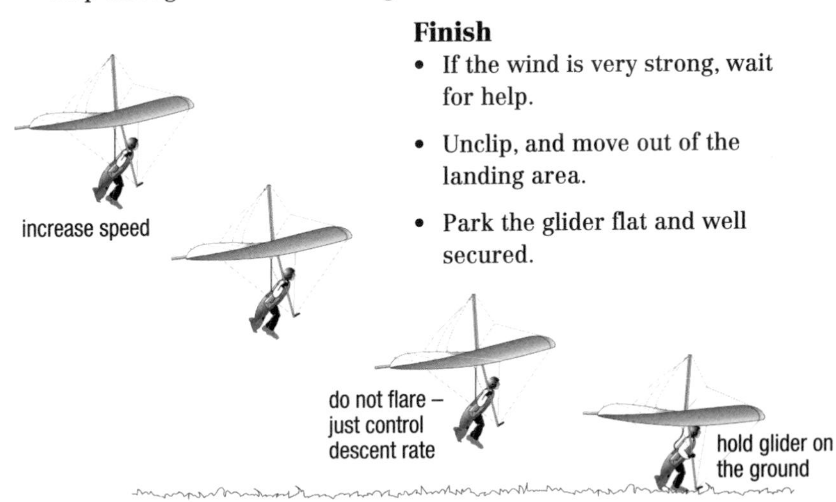

Figure 11.4 *Strong-wind landing sequence*

Common faults

- Allowing the glider to be turned out of wind on the approach (ouch!).
- Trying to achieve a very gentle touchdown. This results in either:
  - the glider waffling about just above the ground at the mercy of gusts and turbulence
  - or the glider being ground-looped when your weight transfers to the ground.
- Flaring out – new pilots tend to do this on early strong-wind landings as a reflex reaction to their feet touching the ground. It's very dramatic, very painful and very expensive, as the glider tries to do a backward somersault.
- Relaxing after touchdown – this is the most dangerous phase. You should land the glider, lower it so the base-bar is on the ground, and grab the front wires – all in one continuous movement using the slight forward momentum of the glider. Don't under any circumstances stand there, clipped in, with the glider's nose in the air.

Stalling

To fly, the wing must produce sufficient lift to support the weight of the aircraft and its load. This is achieved by flying the wing at an angle of attack to the airflow. If the angle of attack is increased (such as when a pilot tries to fly very slowly) then eventually a point is reached at which the airflow can no longer flow smoothly around the contours of the wing. The flow breaks away into turbulence – and to all intents and purposes the wing stops producing lift. This is a stall. A hang glider will recover itself from a stall, but it will lose perhaps 15m (50ft) or even 23m (75ft) of height in the process, depending on the severity of the stall, the glider design and the recovery technique used.

Practising stalling

Stalling a hang glider when there is sufficient height to recover is not dangerous, and it is something all pilots should practise from time to time, so that they are reminded what the aircraft feels like when it is being flown too slowly.

At a safe height of 150m (500ft) or more, practise flying very close to the stall, and then stalling, but do it gently; the object is not just to do stalls, but to learn to recognise the warning signals that you are being given just before the glider stalls. Practise this regularly. If you are thoroughly familiar with these signals, you will be able to avoid stalling by mistake. Stalling by mistake, when close to the ground, is very dangerous.

Recognising when you are about to stall

The symptoms of the approaching stall include:

- Reduced airflow on your face
- 'Bar out' control position
- Alteration or reduction in airflow noise
- Increase in the sink rate – this is easy to miss
- The control feels different and heavier
- Control becomes imprecise
- Possible buffeting or shaking of the sail

If any of these occur, you should increase your airspeed at once.

Reasons for stalling

The most likely reasons for stalling inadvertently and without enough height to recover are:

- trying desperately to stay up when ridge-soaring in marginal conditions
- making a landing approach without enough reserve speed in windy conditions
- mistaking groundspeed for airspeed (especially when flying downwind close to the ground)
- unfamiliarity with the type of glider and the warning signs of an impending stall.

If the glider stalls in a turn, one wing will drop, and the glider may spin. In conventional aircraft if would be exceptional if it did not, at least, enter an incipient spin. With a hang glider, when ridge-soaring without much height, stalling in a turn invariably means turning into the hill and hitting it. This is an undesirable flying manoeuvre, and is best avoided!

The reason why a glider drops one wing when stalled in a turn is that the angles of attack of the inner and outer wings are different. The inner wing has a greater angle of attack than the outer, because it is travelling less distance for the same descent rate. If the glider is slowed down, the point will come when the inner wing stalls while the outer wing is still flying properly.

There are also circumstances in which the two wing-tips may be travelling at different airspeeds even when the aircraft is being flown straight: this situation can occur in the wind gradient close to the hill face, or close to the ground, or in sudden gusts. This is why, when ridge-soaring, you should fly the glider with an adequate margin of speed, particularly if the hill face is broken or covered with trees or other obstructions, which will create turbulence.

Chapter 12: Paragliding techniques

Launches

Before every successful flight there must be a successful launch. Leaving the ground in a controlled and elegant fashion is the product of a series of actions known as ground-handling. Good ground-handling makes taking off easy in any flyable weather conditions.

Clean launches depend on lots and lots of practice. The combination of using the controls, risers, body weight and movement to control the canopy does not come automatically. If you find that you often make multiple unsuccessful attempts at getting into the air before getting it right, you should arrange some concentrated practice under the guidance of a coach or instructor.

Which technique?

There are two basic techniques, depending on the wind speed: the forward launch and the reverse launch.

- If the wind is a light breeze or less – rough guide: less than 13kph (8mph) – use the forward launch.
- If the wind is fresher than this, use the reverse launch.

Winds above 26kph (16mph) should be treated with extra caution, and the skilled use of a continuous-control take-off technique is strongly recommended – see the section on 'Taking off in strong winds' on page 112.

Control with sensitivity

Whichever technique you use, you must be in control of the canopy at all times. Use your senses to monitor what is happening – the look and feel of the canopy, risers and lines. Balance the tension in the risers, and modify your actions according to the wind speed and the feedback you get from the canopy. Be sensitive. You should be relaxed but able to apply sufficient force to have the desired effect. You must know what you want the canopy to do – it is no good allowing it to overpower you.

The forward launch

To begin with, choose a suitable launch site with no obstacles. There should be enough room to lay the glider out fully, and enough runway to enable the glider to inflate and gain enough airspeed to fly.

Carefully lay the canopy out in a crescent shape. Ideally the centre cells can be made to sit up, as the idea is for the centre section to inflate first, ensuring an even inflation. At the tips, make sure that no lines are underneath the canopy. Now carefully check that all the lines are clear, by lifting all the risers on one side and then clearing the lines riser by riser, starting from the bottom. Repeat this process for the other riser set.

When you are ready, move your harness a few steps closer to the wing, so that you do not inadvertently tension any lines, and put it on. As soon as you have completed all your pre-flight checks (see Chapter 3), position yourself in front of the centre of the canopy, facing forwards with the controls in the appropriate hands and the risers arranged in the crook of your elbows. You should very lightly hold the 'A'-riser maillons. Move forward until you have just a hint of tension in the 'A'-lines. Your arms should be back and down along the risers (like a child playing jet fighters), ready to guide the 'A's.

Rock your weight onto your back foot, then lean forwards, putting pressure on the risers using your upper body. Make a good, smooth, committed, progressively accelerating run, aiming (and looking) at your pre-selected reference point. As you run forwards, use your hands to guide the 'A'-risers upwards, with the palms open (to ensure that you don't inadvertently pull the risers).

The canopy will slow your run, but you should continue to apply a steady smooth pull from the harness. As the canopy comes above your head, stop guiding the risers, have a quick look to check the canopy, while applying control as necessary to prevent any overshooting. Continue running, leaning and looking forward at your reference point. Keep your hands up, so no control is applied and you can maximise airspeed, and keep running until the canopy lifts you off the ground, when you can return the controls to the normal flying position. Keep a good lookout at all times.

Common faults

- Canopy not spread in a neat crescent shape directly into wind; this usually results in a failed launch. A couple of minutes spent arranging the canopy correctly will save time in the long run.

- Uneven pressure on the risers during launch, which causes the canopy to inflate asymmetrically and turn to one side. To avoid this, make sure that all the harness straps and adjustments are symmetrical, and that you apply the pressure evenly. This takes lots of practice.
- Releasing the risers too soon. This results in the canopy 'hanging back', preventing you from gaining airspeed.
- Releasing the risers too late. This will usually result in a frontal collapse. (Using the 'open palm' method to ease the 'A'-risers up helps to avoid releasing the risers too soon or too late.)
- Stopping the run when checking the canopy.
- Failure to remain directly under the centre of the canopy before launching. This results in the canopy turning off the intended launch path, making the launch difficult if not impossible. The correct technique for making corrective inputs is – while still accelerating forward – to move under the canopy while applying control to the other side. The quicker you are able to move under the canopy, the less control input is needed. It is common for inexperienced pilots to pull against the canopy instead of moving under it, which prevents the canopy from coming straight.
- Not looking ahead on the launch run. For obvious reasons it is essential to be looking where you're going when on the launch run.
- 'Jumping' into the seat before the glider is fully flying. This often means you have to come out of the seat again to resume running in order to rebuild the airspeed that has been lost. This causes the canopy to pitch forward, leading to a frontal collapse. Jumping off a hill with a semi-stalled glider is not recommended! Always keep accelerating until the glider lifts you off the ground.

While on the ground your attention will have been focused on the canopy. As soon as you launch you must re-focus onto your flight plan.

The reverse launch

Preparation

As with the forward launch, a good reverse launch comes about as a result of thorough preparation beforehand. This begins with choosing the right day and the right site. Having checked the wind and weather on site, choose an appropriate launch spot, free from obstacles. This will usually be only a short distance back from the crest of the hill, so that the task of moving forward to launch once the canopy is above your head is not made unnecessarily prolonged or difficult. Don't forget to leave space behind just in case you get blown backwards while ground-handling.

Complete your Daily Inspection before laying the canopy out on its back, with the trailing edge upwind. Standing upwind of the canopy, move the risers several paces back towards the canopy so that the lines are completely slack. Now don your helmet and harness. If they are not already connected, attach the main risers to the harness. Now complete your pre-flight checks (see Chapter 3).

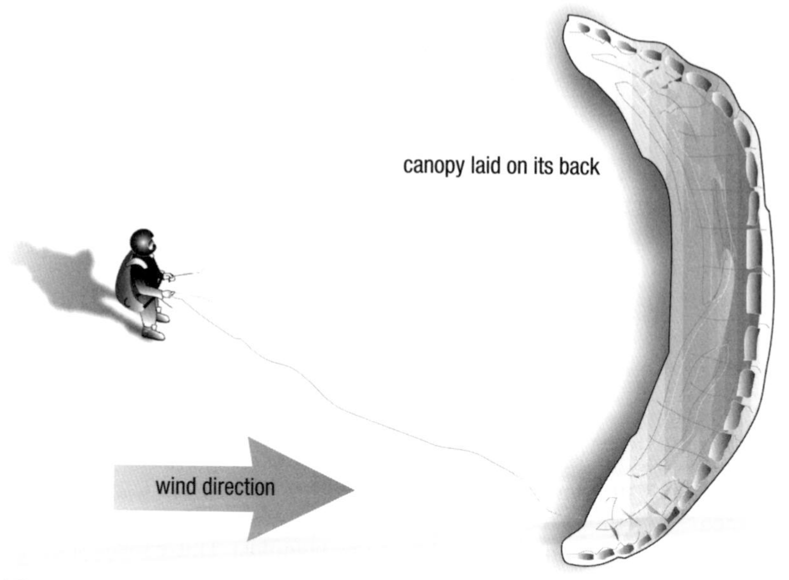

Figure 12.1 *Reverse-launch preparation*

Building the wall

Turn to face the canopy and check that there are no tangles in the risers or lines. The risers will be crossed in front of you. Check that the top riser leads to the shoulder that you will naturally prefer to go back when you turn around. (We'll assume that this is your right shoulder.)

Slide your right hand along the upper set of risers and unclip the control and bring your hand back to your side. Slide your left hand along the bottom risers and take that control from underneath.

When facing the canopy your right hand will be holding the control that steers the left side of the wing (as you look at it) and vice versa. With your right hand grasp the right hand 'A'-riser just under the maillon (i.e.

the riser connected to the right side of the wing as you look at it). With your left hand grasp the left 'A' riser.

Now lean back so that your harness applies some tension to the lines, and by gently teasing the 'A'-risers (and judicious use of the control handles) you will be able to inflate the front portion of the canopy evenly while the trailing-edge portion remains firmly on the ground. This is 'the wall'. If it starts to rise, walk towards it to de-tension the lines.

Apart from readying the canopy for launch, the wall serves other equally important purposes. A good wall allows you to check for snags and twists in the lines and risers; it also shows the exact wind direction, strength and gustiness. You determine the height of the wall in accordance with the strength of the wind: light wind = large wall, stronger wind = smaller wall. Run through the entire pre-flight checklist again at this point.

When building the wall, make sure it's directly into wind with an imaginary line drawn between the centre of your glider through your back and into the wind. By moving your body from side to side you will get an even leading edge when your back is directly into wind.

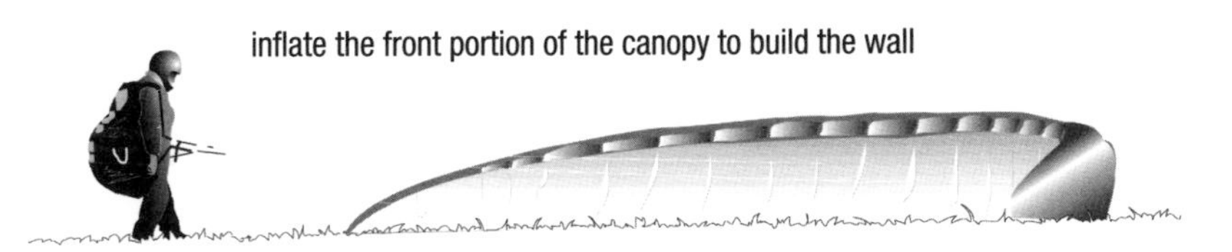

Figure 12.2 *Starting to build the wall*

Inflating the canopy

Check that the airspace around you is clear and then, with a firm foothold, chest/shoulders parallel to the wing, ease the canopy up by leaning back, using your upper body to put pressure on the risers. The amount of pressure required will depend on the wind strength – with practice you will be able to judge this. Too little and the canopy won't come up all the way: too much and it will fly up and lift you off your feet before dumping you ignominiously on your backside! The 'A' risers are guided up using your open hands, keeping the risers at full length. Don't pull the risers towards you or you will distort the canopy. Be prepared to move towards and underneath the ascending canopy. If the canopy is not coming up straight, move towards it to lower it back down and start again. If it does come up straight (and it should if your wall was good and your technique is even) then be ready to apply a little control to prevent it overshooting, if necessary. Once the canopy is overhead, stabilise it and make a final line-check.

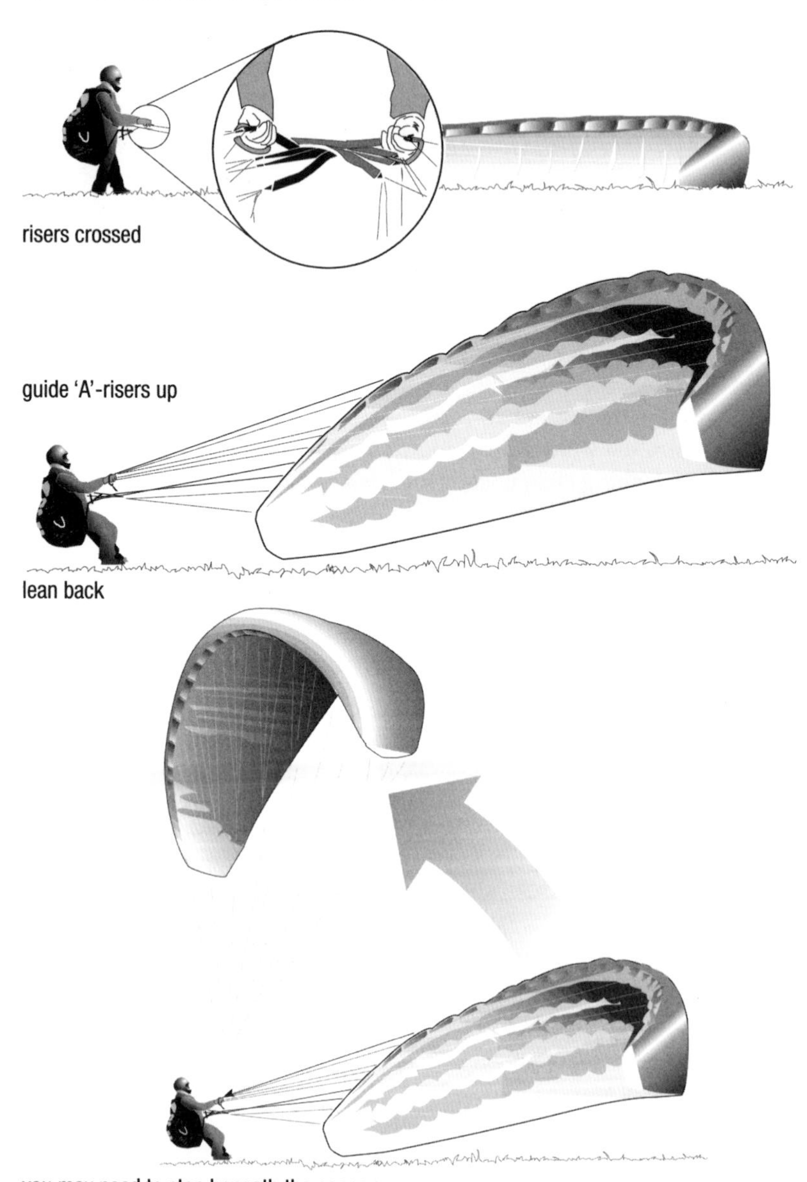

Figure 12.3 *Inflating the canopy*

Turn around

Once the glider is above you do not be in a hurry to turn. Get the glider stable and check the lines.

As you turn around step back into wind, this keeps the glider loaded. A common mistake is to turn on the one spot or to turn and immediately step backwards - which makes the lines go slack, creating a front tuck.

Step calmly into wind keeping your body leaning forward so the pressure still comes from your harness. If there is enough wind practice standing with the glider above your head feeling the paraglider through your brakes. Try not to look at it. If it drops down to one side move under the centre of the glider and pull on the opposite brake whilst keeping the pressure on the wing. Don't pull too much brake or the glider will pull you backwards and stall.

Make the final wind and airspace checks.

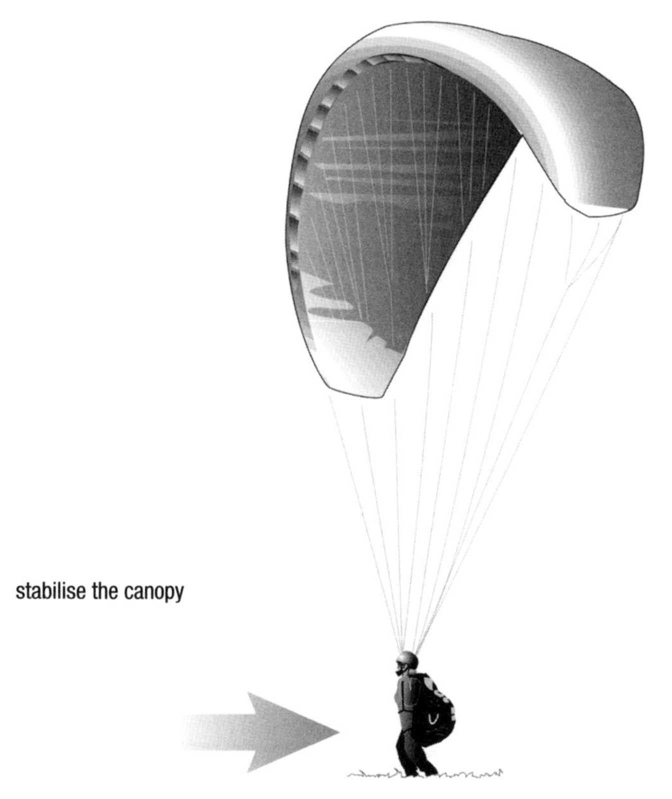

Figure 12.4 *Ready for take-off*

Take-off

Run forwards, looking ahead with the controls held high, until the canopy lifts you off the ground. Don't jump! Steer, control your airspeed and follow your flight plan. Once safely away from the hill, sit back into your harness.

Common faults

Some of the faults associated with reverse launches are similar to those in forward launches. These include uneven pressure on risers, releasing the risers too late or too soon, not remaining under the centre of the canopy when ground-handling, and jumping into your seat on launch. The remedies for these faults are the same as detailed in the forward-launch 'Common faults' section (see page 104).

Other faults, specific to reverse launches, include:

- Pulling the canopy up with the arms rather than the upper body. Apart from being inefficient, this usually means that the risers are pulled towards your body, effectively shortening them. When the canopy is overhead and the risers are released they revert to their normal length. This can cause the front ports to partially close, which usually results in a frontal collapse.
- Turning the wrong way after having inflated the canopy. This is potentially very dangerous as it could cause you to be out of control just after take-off while the risers untwist themselves. The simple way to avoid this happening is always to turn the same way, so that it becomes second nature. Always check before inflating the canopy that your natural turn direction is the one required. The easiest way to do this is to check the risers while facing the canopy ready for the reverse launch. If the right riser is on top when they are crossed in front of you, then the right shoulder goes back to start the turn. If the uppermost riser does not happen to suit your normal turn direction, then rotate until it does.

The 'Traditional' reverse launch

It is possible that you learnt the 'traditional' reverse launch. With this method you initially face the canopy with the control handles in the 'wrong' hands. After inflating the canopy and stabilising it, as you then turn to face forwards you therefore have to swap the controls over to the 'correct' hands. This 'swapping over' produces a period of minimal control at what can be a critical period. To avoid this, 'continuous control' reverse-launch methods such as the 'cross brakes' (sometimes called 'cross control') method detailed above have evolved, and these are generally preferred.

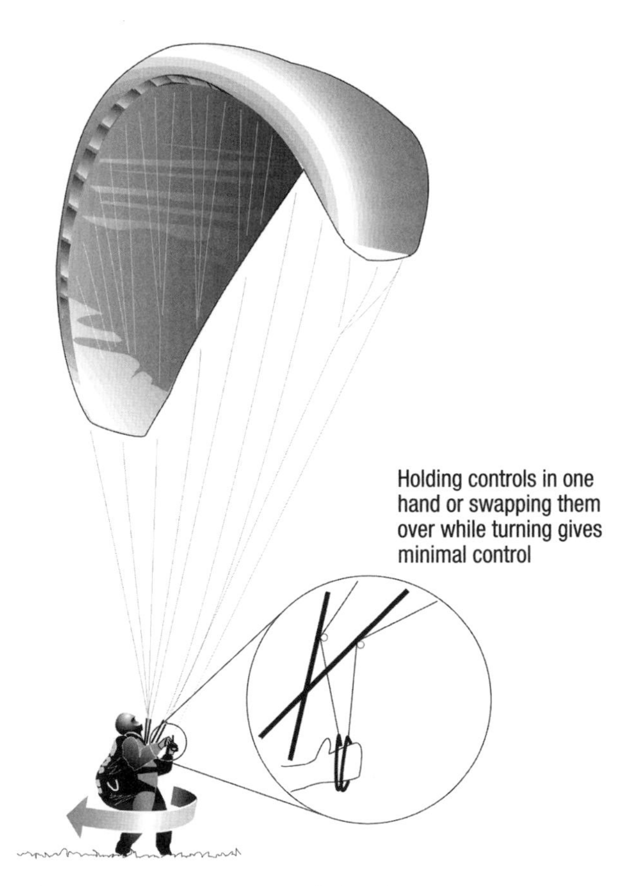

Figure 12.5 *The 'Traditional' reverse launch involved poor control at a critical moment*

The 'Cross Hands' reverse launch

The **cross-hand** method is a simple variation on the cross-control method. Prepare exactly as above, but when it comes to grasping the 'A'-risers, cross your hands (right over left if you usually turn your right shoulder back) and grasp the opposite 'A'-riser. Your right hand will now be holding the control handle and riser for the left side of the wing (as you look at it) and vice versa. (The advantage of this method is that the lines do not run over the risers. A disadvantage is that with your arms crossed you have a reduced range of movement.)

Changing your technique

Changing your technique requires many hours of practice in order for the new technique to become second nature. This is particularly true when changing from the traditional reverse launch to a continuous-control method. The top of an unfamiliar site on a breezy day is not the place to make your first attempt. Practise in a stress-free environment (i.e. gentle winds, gentle slope) so you can concentrate solely on the technique. When you are getting to grips with the technique, try it on the hill in easy conditions. By the time you come to use the technique in more windy conditions there should be no problems, assuming you've done enough practising!

Taking off in strong winds

For paraglider pilots, winds of more than 26kph (16mph) should be treated as 'strong'. With practice, an experienced, competent pilot using a fast canopy may find it possible to take off in winds of up to 30kph (18mph). In 'strong' winds it is essential to be completely familiar with the launch characteristics of your canopy. It is even more important to be sure of the wisdom of such a launch: can you be sure the wind will not increase to a level where forward flight is impossible? Can you guarantee finding a landing area free from the rotors and turbulence usual in strong winds? Remember the old aviation saying: 'It is much better to be down here wishing you were up there, than up there wishing you were down here.'

Possibly the most important factor in the technique for taking off in strong winds is choosing the right part of the hill for launch. Taking off at the top of the hill is by far the safest option, as it allows you to assess the true conditions – i.e. wind strength and gustiness. This should be done by briefly ground-handling with the canopy set at standard trim speed and with the use of a good-quality anemometer if you have one. (Launching solely on the evidence of wind-measuring devices is not recommended, as they do not give the degree of 'feel' that you can get by actually ground-handling the canopy.)

If you cannot handle the canopy and launch from the top of the hill, then **it is too windy for *you* to fly**!

When assessing conditions at the top of the hill, it is essential that there is enough room for you to be dragged back if it all goes wrong. The hang glider pilots will not be pleased if you end up wrapped around their kit!

Taking off from below the top of the hill – where the slope is steeper and the wind appears less strong – is **not recommended**, because from this position it is impossible to make an accurate assessment of the true wind conditions further up. Also, launching from the slope will result in an immediate and rapid take-off, allowing no time to check for line snags or to make corrective inputs to the canopy should it not come up straight. And remember that aborting the launch will be almost impossible once you have started, as you will be airborne as soon as the canopy comes overhead and will invariably be facing backwards. If you have assessed the wind strength incorrectly, this can quite easily result in your gaining height rapidly and then being blown back over the top of the hill, with unpleasant consequences!

Strong-wind techniques

Building a wall in strong winds is a difficult balance between having the wall too high and having it not high enough (not enough wing off the ground to aerodynamically pin the canopy down and stop the trailing edge from lifting off). The most common ground-handling mistake is the latter, pulling too much control and not letting the canopy pin itself to the ground.

From 'wall' to 'canopy above head' should be one quick, flowing movement, so prepare well before pulling the canopy up. A thorough pre-flight check is essential at this point as there will be little or no time for corrections once the launch is initiated. Make sure you are exactly into wind and that the wind is not too crossed on the slope. If the canopy does not come up straight when you start to inflate it, ground it immediately and start again.

Assuming you have prepared well and the canopy is coming up straight, the most important thing is to control the rate of ascent of the canopy. Let the canopy 'ride up' by keeping gentle tension on the 'A'-lines. Avoid giving the canopy a hard pull, as this will cause it to pass the critical angle of attack with so much energy that you will be lifted off the ground out of control (and normally dumped back down on your backside!). Be prepared to move towards the canopy as it comes up, to control the rate of ascent (this is a positive movement towards the canopy, not to be confused with being dragged towards the canopy). At these wind speeds, no control input will be needed to stabilise the canopy. If you pull the controls at all, there is great danger that the sudden extra lift this generates will take you off the ground far too soon. This inflation technique is easy with practice at the top of the hill where it is relatively flat, but extremely difficult on steep slopes!

On turning to face into wind, lean forwards to put as much body weight as possible on the chest strap to 'load' the glider, and drive forwards from the toes. **Look where you're going!**

Safety note

When launching in strong winds you must be prepared to find yourself taking off prematurely, before you have completed the turn. For this reason, you should not attempt to launch in such conditions until you have mastered a continuous-control technique.

Landings

A good landing is always the result of a good approach. Read the section on 'Approaches' in Chapter 13, and make sure you understand how to set up a good approach to a selected landing area.

Landing in light winds

Start your final approach at a minimum of 15m (50ft) above the ground. You must be into wind, sitting forward in the harness, and with your approach speed stabilised. (This should be with just a little control applied.) Keep looking forward (not down). As you reach the ground, flare smoothly, reach for the ground with your forward foot, and run off any excess speed. The idea of the flare is to reduce your speed over the ground to a figure that your undercarriage (legs) can easily cope with, so the actual amount of flare, if any, will be determined by the wind strength. In very light winds the flare will need to be full, with the controls extended below your backside. As you trot off the excess speed, the canopy will drop to the ground behind you.

Landing in moderate winds (e.g. normal top-landing)

Proceed as for light winds, except with the important difference that hardly any flare will be required. After touchdown, keep the canopy flying above your head, into wind and loaded as much as possible, so preventing it from dropping back and acting as a spinnaker while you are still facing forward. The next step is to turn and face the canopy and then collapse it in a controlled manner.

There are a number of options for collapsing the canopy. The choice will depend largely on the characteristics of the canopy, so it goes without saying that **you must know your canopy!** Check the user manual, and consider practising in a large open field to see which is the most effective method for you and your particular canopy.

1. Pull down sharply on the rear risers, then run towards and to the side of the canopy while maintaining the pull.
2. Pull down sharply on the 'C'-risers (assuming a four-riser setup), then run towards and to the side of the canopy while maintaining the pull.

3 Pull down sharply on the controls (with a wrap or two if necessary) then run towards and to the side of the canopy while maintaining the pull.

4 Pull down sharply on the 'B'-risers (for a three- or four-riser setup), then run towards and to the side of the canopy while maintaining the pull.

Once the canopy is on the ground and under control, gather it together and make it as small as possible to prevent re-inflation. Don't just stand there in the way; clear the landing area.

Landing in strong winds (emergencies)

In stronger winds the descent may be vertical or even backwards. This is not a good situation at all, and the chances of escaping unscathed are small!

1 If you have a high vertical or horizontal speed, carry out a PLF (see page 11). Once safely on the ground (after your PLF), be prepared to use the standard drag-back technique of pulling in one of the control lines or rear risers hand over hand until the canopy is under control.

2 If a controlled arrival seems possible, turn into wind and adopt an upright position in the harness at a minimum of 15m (50ft) above the ground. Assume the PLF position (just in case). Concentrate on keeping the glider into wind and overhead. Fly as fast as possible on standard trim while guarding against possible turbulence and wind gradient by applying just enough control to 'feel' the glider and maintain correct pitch. (Do not use a speed system at this height and wind speed: it may induce an asymmetric or symmetric collapse.) At 50-100cm (2-3ft) – assuming a sensible descent rate – put one foot just in front of the other. At the instant you reach the ground, you need to do three things simultaneously: pivot on the rear foot to face the glider, and collapse the wing while running in an arc to the side of it. Gather it in carefully, and make yourself a promise never to get caught out again!

Slope-landing

Slope-landing can save a long walk from the bottom landing field on those light and scratchy days, and can be an invaluable technique when landing out after a cross-country in areas where the terrain is not perfectly flat.

Choosing the right place

Select a hill where the slope is not too steep – i.e. one where it is possible to walk easily without the need to use your hands for support. It should be clear of rocks and other obstacles that might cause you to trip on landing. There should be a bottom-landing within easy reach in case it should prove necessary to abort the slope-landing.

Conditions

For your first attempts, choose a day when the winds are on the light side for ridge-soaring and the air is not thermic. This will make it easier to judge the approach and to control the canopy after landing.

Approach and landing

Given that it may not be possible to soar, you must assess the wind direction before taking off. As you will be landing crosswind, your groundspeed will be higher than normal. It is therefore essential to land on the more into-wind beat, so that your groundspeed is minimised. If the wind is at exactly 90 degrees to the slope then landings can be practised in both directions. If it is possible to maintain height after taking off, then do a few beats to assess the wind direction. Keep an eye on the windsock, as the wind may change, forcing you to alter your flight plan.

The basis of the slope landing is that you fly increasingly close to the hill at a very shallow angle until your feet eventually touch the slope. Having determined your approach direction, you should set up this very shallow angle approach towards your chosen part of the hill, which should be clear and unobstructed.

Avoid any large control inputs – these will induce roll oscillations which would make a controlled arrival impossible. The aim is to achieve a very steady, stabilised flight-path. Get out of your seat (legs down) early. Fly fast (controls up) so that there is energy for the flare, and so that you have good control if you need to turn away from the hill because you are not happy with the approach. You may find that it is best to loop the control lines once (or even twice) around your hands ('take a wrap') to ensure that you have sufficient control immediately available for the flare, and to collapse the canopy after landing – **but discuss taking a wrap with your instructor beforehand.**

As you near your chosen spot, constantly assess your horizontal and vertical closure rate – **if you are in any doubt, turn away**. If all goes according to plan, flare hard as your feet touch – be prepared to run across and up the slope – and then concentrate on ensuring that the canopy collapses onto the slope so that you do not inadvertently take off again (this could be very dangerous with an unloaded wing).

It is very unlikely that you will have time and space to turn to face the canopy, so the collapse is best managed by further depressing the control on the side nearest the slope – to make sure the canopy falls sideways toward the slope – and then controlling the collapse with the other control (the one furthest from the slope), to stop the canopy from rotating and hitting the slope cell-openings first. This would not only risk damaging the canopy, but – more immediately important – would make it extremely difficult to collapse the canopy if it started to drag you.

You should now walk up the hill to one side of the canopy – being careful not to stand on any lines or trip over them – until you are level with it or slightly above it. Then carefully gather the canopy up. In this way you minimise the risk of inadvertently re-inflating it.

Common faults

- Attempting to land on a 'downwind' beat.
- Carrying on with a bad approach instead of giving up on it and either setting up again further down the hill or bottom-landing.
- Deliberately re-inflating the canopy to walk it back up the hill. Do not do this! Besides endangering yourself, other pilots taking off will not expect an obstacle to appear suddenly from below.

Weightshift turning

Weightshifting is a way of improving the efficiency of the canopy in turning flight, by reducing the need for large conventional control inputs. Once familiar with the technique you will find you use it almost all the time.

As the name suggests, weightshifting involves transferring your body weight towards one side of the canopy by shifting your weight in the harness seat. In order to do this effectively, your cross-bracing must be fairly slack to allow the harness to tilt, and your chest strap must be set to the correct distance (see the section on 'Harnesses' in Chapter 8). To weightshift to the left, lean your weight to the left and the glider will turn to the left; and vice versa for turning to the right. Some people prefer to cross their legs to achieve the weightshift; others simply lean over in the harness.

Whichever method you prefer to use, the aim is to get as much weight as possible onto one set of risers.

Efficient co-ordinated turns are achieved through a combination of weightshift and control input. Generally, the better your weightshift technique, the less control input is needed, and the more efficient the turn.

Slow flight

There may be a number of reasons why you might want to fly slowly, the most common being to achieve a better sink rate and to enable you to make efficient flat turns. Whether scratching at your local hill or making the most of patchy lift at cloudbase, flying at minimum-sink speed will usually achieve the best results. However, on today's canopies there is not a lot to be gained from flying particularly slowly as the minimum-sink speed is usually quite close to the 'controls up' trim speed.

There are problems with flying too slowly. Flying slowly means that the glider is close to the stall. If you encounter a gust while scratching round a hilltop or ridge at slow airspeeds, there is little or no time (or space) for corrective action. Being stalled high up is nearly as undesirable, and you will certainly have lost the height you were trying to gain in the first place... is it worth it?

It is very easy to fly more slowly than the minimum-sink speed, but you should realise that the sink rate will actually be higher – and you will be much closer to the stall. This is not a safe speed to fly at! Read your user manual, and practise flying at minimum-sink speed in smooth, stable conditions.

Rapid-descent techniques

As the title suggests, the following techniques enable you and your canopy to descend quickly in emergency situations. These could include finding yourself in danger of being sucked into cloud, or experiencing deteriorating weather conditions that make a prompt return to terra firma highly desirable.

All the techniques mentioned cause increased stress to the paraglider lines and fabric. None of them should be attempted near the ground, and once mastered they should be used only when really necessary! Your initial attempts should be under the guidance of an instructor, in calm air and with sufficient height to deal with any problems.

You should check your paraglider's user manual to see which method is recommended.

'Big ears'

'Big ears' is a rapid-descent technique that involves deliberately collapsing the wing-tips of the paraglider. The resulting combination of increased drag and increased wing-loading produces a significantly increased descent rate. Unlike the 'B'-line stall and the spiral dive (described later), in 'big ears' the paraglider still has approximately its normal forward speed, and you can control its direction of travel.

Getting into 'big ears'

The correct technique is to reach up and (without letting go of the control handles) grasp the outermost 'A'-line at each side with your thumbs downward. Then by rotating your hand you can twist the lines outwards and down, so collapsing the outer 20-30 percent of each wing. Some manufacturers have made applying 'big ears' easy by splitting each 'A'- riser so that the outer line is attached to its own sub-riser.

On some gliders (generally those with at least four 'A'-lines on each side) the user manual may advise twisting down the outer two lines at each side: in these cases it is especially important that you are careful not to pull the lines down, as you could inadvertently induce a full front collapse.

As the 'ears' are applied there is a sudden increase in drag. Applying both ears at once can rock the glider back into a stall. For this reason, on most gliders it is much safer to gently apply one ear at a time. (However, there are a few gliders where it is better to apply the ears simultaneously: check your user manual for advice.)

While in 'big ears'

On some gliders the ears stay in on their own: on others you need to hold them in. Either way, you will not be able to use the controls for steering, as any application of control will force out the ear on that side. Instead you must rely on weightshift steering. This is adequate for maintaining a general course while well clear of the ground.

The glider adopts a steeper flight-path with no change of attitude, so the wing is operating at a higher angle of attack. This makes the glider less susceptible to tucks, but more susceptible to stalling. Using the speed-bar to lower the angle of attack a little (once safely established in 'big ears') can provide an increased safety margin above the stall, and will also increase the horizontal speed and descent rate.

The use of other manoeuvres (e.g. tight turns) must be restricted, as there is a very real danger of overloading the lines. The flying loads are being taken by far fewer lines. Anything that might further increase the loads on them is to be avoided.

Getting out of 'big ears'

As already mentioned, in 'big ears' the glider is operating at an increased angle of attack, and this means that care must be taken not to provoke a stall. Unfortunately, several serious accidents have occurred when pilots have used the old 'pumping out' technique to recover both 'ears' simultaneously, and have inadvertently stalled the wing. This risk is greater when descending through wind shears such as those likely to be found when top-landing.

The best policy for recovery from 'big ears' is to let the ears pop out on their own, one at a time, with just a tickle of control application if necessary to help them. Do not use big pumps on the controls, and never exit 'big ears' by using big pumps on both controls together!

Spiral dive

There are two types of spiral dive that can be performed on a paraglider. The first is a continuous, tight, high-speed 360 degree turn, with a bank angle of approximately 45 degrees. This spiral is easily controlled and can produce descent rates of around 10m/s. Due to the energy built up, some care should be taken when recovering to normal flight: a gradual exit by completing another, wider, circle in the initial direction is the best policy.

The second type (or 'mode') of paraglider spiral dive is the 'nose-down spiral'. This is a continuous, tight, nose-nearly-vertically-down 360-degree 'corkscrew' turn in which the pilot swings out level with the canopy. This results in extremely high rates of descent –14 to 27m/s (approximately 30 to 60mph straight down).

Due to the very rapid height loss, rapid disorientating rate of rotation, high speed, high g force and the potential for the recovery to go wrong (due to the amount of energy) the nose-down spiral is a **dangerous manoeuvre**: recovery should always be completed at least 300m (1,000ft) above ground level.

Getting into a nose-down spiral dive

Make sure that you have sufficient height – several thousand feet! On most canopies entry is achieved by setting up a 360-degree turn and progressively tightening it until the desired degree of spiral is obtained. The ease with which this is initiated varies from canopy to canopy. Most will enter a nose-down spiral if you simply apply control and weightshift in the desired direction of turn and maintain the inside control. A few canopy types may need an additional abrupt application of inside control after the first 360, to rotate the nose down. Read your user's manual carefully.

While in a nose-down spiral dive

Some canopies require the inner control line to be held down in order to maintain the spiral, while others will stay in the spiral when the controls have been returned to their normal flying position. It is also the case that, if the severity of the spiral is allowed to increase, canopies will often become increasingly 'locked-in'. It may be necessary to apply a little outside brake and weightshift to control the rate of spiral. Wing-loading is increased dramatically and high 'g' forces can be reached, putting potentially catastrophic stresses on both fabric and lines. Spiral dives have caused a number of fatalities involving canopy failure. There are also reports of pilot 'greying out' / 'blacking out' due to the high 'g' forces.

You will drift downwind during the spiral, so ensure that you have enough space to recover. It is easy to become disoriented and dizzy when in a spiral, and this can even cause you to spiral into the ground. Again several fatalities have occurred this way. Monitor your height and initiate the recovery early.

Getting out of a nose-down spiral dive

This is achieved by gradually releasing the control that is maintaining the spiral, or in the case of canopies that stay in the spiral without continued input, by applying outside brake and weightshift. Considerable force may be required on the controls. Often slowing the canopy first by applying both controls is the best strategy. Exit the spiral gradually – completing another, wider, circle in the initial direction is a good way of dissipating the energy. Avoid exiting immediately to straight flight as you will have considerable airspeed and energy, and this will result in a surging climb followed by a dive which must be 'damped' out to prevent a possible collapse.

NB: Low aspect ratio wings (generally EN A, B, LTF 1, 1 / 2 grades) tend to be particularly prone to 'locking in' to nose-down spirals if allowed, and will then require very positive pilot action to exit. They will not 'self-recover'. You should only experiment with nose-down spirals over water, under the guidance of a suitably experienced SIV Instructor with full safety back-up.

'B'-line stall

The 'B'-line stall involves forming a large spanwise crease in the canopy. This destroys the normal airflow around the wing and induces a stall. Descent rates can be high, with the canopy remaining in a relatively stable position above the pilot's head. For you to be able to induce a 'B'-line stall, your canopy must have at least three risers on each side. Check your user manual.

Inducing a 'B'-line stall

Reach up, with the controls in your hands, and take hold of the 'B'-risers at the point where they connect to the lines. Pull down smoothly and symmetrically until you feel the canopy drop back into the stall. Then allow yourself to stabilise underneath it before attempting to release the risers.

While in a 'B'-line stall

As in the spiral dive, you will drift with the wind, so ensure you have plenty of space in which to carry out the manoeuvre.

You can control your rate of descent to an extent by varying the degree of pull on the risers, the further you pull down the faster you drop. However, some canopies become unstable and thrash about if the 'B'-risers are pulled down too far. This can lead to the canopy not recovering evenly, resulting in a spin.

'B'-lining distorts the canopy, putting uneven and increased stress on both fabric and lines.

Getting out of a 'B'-line stall

The object is to restore the shape of the canopy and to recover its normal flying speed. If the speed is not regained, the glider is said to be in a parachutal stall (see page 126).

The normal method of recovering from 'B'-lining is gradually to raise the risers until they are 15cm (6in) from their normal flying position. Then you quickly release them fully, allowing the canopy to snap back into shape. This must be done symmetrically to prevent a spin.

The alternative is to release the risers fully from the stall position without first raising them. This will give a more vigorous inflation, which could put more stress on the canopy but should be less likely to result in a parachutal stall. The canopy should then regain airspeed and surge forward as it begins to fly, so be prepared to 'damp' out this surge if necessary.

It is not uncommon for a canopy to remain in a parachutal state once the risers have been released. In this state the canopy is stalled, yet fully inflated overhead, and appears normal. However, you will still have a high sink rate (which will be obvious if you look at the horizon), and you will not be able to feel the airflow on your face as in normal flight. To recover from this parachutal stall, pull down firmly on both controls and then quickly release them. This causes the canopy to rock backwards and then forwards: as it rocks forwards it will regain normal flight.

Full stall

The full stall is the most radical and dangerous of all the rapid-descent techniques. It is mentioned here for the sake of completeness, but not described. **This technique must only be practised over water under the guidance of a suitably experienced SIV instructor with full safety backup.**

Instability and active flying

Instability/ in-sta-bil'i-ti /n Want of stability; inconstancy; fickleness This dictionary definition of the word 'instability' quite nicely gives a flavour of the less desirable paraglider behaviour that will be discussed in this section.

Causes of instability

With virtually all winged aircraft, including paragliders, the dangers of stalling and spinning are ready to trip the imprudent pilot. But in addition to these potential problems, the use of a non-rigid wing gives paragliders a unique capacity for other types of uncontrolled flight!

During normal flight a paraglider is held in shape by tension in the lines: the wing generates aerodynamic forces which normally act away from the pilot, and gravity provides a force on the pilot's mass which normally acts away from the wing. If this tension is lost, either by the wing moving toward the pilot, or the pilot moving toward the wing – both of which can happen in turbulence – then the paraglider may partially collapse and the pilot will experience a greater or lesser degree of loss of control.

During the certification testing of paragliders, great attention is paid to the design's stability characteristics, specifically its resistance to getting into these abnormal flight situations and the ease with which it can be recovered (see page 29). So a very important part of avoiding instability problems is to fly wings certified in the 'safer' categories. But nevertheless it is also important for you to gain skill at avoiding departures from normal flight and at recovery from such departures.

Collapses are avoided by two linked strategies: steer clear of turbulence, and fly **actively**.

The problem with avoiding turbulent air is that you can't see it; you can, however, anticipate it. If the sky is full of cumulus then it will be turbulent. If the wind is fresh and blowing over broken ground there will be turbulence. If you fly in the lee of a spur in any wind you will find turbulence. Carefully assessing the site and conditions, and exercising your ability to say 'Not today, thank you', will keep you clear of most problems.

The second element of avoiding collapses is called **active flying**. Collapses will occur if the angle of attack gets too low, and this tends to happen if the canopy surges forward ahead of you. Active flying is all about exercising constant accurate pitch control to keep the canopy directly above your head. Keep a little pressure on the controls at all times so that you can feel what is going on with your wing: this also allows you to speed the canopy up or slow it down as necessary. If you feel the canopy start to rock forward, then apply a little control to slow it down. If you feel it dropping back, raise the controls to speed it up. If pressure begins to reduce in one of the controls, smoothly pull down on that control until the canopy can be 'felt' again. (It may be necessary to apply some control to the opposite side to maintain direction.) Try to react quickly, enabling the use of minimal input. The quicker, smoother and more instinctively these reactions can be achieved, the less likely the chance of having a major wing closure.

Recovery techniques

As outlined above, flying a 'safe' glider and using the linked strategies of avoiding turbulence and flying actively will keep you clear of most instability problems, and this will always be better than having to execute dramatic recoveries. But you must also know the basic recovery techniques, just in case.

This section outlines the major instability situations and gives a brief description of the 'standard' recovery techniques. (You should always check your glider's 'User's Manual' to see if any specific techniques are recommended.) However, in the real world there are many factors that could dramatically affect the ease with which you can achieve a recovery. These factors include the glider type, the harness type, your skill-level, your weight, the extent of the collapse, air conditions and so on. Because of this it is vital that you monitor your proximity to the ground: if you are out of control and losing height rapidly, the correct recovery technique is to use your emergency parachute!

Two fundamental points that apply to recovery from any unstable situation:

- Don't overreact.
- Maintain orientation. Glance at your wing from time to time to see what's happening, but don't gaze at it all the time; check your height and distance from obstacles, and monitor some reference point in the distance to maintain your orientation.

Asymmetric collapse

This is the most common type of collapse, where one side of the canopy has deflated, effectively forming one 'big ear' (though it may be disconcertingly large!). Most paragliders, depending on the size of the collapse, will enter a turn towards the collapsed side. The general principle of dealing with it is to maintain some directional control by using weightshift and opposite control, and then to deal with the deflation with a firm, smooth pump or pumps on the control on the deflated side. Never hold the control down when pumping, as this could result in a stall. Return the controls to the trim position immediately.

With most modern canopies particular care must be taken when maintaining direction during a large asymmetric closure. **Excessive input to correct the turn may cause the side that is still flying to stall.** Unless there is a danger of crashing into something, it is sufficient to slow down the turn – thus preventing it from becoming a spiral – while the collapse is pumped out. If the collapse is a large one (65 percent or more), allowing the canopy to roll slightly into the turn can help re-inflation. It may sometimes be necessary to pump both sides simultaneously, but again be very careful not to stall the wing.

Symmetric collapse

This is where the whole leading edge collapses. It usually occurs when the canopy is at a shallow angle of attack such as when using the speed-bar. It feels radical, yet recovery is usually straightforward. If the collapse was caused by excessive use of the speed-bar then the first move is to release the bar, quickly followed by a rapid firm pump on both controls. This should be enough to sort out the collapse. In severe cases the canopy will drop behind you and then dive forward as you swing underneath it. This dive forward will re-inflate the canopy naturally, leaving you to control the dive by judicious use of the controls.

Spins

A spin is a rapid descending rotation where one side of the wing is stalled and the other side remains flying. Spins are often confused with spiral dives, but they are fundamentally different. In a spiral the whole wing is flying and is turning about an axis beyond the span of the canopy; in a spin not all the wing is flying and the axis is within the span of the canopy. It is important to be able to tell the difference, to ensure you react appropriately.

A spin can be entered inadvertently if, when flying slowly, you further depress one of the controls and cause that side of the wing to stall; or if, when flying at normal speed, you suddenly apply a large control movement on one side, which can again stall one side of the wing. The resulting spins (which have rather different motions) are called 'flat spins' and 'maximum-amplitude spins' respectively. The recovery action for both is to get your hands up immediately, and then counter the ensuing dive with a judicious application of the controls. The faster you react in getting both controls up, the easier it will be to recover the canopy. If a spin is not recovered quickly then it is possible for risers, lines and controls to become twisted, and in this situation your emergency parachute is likely to be the only option!

Parachutal stall

In this situation the canopy is inflated as normal above your head, but rather than flying on a normal trajectory, it descends like a parachute, quite rapidly, more or less vertically. The parachutal stall is best recognised by looking at the horizon, which will show you the high rate of descent. You will also notice a lack of airflow on your face. A parachutal stall can be entered inadvertently when a gust rocks the wing back, increasing the angle of attack beyond the stall point. Usually the canopy will regain normal flight as it dives forward again, without your needing to do anything. If the canopy remains in the stall, then pull down firmly on both controls and quickly release them: this will cause the canopy to rock back and then forwards. As the canopy rocks forwards it will regain normal flight.

Full stall

The full stall can only be induced by the pilot depressing both controls fully. It does not occur without pilot input, and as such is different from the other forms of instability. The full stall is covered here because it can be used as a 'last ditch' method to recover from some of the other instability situations such as the cravat (see below). It should be borne in mind that the recovery from a full stall can be very unpredictable, and any degree of canopy asymmetry will result in it entering a 'cascade' of uncontrolled manoeuvres.

To induce a full stall, depress both controls firmly and evenly until your hands are 'locked' under the harness. You may even need to loop the control lines once around your hands ('take a wrap') to gain extra control travel. The glider will drop back into the stall (usually forming a 'horseshoe' shape), and you will swing back underneath it. It is essential to hold the controls down until you have stabilised underneath the wing. The wing will now be lurching back and forth as it tries to regain normal flight. To recover, you need to release the controls smoothly and symmetrically when the canopy is fully forward. This will allow the canopy to inflate and then dive forward. Damp down the dive, and then fly off. If the controls are released when the canopy is back, then when it inflates it could dive forward with enough energy to swing in front of or even underneath you – possibly causing you to fall into the canopy.

To exit from a full stall with any degree of safety, the controls must be released simultaneously. If they are not, a very fast spin follows.

Cravats

'Cravat' is the term used for a collapsed wingtip that has become trapped in the lines. Such events are thankfully quite rare. Cravats may occur when a glider dives while yawed, and the lower tip collapses and becomes caught in the lines. They can also occur as a result of attempts to recover from other unstable manoeuvres. A small cravat can be no more than a nuisance, with the paraglider remaining easily controlled. A major cravat causes a massive amount of drag on the collapsed side of the wing: the trick is to counter the resulting turn quickly, otherwise it can rapidly develop into a fast spiral dive.

Prevent the turn from tightening by using weightshift and opposite control. From then on the recovery is an inexact art: a minor cravat may be cleared by pumping it out (using first one, then both controls), or teased out by pulling the 'A'-lines that lead to the wingtip, or pulling an 'A'-line inboard of the cravat. This last action may also clear a bigger cravat, but if not, grasping the 'A'-riser on the collapsed side and pulling in an asymmetric collapse should leave you only needing to complete a straightforward asymmetric collapse recovery. If none of this works, and you have lots of height, you might try slowing the glider down until it almost stalls; this may force the cravat out.

If the cravat is a bad one, and the paraglider has immediately rotated into a spiral dive, recovery may be very difficult. To counter the turn you must pull on the opposite control: due to the very high forces you may need to use both hands on one control (without releasing the other). This will probably result in a full stall, in which case you may swing back quite violently. If this happens it is important to get your hands 'locked' down under the seat and hold them there until the stall has stabilised. Then recover as for the full stall.

Summary

This section includes descriptions of some rather daunting situations. As stated earlier, if you fly a stable canopy in sensible conditions, and fly actively, you are unlikely to encounter any of them. Even if you are a keen cross-country pilot and fly in more thermic air you are unlikely to experience anything other than the occasional asymmetric collapse, which is easily dealt with. But forewarned is forearmed.

It is also important to realise that recovery from the worst situations often requires a great deal of height (highly experienced test pilots have been known to fall thousands of feet attempting to recover from instability situations). **Monitor your height! If in doubt, deploy your emergency parachute.**

SIV

A possible way of learning to deal with unstable situations is to attend an SIV course run by experienced SIV instructors. SIV stands for '*simulation d'incident en vol*', which roughly translated means simulating unstable situations in flight. Here you can learn about the way your particular canopy handles and how to make the correct inputs, progressively building up to more radical manoeuvres. This must all be done over water with the use of buoyancy aids, radios, video equipment, support boats and a rescue crew.

It is arguable whether attending an SIV course is fundamental to a pilot's development. Establishing good 'active flying' skills is more important, as this will prevent the majority of collapses in the first place. Flying an appropriate wing, certified in the more 'forgiving' categories, will also help keep you out of trouble. Having said that, a good, well run SIV course, with plenty of feedback (including video), can teach you a lot about your wing and how it feels at the onset of a spin, stall or other unusual flight-mode. The course should be geared to your individual needs and experience, and the manoeuvres should be progressive. A badly run course will teach you nothing and may have a detrimental effect on your development as a pilot.

The BHPA has no direct input into the running of SIV courses, so you should carefully check the credentials of those running any course that you may be considering. To help with this the BHPA produces an information leaflet that outlines what to expect on an SIV course and contains a detailed syllabus that the instructors should adhere to. This is available from the BHPA office and at www.bhpa.co.uk/members/documents/index.php.

Chapter 13: 360s and approaches (hang gliders and paragliders)

360-degree turns

The 360-degree turn is a simple enough manoeuvre, yet several pilots have come to grief during their early attempts. The problem is that for half of the 360 degrees you will be flying more or less downwind with a high groundspeed. There is an obvious danger of flying back into the hill, or over it into a dangerous position. Less obviously, there is also the danger of confusing the high groundspeed (on the downwind part of the manoeuvre) with high airspeed. Many pilots have slowed their gliders down and stalled into the ground because of this confusion. To lessen these risks you need to be as far away from the ground as possible when you make your first attempts.

For hang-glider pilots, an aerotowed dual flight with an instructor will give you the best situation from which to attempt your first 360s. For paraglider pilots and less fortunate hang-glider pilots a winch-launch can provide an opportunity that is almost as good – 300 metres (1,000ft) or so of clear space to play with. That said, it is possible to learn to 360 from a ridge as long as you take due care. Do not attempt your first 360-degree turn unless you have these minimum conditions:

- You have a few hours of soaring logged, and are familiar with your glider and equipment.
- You are capable of completing smoothly controlled 180-degree turns.
- You are at least 150m (500ft) clear of all obstacles, vertically and horizontally.

Before starting the turn, note some landmark upwind which will help you determine when to come out of the turn. Have a really good look around for other traffic; if it is clear, apply control to achieve a moderate bank angle (similar to that used for 180-degree turns). With most hang gliders, once the turn is established you will need to centralise the controls, and perhaps push out a tiny bit to stop the nose from dropping. With most paragliders, you need to hold some control on as you go into the turn, otherwise the glider will straighten up. You may also need a little opposite control to stop the turn tightening.

Maintain a good lookout at all times. Keep looking in the direction you are going, but also keep checking – over your shoulder – the area into which your turn is taking you. As your landmark comes into view, roll the glider level and stabilise your airspeed.

Disorientation

Some pilots quickly feel disorientated when doing their first 360-degree turns. To begin with, only do one. Straighten up and fly level for a while before checking you have adequate space to attempt another. When you do come to attempt multiple 360s, hang glider pilots must remember that the correct way to recover is to take off bank first and then control the airspeed – don't start by trying to slow the glider by pushing out as this will only tighten the turn. Paraglider pilots should recover by using outside brake and weightshift.

Approaches

A good approach is the key to a good landing. In this section the term 'approach' is used for that portion of the flight that gets you from many hundreds of feet up, in the general vicinity of a landing field, to a very precise 'final approach' position that leaves you with only a few seconds' worth of straight flight and the landing itself to perform– and with every chance of getting it right.

The **ideal final-approach position** is:

- 15m (50ft) up
- lined up with your chosen landing area
- heading into wind
- wings level
- in the field (or above the boundary – but not behind it!)
- good controlled airspeed
- body positioned ready for landing.

From this position making a good landing should be a formality. (If it isn't, re-read the appropriate earlier section on landings – in Chapter 11 or 12 – and consider getting help from an instructor or coach.)

The recommended technique for getting to that 'ideal final-approach position' is called the **constant-aspect approach**. This method works equally well for paragliders and hang gliders, in light winds and fresh winds, for top-landings, bottom-landings and landings into unfamiliar fields after cross-countries. (Hang gliders will tend to fly a larger version of the pattern than paragliders, because they have greater speed and flatter glide.)

The constant-aspect approach – for bottom- or cross-country landings

The basic plan is to fly a slightly rounded hook-shaped pattern ('circuit'), starting at the top of the hook's spine upwind and slightly offset to the field, and ending at your landing-point just off the point of the hook. In doing this, you are within easy range of your field at all times, you can see your chosen landing-point at all times, you only make one extended progressive turn, which is finished while you are still more than 15m (50ft) up, and you should have plenty of time to spare to look out for other traffic.

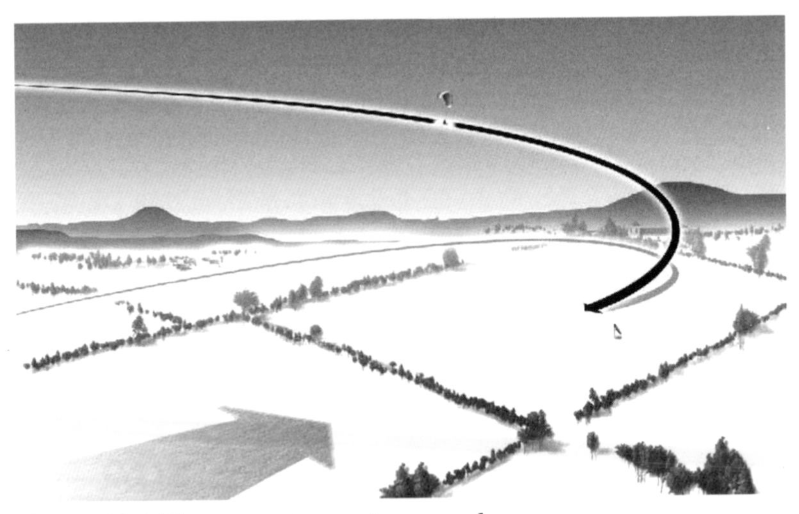

Figure 13.1 *The constant-aspect approach*

Planning the approach pattern

The first stage is to select your landing-spot within the chosen landing-field, having due regard to the wind strength, wind direction, and any peculiarities of the field. (For advice on 'Choosing a field' see the end of Chapter 15.) Usually you will choose a landing-spot near the middle of the field.

Next consider the likely location of your 'ideal final-approach position': by using the constant-aspect technique this automatically positions itself, but it is useful to have some idea in advance. Obviously it will be slightly downwind of your chosen landing-spot, but this distance will vary according to the wind strength and the type of craft you are flying. If you are paragliding and landing into a good breeze, then expect your ideal final-approach position to be a few paces back from your landing target. If there is very little wind and you are flying a hang glider, then expect it to be a good way back. Your 'ideal final-approach position' should always be within the field, or at worst above the boundary – never give yourself obstacles to clear on the final approach.

Now decide whether to make a left-hand or right-hand circuit, taking into account local factors such as a line of trees along one side of the field, which you wouldn't want to have to clear if you're running out of height – in this case fly the circuit from the other side.

Finally, decide on an area (upwind of and slightly offset from the field) in which to lose any excess height and complete your preparations before starting your circuit. This is your 'set-up zone'.

You should now have a full mental picture of your approach pattern. In practice this planning should take no more than a few seconds of mental activity.

Flying the approach

Now position yourself for the start of the circuit in your set-up zone. (By this stage if you are flying a hang glider you should unzip your harness.)

Lose excess height until you are down to the correct height to start the approach pattern – this will usually be around 110-140m (350-450ft) above the field, but the main point is that you should position yourself at a reasonable glide angle from your 'ideal position'. Imagine extending your arm horizontally, and then lowering it until it is 35-40 degrees below the horizontal. Your landing target should be at that same relative angle below the horizon. The basis of the constant-aspect approach technique is that, from this stage onwards, you concentrate on keeping this angle – and therefore the field's 'aspect' – constant: as you get lower this will bring you closer and closer to your target, until you finally land on it. Perfect!

Start your approach pattern by flying downwind, off to the field's side. Keep monitoring the field's aspect: adjust your track to keep the aspect constant by edging out a little or edging in a little as necessary. (Such corrections will certainly be required if you encounter rising or sinking air.) It may help to imagine that you are flying down the thread near the point of a screw. You should be flying at maximum-glide airspeed. And of course you should be keeping a good eye out for other traffic.

As you reach the position where your chosen landing-spot is under your left wing-tip (assuming you are doing a left-hand approach pattern), you should start on a gentle curving turn towards it. This will take you from a downwind track through crosswind and eventually into wind. Keep monitoring your angle relative to your chosen landing-spot, adjusting your track to keep it constant – and so automatically adjusting for more or less wind and lift or sink. Maintain at least maximum-glide airspeed throughout. As you come around into wind, level your wings, adopt a suitable body position for the landing, increase your speed as necessary for the final approach, and commence your landing procedure.

If at any stage you encounter massive sink, and – despite the turning towards the landing-area that is automatically required to keep the aspect constant – realise that you will run out of height before reaching the chosen landing-spot, turn in towards the field early and complete a good landing in another part of the field. The fact that the field is always in easy range, allowing you to do just this, is one of the major benefits of this approach method.

NB It may well be that you do not have enough experience to safely fly this full pattern with the downwind leg. If this is the case, modify the pattern by completing your setting-up to one side, and then completing a curving crosswind leg along the downwind boundary of the field, followed by the final approach. If obstructions prevent this, then you should reconsider whether the field is suitable.

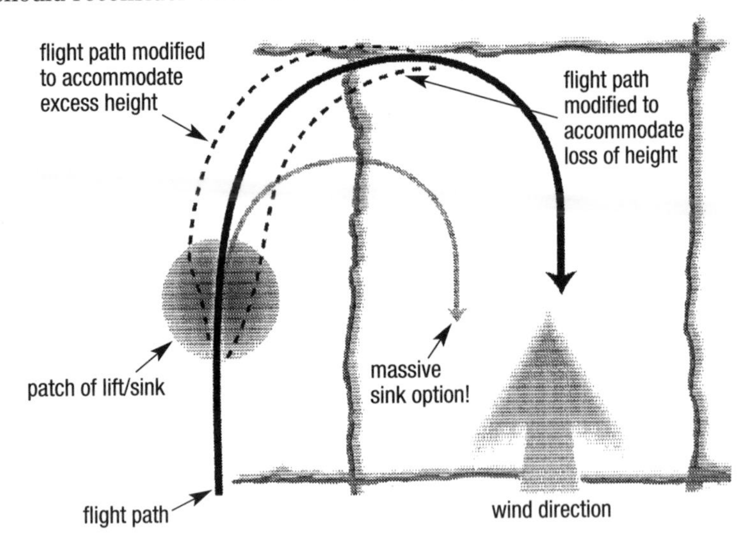

Figure 13.2 *Constant-aspect approach – adjusting the flight path for lift or sink*

'S'-turns

In the past, many pilots would simply fly directly to the downwind end of the chosen field, and use up their excess height by making a series of short beats ('S'-turns). This method can work, especially if you are flying low-performance gliders into large fields, and if there is a breeze. It does, however, have many drawbacks. These include:

- the dangers inherent in completing multiple high-bank turns at low level (especially if there is wind gradient or low-level turbulence)
- the difficulties of keeping a good lookout for other gliders while so engaged
- the difficulties you cause to other gliders that may be trying to get past you into the landing-field
- the problems of monitoring your height above the field (especially when your airspeed will probably be varying significantly during the manoeuvres)
- the fact that it is very difficult to stop yourself creeping up the field in light winds, which results in overshooting.

The crosswind approach – for top-landings

This approach method is really just a variation on the last stages of the full constant-aspect approach. Again it gives lots of opportunity for adjustments to your track to soak up any unexpected gains or losses of height, while being a simple figure to fly.

A top landing is possible only when there is enough lift to allow a planned approach, well above the hilltop, to a suitable unobstructed landing-place. This usually means that the actual landing will be a fresh-wind landing. (See the sections on landings in Chapters 11 and 12.) It also means that the approach will involve descending through a pronounced wind-gradient with associated turbulence. Depending on the shape of the hill and the wind-strength, this turbulence may be completely unmanageable. It is therefore vital that you carefully evaluate possible top-landing areas before attempting an approach and landing. At well-established sites the characteristics will be well known, so seek experienced local advice. But you should acquire the skill and habit of making your own judgement – one day you will need to put down in a less 'well-trodden' location, and so will have to rely on your own assessment.

Assessing potential top-landing areas

The hilltop should have a smooth, rounded edge with a flat top that extends back far enough to allow a turbulence-free final leg. Avoid hilltops that fall away immediately behind the crest. The hill should be free of upwind obstacles that may produce turbulence. The landing-area and possible approaches should also be clear of obstacles, including other gliders. Walk back over the landing-area, away from the hill edge, to ensure that there is no turbulence further back. Watch other pilots and talk to them.

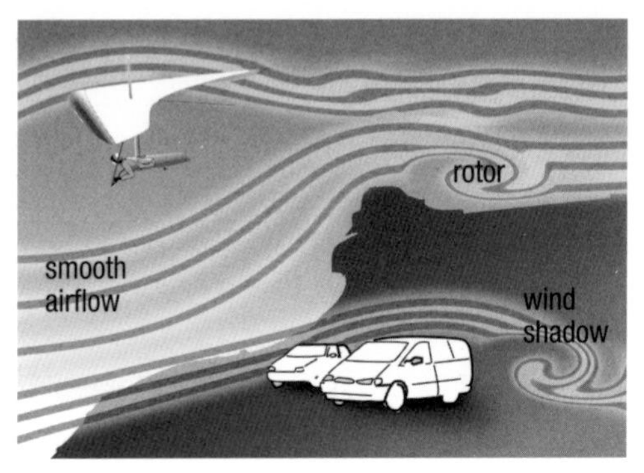

Figure 13.3 *Hilltop sources of turbulence*

Cliff or crag-top sites

Turbulence around cliff sites can be extreme, and for this reason very few are suitable for top-landing. Landings should never be attempted behind a sheer cliff (Figure 13.4a) or even a steep cliff that drops away at the top. The only type of cliff that is safe for normal top-landing is one that has a rounded slope on the top of the cliff, and a landing-area rising away from the edge (b).

a

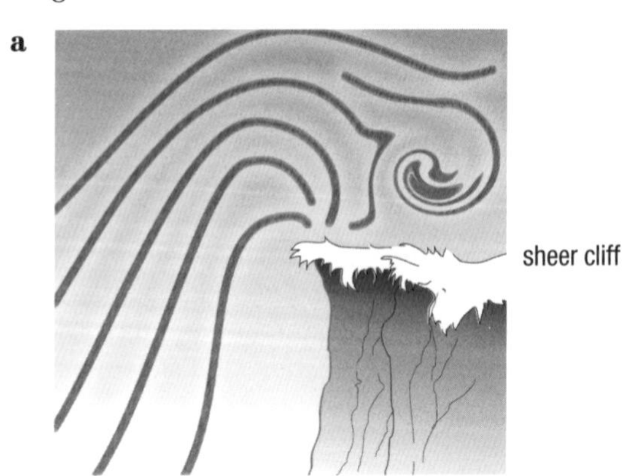

Figure 13.4 *Top-landings near (a) will have unpleasant consequences owing to the abrupt edge. If the cliff has a rounded top section (b) you could be a little safer*

One method to check for rotor turbulence is to park a rigged hang glider (or to ground-handle a paraglider) at the anticipated landing-area. If the glider shows signs of pitching about or being inflated from the rear, forget all about top-landings. You should watch the glider for several minutes in its parked position for gusts and periodic surges.

This method will only detect rotor below 2.5m (8ft). You must give further consideration to the air above this height which will be encountered on the approach path. There is no easy way to do this, apart from asking and watching experienced pilots. If in doubt, don't: there's always another day.

Attempt your first top-landings on a known and easy site, and make sure you receive proper advice and a briefing from a coach or instructor familiar with the site. Later on in your flying career, when you fly new sites, carefully examine the top-landing areas to be sure that you will be able to cope with them.

First attempts

The wind should be steady, and providing easy soaring conditions such that you can maintain a steady height above the ridge. For hang gliders this will need to be 45m (150ft) or more. For paragliders a little less is needed.

Check that the wind is either directly onto the face of the hill, or only at a slight angle to it. Decide where you intend to land. Make sure that there is a clear overshoot zone (which will usually be an escape route back into the ridge lift) and an undershoot zone. Basically, make sure that there is lots of room for error!

Begin by flying several beats to get a feel for the wind speed and direction. Identify the soaring beat that is most into wind – that is the beat that will be modified into your approach path. This will give you the lowest groundspeed and the smallest final turn.

Keep flying beats along the ridge over and past the chosen landing-place, and practise edging back over the crest to get a feel for the behaviour of the air, the boundaries of the lift, and the ease of penetration out into the lift-band again. Hang-glider pilots should unzip the harness at this stage.

When you are happy, and your landing-area and the approach are clear, adjust your height – if necessary by flying upwind out of the lift-band – before positioning to start the crosswind leg.

Figure 13.5 *Crabbing top-landing approach*

While 'crabbing' along the approach track, hang-glider pilots should fly at just above maximum-glide airspeed (5-8cm/2-3in pulled in from trim), while paraglider pilots should keep just a small amount of control applied. Keep monitoring your vertical angle relative to your chosen landing-spot, adjusting your track and crabbing angle to keep this constant. If you feel you are getting too low, turn into wind and penetrate back out into the lift-band if you can. If you are really low, you may have to land where you are – but ideally you should not allow yourself to get into this situation!

If all is going according to plan, make your final turn into wind downwind of your chosen landing-area. Hang-glider pilots should come out of prone; paraglider pilots should get their legs down and adopt the PLF position. Increase your airspeed to your final approach speed, and commence your fresh-wind landing procedure. After landing, don't just stand there in the way – clear the landing area.

After your final turn, if you find that you are not going to get your feet on the ground before reaching the edge of the hill, concentrate on penetrating back out into the lift-band with plenty of airspeed. You can then regain your height, marshal your thoughts, and set up a new approach. If it seems too difficult, the safe bottom-landing field is always available. When practising, make your first approaches a little too high, and overshoot as necessary. This will allow you to work towards the correct approach height. Top-landing approach accidents are usually caused by low approaches which result in an incomplete final turn or in a crosswind or downwind impact with the hill.

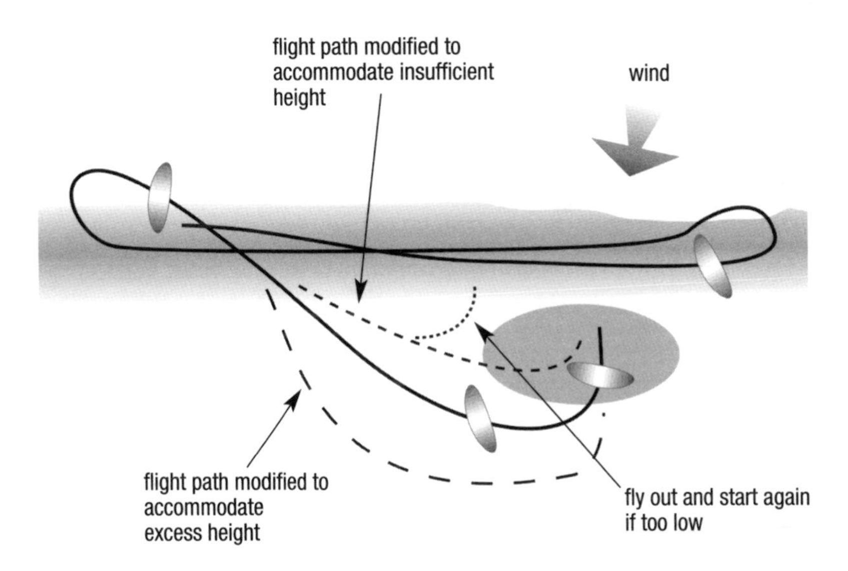

Figure 13.6 *Plan view of top-landing approaches*

Chapter 14: Tow-launching

Introduction

Tow-launching covers being launched with a ground-based line using a winch or vehicle, or being pulled up by another aircraft (aerotowing). Ground-based towing from large sites can produce launch heights of over 600m (2,000ft) – if allowed by the CAA tow-site permission – and this is more than enough to get started on a thermal soaring flight.

With hang gliders, the option of aerotowing gives even greater advantages – not only can you be towed to more or less any height you wish, but the tug can tow you towards likely-looking clouds. The tug pilot will then search out some lift and wave you off when you are in it! There are various types of tow unit and operation. These include:

- **Vehicle/fixed line** Here a vehicle pulls a fixed length of towline. (Parascending clubs invariably use this method.)
- **Pay-out winch** Here the towline is on a drum that is mounted on a tow vehicle. A short towline length is laid out to start the tow, and as the vehicle drives along (at a speed just greater than the glider airspeed) additional line is paid out at a pre-set tension.
- **Static winch** Here the winch unit (effectively a motorised drum) is anchored at the upwind end of the tow field. It draws in the towline and winds it onto the drum. (A retrieve motorcycle then drags the line back out ready for the next launch.)
- **Aerotow tug** A specialised microlight aircraft tows hang gliders into the air using a short fixed line.

Training

While some pilots will have been trained as winch-tow pilots, and so need to complete a hill endorsement (see Chapter 31) before flying in the hills, hill-trained pilots will need to complete a tow-endorsement course to gain a basic proficiency in the art. To enrol on the course you must hold a CP (hill) or higher rating and have at least ten hours logged. You will need a tow-release correctly mounted on your harness. All your equipment should be checked and approved by the senior tow coach (or tow instructor) who will be converting you. Hang-glider pilots also need wheels for the glider base-bar.

The situation is similar with hang-glider aerotowing, where you will need to complete a short aerotow endorsement course as an introduction. For this you first need to hold a 'Pilot' rating or higher. You also need to be able to handle your glider competently at the high speeds at which the tug has to fly (normally about 38mph/61kph), and you need a glider that can easily be flown at these speeds. You also need the equipment mentioned above (tow release, suitable harness and attachments, and wheels).

Tow-launching in general

All tow operations require the presence of a qualified **tow instructor** or **tow coach**, who will ensure that established safe practices are followed (as detailed in the BHPA Technical Manual). Whichever type of tow unit is used, it will be manned by a qualified **operator** who will be able to start or stop the tow (as directed), control the towline tension, and, in emergencies, cut the towline free at the tow-unit end. The tow-unit operator will be in radio contact or visual contact (usually both) with the launch point. A **launch marshal** is in charge at the launch end.

The towline will incorporate a weak link, which will break if the tension on the line exceeds the set value (normally 100kg). Excessive forces can easily be generated when towing, with the danger of the tow line then breaking at such high tension that the glider is catapulted into a dangerous attitude. Structural failure of the glider is also a possibility. The weak link ensures that the tow forces remain within manageable limits, rather like the fuse in a domestic plug. The weak link will not, however, prevent a rotation or lock-out – explained below.

The towline will also incorporate a drogue parachute to control how the line falls and to enable the operator to see clearly that the line has dropped clear of the pilot at release.

Key points for all types of towing

- Make sure that you have completed the required training and that all members of the tow club are properly qualified. Many aspects of towing look deceptively simple – this is because they are in the hands of highly experienced trained persons. There are many examples of fatal accidents involving those attempting a DIY approach.

- Make sure that you are absolutely familiar with the release system you are using. and that it is a simple, foolproof, well-engineered design.

- You must follow the advice of an instructor or tow coach as to how to attach the tow release to your harness properly. With paragliders, you must pay particular attention to avoiding any incorrect loading of the harness-to-canopy connectors.

- Never connect to a towline until the launch marshal authorises you to do so. If there is any delay or sign of confusion, disconnect from the towline. An inadvertent tow when you are not ready must be avoided!
- Be extra careful with your pre-flight checks. One of the greatest dangers in any form of tow-launching is to forget a vital action before the launch. Somehow experienced hill pilots with a well established pre-flight check pattern will clip in to a towline and believe they are ready to launch with no helmet on, or without their leg loops fastened (or in the case of hang gliding, not clipped in to the glider). To guard against this danger, in the aerotow clubs the launch marshal is required to use a written checklist. (Some winch operations have also adopted this idea, which is to be encouraged.)
- If a launch is interrupted for some reason, the whole procedure must start again from the very beginning. (One cause of accidents has been failed hang-glider tow-launch attempts: the pilot unclips to carry his glider back to the launch point and then forgets to clip back in before commencing the next attempt.)
- If there is any significant crosswind, split the angle between the towline and the direction of the wind. (In anything other than very light winds, the wind should be no more than 45 degrees off the direction of tow.) Carefully monitor the windsock for changes in wind direction, particularly on low-wind days.
- Once airborne, **do not try to counteract any crosswind.** It is imperative that you keep your glider correctly aligned with the towline, flying in the direction of the tow force – down the line, regardless of any drifting relative to the ground. Do **not** angle off into wind so that you crab along the initial 'runway' line, or for any other reason allow the glider to be facing other than at 90 degrees to the towline. The danger with being 'off-line' is that the tow tension will start to apply a sideways component, and this will cause the glider to roll further off course. This increases the tow force, which accelerates the turn, and if it is not corrected quickly a rotation (or 'lock-out') will result. This can happen very rapidly, and in an extreme case the forces involved may become so great that you will be unable to steer back on-line, and a disaster is likely.

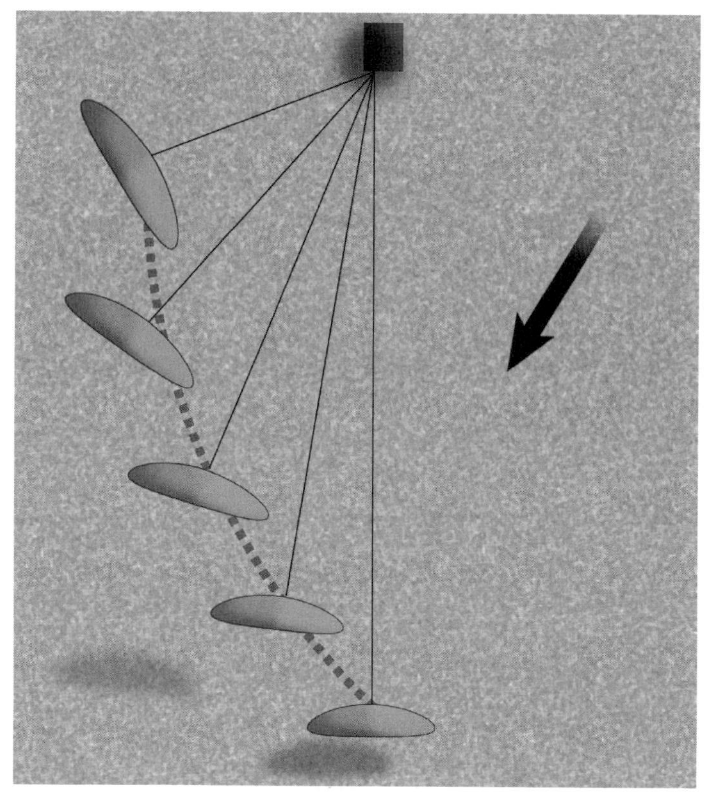

Figure 14.1 *Correct 90 degree alignment with the towline*

- To prevent this, the alert winch operator will reduce the tow force if you let your heading drift off alignment with the towline. This reduction in power should act as a signal to you that something is wrong, and also makes it easier for you to recover your course. Power will not be restored until you get back correctly in line.
- If the situation continues to worsen, the winch operator can totally remove all line tension, and as a last resort he can guillotine the line. As well as being costly and time-consuming to repair the line, guillotining can create its own problems – the sudden release of tension could at worst stall the glider (or collapse the canopy in the case of a paraglider). At best, it leaves the pilot trailing a considerable amount of line hanging below him – which is a major hazard.
- Dealing with a trailing line. This situation can arise if the line breaks, or if it is released from the tow-unit end because you have

got out of position or have experienced a release failure. It is imperative that the trailing end is not allowed to snag on any ground feature, as this 'anchoring' can lead to the glider 'down-planing' and flying straight into the ground.

- Exactly what you should do depends on the length of towline, your height, and the precise problem. The priority is to make sure that the line is not still attached to the release, especially if the lower end is within a few hundred feet of the ground. Remove it from the release, hold it loosely in one hand (that way if it snags it will pull out of your hand) and drop it over a clear area, long before the bottom end gets anywhere near the ground. If the bottom end of the line is close to the ground to start with, then never mind the niceties: just drop the line! If you cannot release the line, you must set up a gentle 'S'-turn pattern over a clear area, so as to lay the line down clear of any obstructions. Land right there – and find out what went wrong!
- You should avoid getting fixated with trying always to land back at the launch point, especially if your height becomes marginal. The glider should be turned into wind at a safe height well before landing, even if that landing has to be well up the field.
- If at any time during the launch any member of the launch crew spots anything which makes the proposed launch potentially unsafe, they must shout **'Stop – stop – stop'**.
- You are free to release the glider at any stage of the tow, and should do if you are experiencing any difficulty or if the tow tension becomes excessive. Most tow situations get worse very rapidly once things start to go wrong. It is far better to release the tow (and fly down safely to wonder if perhaps you could have sorted out the problem) than to be lying in hospital wishing you had released! This is especially important with aerotowing, where you could be jeopardising the tug pilot's safety besides your own.

Signals

The launch marshal relays the pilot's requests to the tow-unit operator either by radio or visually. For visual signalling a brightly-coloured signalling bat (shaped like an over-sized tennis racket) is used. Not all the signals are used on every launch in every discipline.

'Take up slack'

The spoken signal is **'Take up slack'** (sometimes this is abbreviated to simply **'Take up'** or **'Up slack'**). The visual signal is swinging the signalling bat from left to right, underhand (4 o'clock to 8 o'clock).

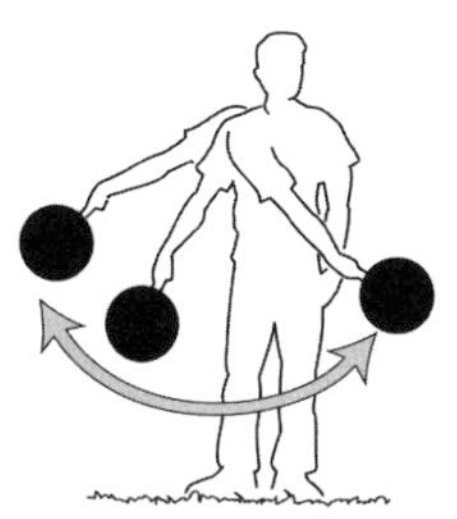

Figure 14.2 *Take up slack*

'Stand by'

The spoken signal is **'Stand by'** (in some clubs the word **'Hold'** is used). The visual signal is holding the signalling bat stationary in a horizontal position.

Figure 14.3 *Stand by*

'All out'

The spoken signal given by the launch marshal is **'All out – all out – all out'**, repeated until the tow is fully under way. The visual signal is waving the signalling bat overhead, left–right–left (10 o'clock to 2 o'clock), which continues until the pilot is airborne.

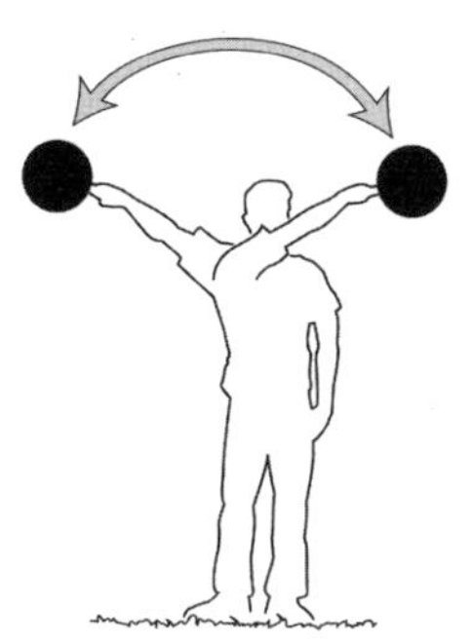

Figure 14.4 *All out*

'Stop'

The command to stop the tow is **'Stop – stop – stop'**. The visual signal is holding the bat stationary overhead. If a **'Stop'** command is given, then the pilot should release the line. Once the problem is resolved the tow can start again, right from the beginning.

Figure 14.5 *Stop*

'Stop, I want to release' (in-flight signal: winch-launching)
The signal for this is for the pilot to hold his legs spread wide. This position must be held until the winch operator has responded and the line-tension has been reduced.

'Release immediately' (in-flight signal: aerotow-launching)
The tug pilot waves his arm clearly up and down, which means that the hang-glider pilot must release immediately.

'Unable to release'(in-flight signal: aerotow-launching)
If the hang-glider pilot's tow-release fails, the pilot should lower his legs. The tug pilot will then tow the glider to within easy gliding range of a large suitable landing area before releasing the line. (You should carry a webbing cutter to use in these circumstances.)

Winch-launching hang gliders

The key aspects for the pilot are making smooth transitions between the various stages of the launch, maintaining a safe airspeed, and keeping the glider correctly 'on-line' (i.e. pointing along the tow rope).

Carry out your normal Daily Inspection and all your pre-flight checks. When these have been completed, including a check of the release system, you tell the winch operator you are ready for tow by giving the spoken signal **'All checks complete'**. The next stage – to take up the slack in the line – is entirely at the direction of the pilot. Once the winch has been readied by **'All checks complete'**, the winch operator will await the next signal.

Point the glider at the winch and get the wings absolutely level. If there is any significant crosswind, split the angle between the towline and the direction of the wind. (In anything other than very light winds, the wind should be no more than 45 degrees off the direction of tow.) Carefully monitor the windsock for changes in wind direction, particularly on low-wind days.

When absolutely ready, get the launch marshal to confirm that it **is 'All clear above and behind'**. If all is OK, lean back slightly (ready to resist the initial gentle pull) and then clearly ask the launch marshal to signal **'Take up slack'**. This signal will be passed on to the winch operator. The winch operator will gently take the slack out of the line. As the line comes tight, give the command **'Stand by'** or **'All out'** as required.

'Stand by' This optional stage allows you time to make any last-second corrections (e.g. for gusty conditions). Check the windsock, check that your wings are level, get the launch marshal to confirm again that it is still **'All clear above and behind'** – and if all is OK, call clearly **'All out'**, and repeat this command until you are airborne.

'All out' As the tow tension is increased, maintain the glider's angle of attack and move along the line of tow while maintaining some tension on the line to avoid overrunning it. Allow yourself to be pulled along the line of tow as your speed increases towards take-off speed. When the glider has sufficient airspeed and the winch is developing sufficient power, allow the glider to take off.

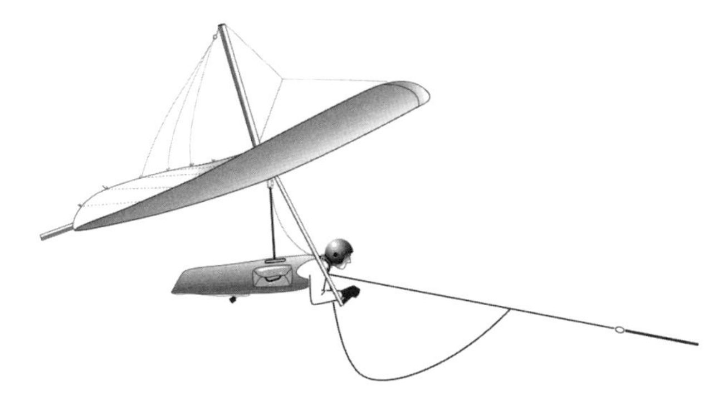

Figure 14.6 *Launch and initial climb using top line*

Keeping plenty of airspeed, adopt a gentle climb. Low rates of climb which keep the glider close to the ground for long periods can be dangerous, particularly on thermic or turbulent days. On the other hand, high rates of climb and a low airspeed could possibly lead to a wing drop or to a dangerously high nose-angle if there is a launch failure or if the towline breaks.

Throughout the following steps, keep the glider correctly aligned with the towline. Go into prone smoothly, without changing the bar position, maintaining a safe airspeed and gentle climb rate. A common mistake when getting into prone is to put your feet into the harness before transferring your hands to the base-bar. This reduces control at a time when it is needed most.

Once above 30m (100ft), prepare to release the top line. Pull on extra speed for a couple of seconds (to reduce line tension and the subsequent jolt to the weak link and towline), move your left hand to the centre of the base-bar and operate the top release with your right hand. There will be a small jolt as the line beneath the base-bar takes up the tension. Using a steady progressive movement (to avoid sudden changes in the line tension), ease the bar out to allow the glider to climb more steeply.

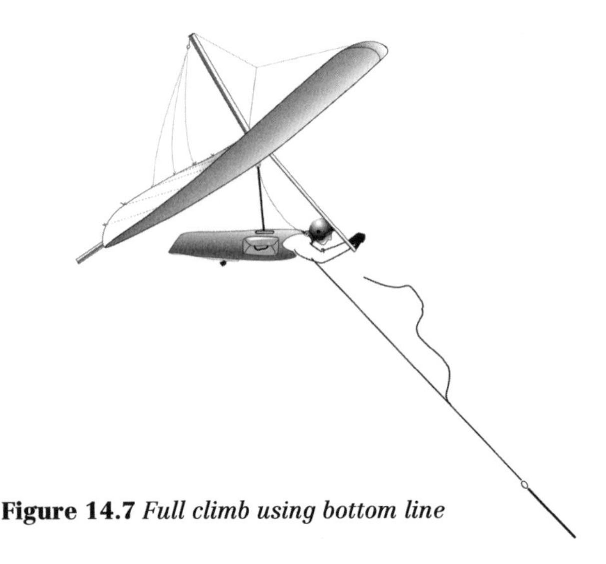

Figure 14.7 *Full climb using bottom line*

As the glider reaches the top of the launch, you will be viewing the tow unit from behind the base-bar. Before reaching a position vertically above the tow unit, you should prepare for release. Pull a little extra speed for a second or two (to reduce line tension), and then operate the release. **Check to make sure that the line has separated from the tow release before flying away.**

Tow-launching paragliders

Launch procedures differ slightly from club to club: At some clubs the pilot calls the commands for the signaller to repeat. At others the launch marshall calls the commands. Make sure that you know exactly the system in place.

Carry out your normal Daily Inspection and all your pre-flight checks. When these have been completed, including a check of the release system, you tell the tow-unit operator you are ready for tow by giving the spoken signal **'All checks complete'**. When you are poised for take-off, you should get the launch marshal to confirm that it is **'All clear above and behind'**. (In tow-launching parascending canopies the launch marshal will ask **'Wing tips ready?'** followed by **'Pilot ready?'**)

If all is OK, you should lean back slightly (ready to resist the initial gentle pull) and then clearly ask the launch marshal to signal **'Take up slack'**. The operator will gently take the slack out of the line. Initially, you should resist this gentle pull, then make a good forward inflation in the direction of the tow force. Check your canopy, and if you are happy to proceed with the launch, shout **'All out'** and repeat this command until you are airborne. (In tow-launching parascending canopies the launch marshal may control the lifting and letting go of the canopy by the wing-tip holders.)

The launch marshal will relay the **'All out'** signal to the operator, and the tow force will be increased gradually. As the force increases, you must run forward, keeping the canopy straight. The winch operator will pull you into the air within a few steps.

In low-wind or nil-wind conditions, the procedure is to take up slack and then call **'Stand by'**. When you are absolutely ready, give the **'All out'** command. Then use the tow pull to launch the canopy and keep moving until off the ground. In these conditions it will not be possible to hold the paraglider overhead, and the launch will have to proceed in one smooth sequence from the **'All out'** command.

In strong winds the paraglider can be inflated under a **'Stand by'** signal, after **'Take up slack'** and before **'All out'**. The operator must be notified at all times that a pilot is attached to the towline, as in these circumstances the paraglider can 'kite up' against a locked and unsupervised drum, which is extremely dangerous. In gusty conditions an anchor person (helmeted and gloved) can be used to steady the line while the canopy is brought overhead, but care must be taken to prevent the anchor person being lifted off. For safety reasons most paraglider tow clubs stop operating if the wind reaches 10mph on the surface.

Once airborne, concentrate on keeping your canopy at 90 degrees to the towline. Keep checking this using the 'nodding dog' technique. (Look up to see that your canopy is pointing the same way as your body and is not banked; look down to see that the wing and your body are at 90 degrees to the line. Keep repeating this movement.)

Do not apply any brake – the winch operator will govern your climb rate: your priority is maintaining a safe airspeed. The only time you need to use the brakes is for small steering corrections. (If you apply brake the canopy will sit back, and the winchman, seeing the canopy sitting back, will think that he is pulling you too hard so will reduce power. Taken to the extreme you will end up deep-stalled on the tow line – it has happened and the results are not pretty!)

The **initial climb** to around 50m (150 feet) will be fairly gentle, with the winch operator keeping the canopy well above your head so that, in the event of any launch failure, transitioning to a glide and landing is straightforward and safe. During this initial climb out, once safely clear of the ground, you should get properly into your harness.

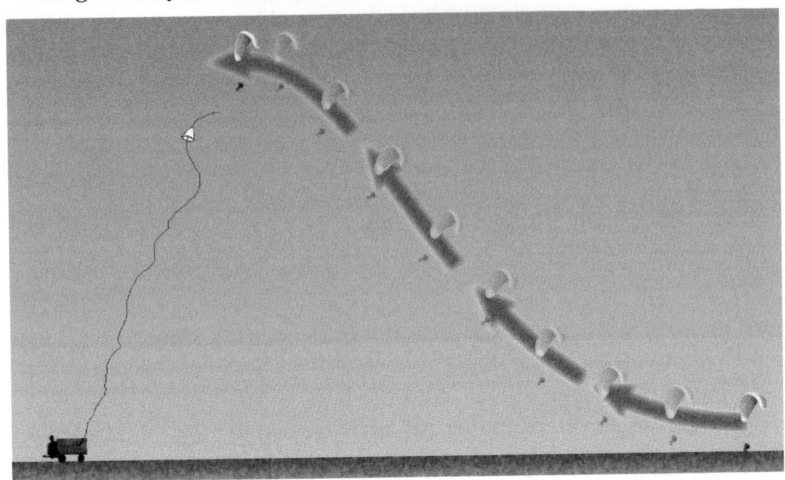

Figure 14.8 *Climb trajectory - full-power climb begins above 50m*

Once safely above 50m (150 feet) the winch operator will go to the **'full climb'** stage and line tension will be increased from around 40kg to perhaps 80kg. The glider will climb quite steeply with the pilot under the leading edge of the canopy. Again the important things to do are to concentrate on keeping the canopy aligned with the tow line – 'nodding dog' - and not applying brake other than for steering corrections.

Signals while on tow

Once airborne, if at any time you wish to stop the tow, use the visual signal (legs spread wide).

Releasing

As the winch operator sees the glider get to a point some 60 to 70 degrees above the launch point he will smoothly back off the power so that the canopy comes back over your head ready for the release. Do not hang on to the tow and try to fly over the winch – no extra height is gained.

When you feel the tow tension decrease, wait for the canopy to stabilise then let go of one control, grasp the release and pull it firmly. Return your hand to the control and resume the normal flying position.

Check to make sure that the line has fallen away from the tow release before flying away.

Common problems

The following are common problems for pilots converting to tow operations from hill-flying.

- **Weightshift under tow** Too much weightshift under tow can be difficult to control. You should adjust your harness cross-bracing to minimise weightshift.
- **Flying too slowly** (too much symmetrical control applied during the tow) There is no need to slow the canopy right down to make it climb. The rate of ascent is controlled from the winch. Over-use of control can stall the paraglider.
- **Over-correcting after a line break** A line break can be disorientating, as the canopy can surge forward; however, you should not damp the surge too much. You should feel and practice this to some degree when the tension is reduced before release on a normal flight.

Aerotow-launching hang gliders

Pre-launch procedure

To guard against the danger of forgetting some vital check or action, the launch marshal uses a written checklist. There is no need to attempt to memorise the checklist (indeed, this may be counter-productive), but for information the order is as follows:

Glider check: has the glider been checked?

Helmet: on and fastened?

Leg loops: engaged?

Hang check: clipped in, correct loops, karabiners locked, bar clearance sufficient?

Bar-clearance check: The pilot, in prone, hooks his thumbs behind the release and pushes down to check that there is still at least 5cm(2 in) clearance above the bar and any ancillary equipment. The pilot also checks that the release is securely attached to the harness.

Release check: The launch marshal attaches the towline and checks that the release is functioning. Take particular care if a release with two levers, as used in winch-towing, is being used for aerotowing: the towline should be connected to the gate which opens when either lever is operated.

Launch sequence

When the checks have been completed you are ready to start the launch sequence.

Assuming that you are now ready to launch immediately, you then reattach the line, taking the opportunity to make a quick visual check of the condition of the weak link, and giving the line a pull to ensure it is correctly held in the tow release.

You then ask the launch marshal to check the airspace above and behind him by asking **'All clear above and behind?'** If it is safe to proceed, you move to the **'Take up slack'** stage. This is simply removing any slack in the towline, either by taking a few steps back or by asking for the tug to ease forward by calling **'Take up'** to the launch marshal.

Once the slack is taken up you may wish to pause (e.g. to rebalance the glider) before going to **'All out'**. In this case you must ask for the tug to cease easing forward by calling **'Stand by'** to the launch marshal.

Once balanced, with the correct angle of attack (slightly higher than for a hill launch), one foot forward ready to run, brain 'on', you call **'All out'** to the launch marshal. This signal literally means: 'the glider pilot is ready if you, the tug pilot, consider it safe to take off'. Sometimes the tug pilot will not respond immediately, perhaps because he has identified a hazard and is waiting for it to clear. If there is any delay, you must remain entirely ready to launch at any time. If this is not possible, then you must tell the launch marshal to signal either **'Stand by'** or **'Stop'** as appropriate. If **'Stop'** is most appropriate, then you should release the line.

On a normal launch the tug will accelerate down the runway more or less immediately the **'All out'** signal is given. You should then allow yourself to be pulled forward, maintaining the correct angle of attack until airborne. The hang glider will lift off before the tug, so after lift-off you should maintain a height of approximately 3m (10ft) until the tug lifts off. As the tug will still be accelerating you will need to increase speed progressively to avoid climbing.

Once the tug lifts off, maintain your position relative to the tug until it becomes possible to use the horizon. Once the horizon comes into view, usually within a few seconds, position the tug's base-bar or kingpost top on the horizon. (Your aerotow club's chief aerotow coach will tell you which positioning is favoured in that particular club.) Make small corrections to maintain this position. With minor lateral excursions, allow the tug to pull the glider back into line. With greater lateral excursions, after making a corrective input, start to straighten up before coming into line behind the tug, otherwise you will overshoot. If at any time you become badly out of position (exceeding or likely to exceed 30 degrees off-line), release at once. Lock-outs or lock-ups will develop very quickly once started.

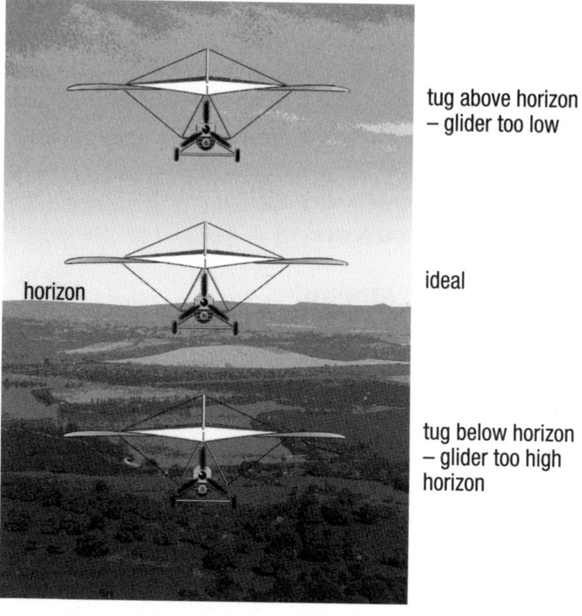

Figure 14.9 *Maintaining position during tow*

Corrections. Keep corrections small and smooth. If you react too slowly and then attempt to sort things out through large corrections, you will only make the situation worse. A typical example would be if you allow yourself to get too low and then push out hard to try to get back into position; this action will draw lots of energy from the towline, which in turn, will slow the tug. The tug will then pitch down to regain airspeed just as you zoom up. Suddenly you are too high, so you pull in rapidly and the situation gets worse and worse. Your actions should be to apply smooth but insistent pressure to remain in line, rather than resorting to radical bar movements.

Turns. If the glider flies directly behind the tug it will cover the same distance. If the glider flies to the outside of the turn it will cover more distance in the same time, and so will travel faster and will try to climb. If the glider flies inside the turn it will travel a smaller distance in the same time, and so will fly more slowly and will tend to sink (or to climb less fast). Fly directly behind the tug unless there is a good (speed) reason not to. Watch the tug pilot and anticipate the tug's movements – turn with it rather than after it.

The release

On release the glider should carry out a climbing left turn. Do not pull in before releasing, as you might do with a winch-launch: firstly you might catch up with the line (your glider will usually have a much higher top speed than the tug), and secondly the tug pilot wants to feel the jerk when you release. That tells him you have gone. Just make sure that you carry on in controlled flight as you operate the release: if you start to go into your climbing left turn as you operate the release, there will be a big problem if the release doesn't work first time!

Approach and landing

On the way back down to the field, make sure you comply with any agreed circuit patterns: many aerotow clubs share microlight airfields, and it is essential that everyone follows agreed safe procedures. Usually you will fly a right-hand pattern (the opposite direction to the tug pattern), using a constant-aspect circuit. Avoid 'S'-turns – they block the approach for tugs and other gliders.

After landing, park your glider somewhere sensible: usually there is a designated area where it will be safe from the hazard of being ripped in half by the towline as the tug lands, and where it doesn't block the landing-area or approach for other gliders wanting to land. In crosswind conditions, gliders should normally park on the upwind side of the approach path so that the towrope is not dragged across them.

Crosswinds

If you are foot-launching in winds of more than 5kph (3mph), the angle between the direction of tow and the wind should be no more than 45 degrees. You should angle slightly into wind at the start of the take-off.

Trolley launch

If the winds are light (less than 5mph/8kph), most aerotow clubs will use a launch trolley. There are extra checks and procedures to be followed when using these, so most clubs use an additional checklist to ensure that nothing is forgotten. Although the trolley launch seems daunting to most pilots at first, after one or two goes it usually becomes the preferred launch technique. Your chief aerotow coach will brief you thoroughly before you use a launch trolley.

Chapter 15: Soaring

Ridge-soaring

Ridge lift

If horizontally moving air ('wind') encounters a ridge, the air is forced to flow upwards over it. As the air is deflected up the face of the ridge there will be a vertical component in the flow. The size of this vertical component (the amount of 'lift' it will provide) is dependent on the steepness of the slope and the strength of the wind. It also depends on the angle at which the wind meets the slope and the stability of the air. Ridge-soaring (also known as hill-soaring) is simply the process of tracking backwards and forwards in front of the ridge, riding this stream of rising air.

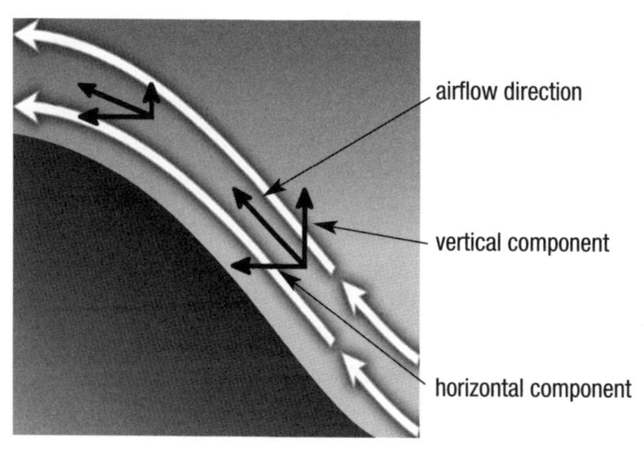

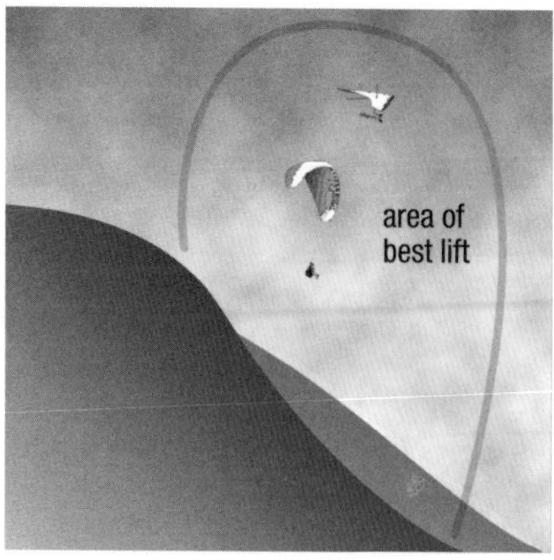

Figure 15.1 *Ridge lift*

Your height gains are likely to be in the region of a few hundred feet (a hundred metres or so), but the beauty of ridge lift is its reliability: for as long as the wind continues to blow onto the face, the lift will be there!

Learning to ridge-soar

Soaring the windward face of a hill is not difficult, but like everything else in flying it needs to be thought about and planned before you try it for the first time. This major step should only be undertaken under the watchful eye of your instructor. (There are special arrangements whereby hang glider pilots may make their first soaring flights under the guidance of a coach. Check the BHPA Student Task Booklet for details.)

The hill

This should be a ridge that is soared frequently and has no nasty characteristics. Talk with other pilots about how best to fly it, and find out about any difficulties it could produce. Before take-off, study the length of the hill that you propose to use, and decide where to turn; walk along the top and see what it looks like close to. The beat should have no marked changes in direction, and should be free of gullies, large trees and telephone wires. Watch other pilots. Ideally your instructor or coach will take you up on a dual glider to show you the soaring beat, but this is not always possible.

The weather

You need a steady, moderate wind, directly onto the hill. Avoid a day of strong thermals, especially one with large cumulus or cumulonimbus developing upwind. If it is a grey day with an inclination to rain or drizzle, watch for the formation of orographic cloud in the slope lift. At the first appearance of any rags of low cloud near the hill, land at once, as such cloud may grow rapidly.

For your first attempt, the wind should be blowing straight onto the face of the hill you intend to soar, and it should be between 22 and 32kph (14-20mph) for hang gliders, 19-26kph (12-16mph) for paragliders, without gusts. If it is a few degrees off the face, note the direction in which you will be flying more into wind with a slower groundspeed, and which direction will be more downwind with higher groundspeed. When in the air, concentrate on airspeed, and do not confuse it with speed over the ground.

Finally, plan how you will reach a good landing-area from any point along the soaring beat, in case you do not stay up as well as you had hoped.

Inform and be informed

Tell other pilots that you will be trying to soar, so that they can give you plenty of space; but do not rely on them to keep clear, and do not fly if the air is crowded. Remind yourself of the anti-collision 'Rules of the Air'. Also make sure you have your red ribbon attached to the kingpost (or harness for paragliders). Before take-off, be sure to discuss your flight plan with your instructor or coach, who will need to be satisfied that your knowledge and understanding are adequate.

The take-off and first turn

By now you should be more than capable of taking off properly. Just do what you've always done – or should have done. Relax, be in control, stay in control and be positive.

Now, immediately after take-off, the glider should lift cleanly up and away from the hill. To stay in the lift-band, you will have to turn along the ridge quite quickly after your feet leave the ground. This turn is crucial – too steep or too quick, and you will end up back on top with bent aluminium (or flapping canopy) all around you. Too gentle, and you will be flying away from the slope and out of the lift-band. The correct turn will enable the glider to track parallel to the ridge. As it does so, and if the conditions are nicely soarable, you should be in front of and higher than the crest. If the wind is not straight onto the hill, but coming, for example, slightly from the left, your first turn should be to the left.

If you fail to soar, perhaps because that first turn was too gentle, it doesn't matter at all. Use the flight to practise your turns at the end of each beat, and finish with a good landing at the bottom. Then go back up and have another go!

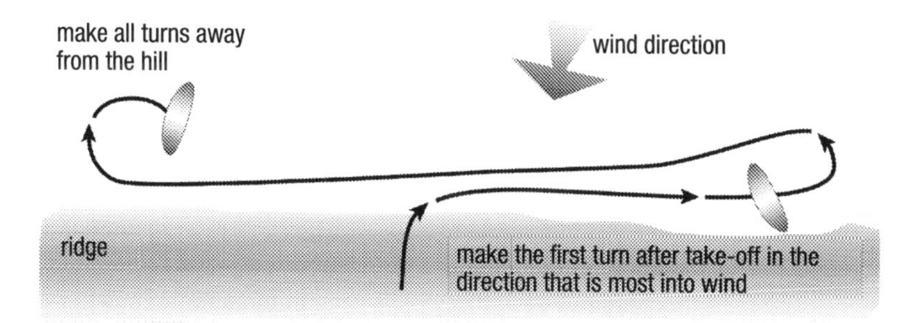

Figure 15.2 *Ridge-soaring flight path*

The flight

If all is going to plan, you will now be above and just in front of the slope. You must keep looking ahead to see where you are going, and sideways to relate your position to the hill, and all around for other traffic! The continuous head movements that are now necessary may seem difficult if you have only been looking forwards in your previous flights.

Continue along the ridge until you approach the place where it is best to turn. Let the glider drift gently in towards the hill so that you will have room to turn without flying out of the lift-band on its upwind side. Check the airspace, and make a positive but gentle turn (away from the ridge), then track back along the ridge, adjusting your position to stay in the best lift. Repeat the process. Do not experiment with new lengths of ridge on this first flight, however well you are doing. Concentrate on flying accurately, smoothly, and at the right airspeed. Do not stay up for longer than 10 to 12 minutes. Obey the 'break right' rule (see Chapter 23). When the hill is on your right, keep close to it. When it is on your left, be prepared to move out from it to give approaching gliders enough space.

If you are finding it difficult to soar and you keep sinking level with or below the hilltop, do not try to defy gravity. Land at the bottom and try again later. However, if you are high up when you decide you should return to earth, the simplest way to reach the usual bottom field is to fly 100m or so (about 330ft) into wind, and then carry on flying a ridge-soaring type pattern. You will no longer be in the lift-band, so you will gradually lose height. Aim to be opposite the take-off point at about hilltop height. From there, the way down to the landing-place will be familiar.

If there are other pilots flying, you will have to watch them closely. Avoid flying close behind another glider, or its wake turbulence will get you! Do not be mesmerised into following someone you think is an expert. Always make all turns outward from the hill.

Soaring in light-wind conditions

In lighter winds the lift-band is small and close to the hill. There is a huge temptation to try to stay up by flying very close to the hill, as slowly as possible. Many pilots have been injured through inadvertently stalling in this situation. The moral of the tale is: don't scrape hills too close and too slowly. Maintain your airspeed, and if you can't stay up, admit defeat and land at the bottom (or slope-land if you are paragliding).

Coastal soaring

Coastal sites can provide very smooth, easy soaring conditions, so can be ideal for gaining airtime and experience. But there are a few important points that must be noted:

Sharp-edged cliff sites (as with inland crag sites) pose special difficulties in taking off, due to the airflow's almost totally vertical component up the cliff face. For hang gliders there is a special take-off technique (see 'Taking off from a sheer cliff or crag (assisted)' on page 91). For paragliders a more suitable location has to be found.

Once airborne, you should make the first turn well out from the edge to be sure the glider is clear of any turbulence. In moderate winds, the lift generated by cliffs is good, and you will soon be well up and clear of the ground. When the wind is light, however, then the lift-band becomes narrow and turbulent, especially if the glider drops below the cliff-top. In this case, you have got to go in close to regain height, and a little extra speed is necessary to deal with the extra turbulence.

If it is obvious you are still going down, you should accept it, as scratching for lift along a cliff face is not a healthy business. The turbulence usually gets much worse from midway to the bottom of the cliff, so be careful. Landing on the beach should be made into the wind, of course, but where will the wind be? If the wind direction at the top is even as little as 5 degrees away from being straight onto the cliff, the predominant wind direction on the beach will be almost parallel to the cliff face.

You should never fly a coastal site if there is no bottom-landing area within easy reach. Landing in the sea is almost invariably fatal.

Thermal soaring

On a good day, heights of several thousand feet are there for the taking by using thermal currents. As this form of lift is not dependent on a particular ground feature like a ridge, it also provides you with a means of breaking away from the ridge and flying cross-country. On many summer days these invisible columns of warm rising air provide opportunities to top up your height as you work your way silently across the countryside. Thermal soaring is perhaps the most exhilarating experience that flying can bring.

What is a thermal?

When the sun beats down, the ground is not warmed uniformly, because different surfaces reflect or absorb heat to varying degrees. For example, the surface of a dry ploughed field will warm up much more quickly than that of a similar area of woodland. The air in contact with these different ground sources will therefore also be heated differentially. When the air over a suitable thermal source is warmed, it becomes less dense and it will start to rise. As this mass, or bubble, of air goes up it will both expand and cool. But it will go on rising as long as it is warmer than the air around it.

Figure 15.3 *Thermal generation*

The pressure and temperature of the surrounding air mass is normally less the higher you go (which helps the thermal maintain the positive temperature difference it needs to continue rising). On average the atmosphere is found to be about 2°C cooler for every 300m (1,000ft) of altitude, but this figure varies from day to day, and at different heights. It is not unusual to find height bands over which the air stays the same temperature (an isothermal layer) or perhaps even gets warmer with height (an inversion). The actual drop in temperature with altitude on any given day is called the **environmental lapse rate** (ELR).

The behaviour of the thermal rising through the atmosphere is more predictable. As this warm air rises, it encounters lower pressure. It expands, and this makes it cool down (remember Boyle's Law at school and those experiments with bicycle pumps?). During this process (in theory at least) it exchanges no heat with the surrounding air. The expansion or contraction of a gas with no input or output of heat is called an *adiabatic* process. The rate of change of temperature with height caused by this process is a fixed physical property of air. This rate is known as **the dry adiabatic lapse rate** (DALR) and is 3°C per 300m (1,000ft). 'Dry' in this context means that all moisture is in its vapour form and has not started to condense. Air that is forced to rise for any reason, such as through thermal activity or flowing over an obstacle, will reduce in temperature at the DALR.

Stability and instability

When a thermal rises it cools at the DALR of 3°C per 300m (1,000ft). If the surrounding air temperature is reducing at a lower rate – the ELR averages 2°C per 300m (1,000ft) – the bubble will soon reach a level where it is as cool as the air surrounding it and will cease to rise. In these conditions the atmosphere is described as being relatively **stable**.

If the surrounding air is cooling at a higher lapse rate – for instance, if the ELR on the day is greater than 3°C per 300m (1,000ft) – then the bubble will continue to be warmer than the surrounding air and it will continue to rise. This condition is described as being **unstable**. Unstable conditions obviously favour the development of thermals, because of the general increase of vertical air movement, although if the atmosphere is too unstable thunderstorms can rapidly form. Moderately unstable conditions make for a good cross-country flying day.

Cloudbase

Usually, in Britain, condensation of the moisture in the thermal air will occur at a few thousand feet when the air has cooled to its **dew point**, with cumulus clouds forming near the top of the up-currents. The act of condensing liberates some heat, and this boosts the thermal, enabling its cloud to grow to greater heights. Saturated air has a lapse rate of 1.5°C per 300m (1,000ft), although this will vary according to the degree of saturation. This figure is known as the **saturated adiabatic lapse rate** (SALR). These can be illustrated by a tephigram (a graph showing temperature and humidity against altitude).

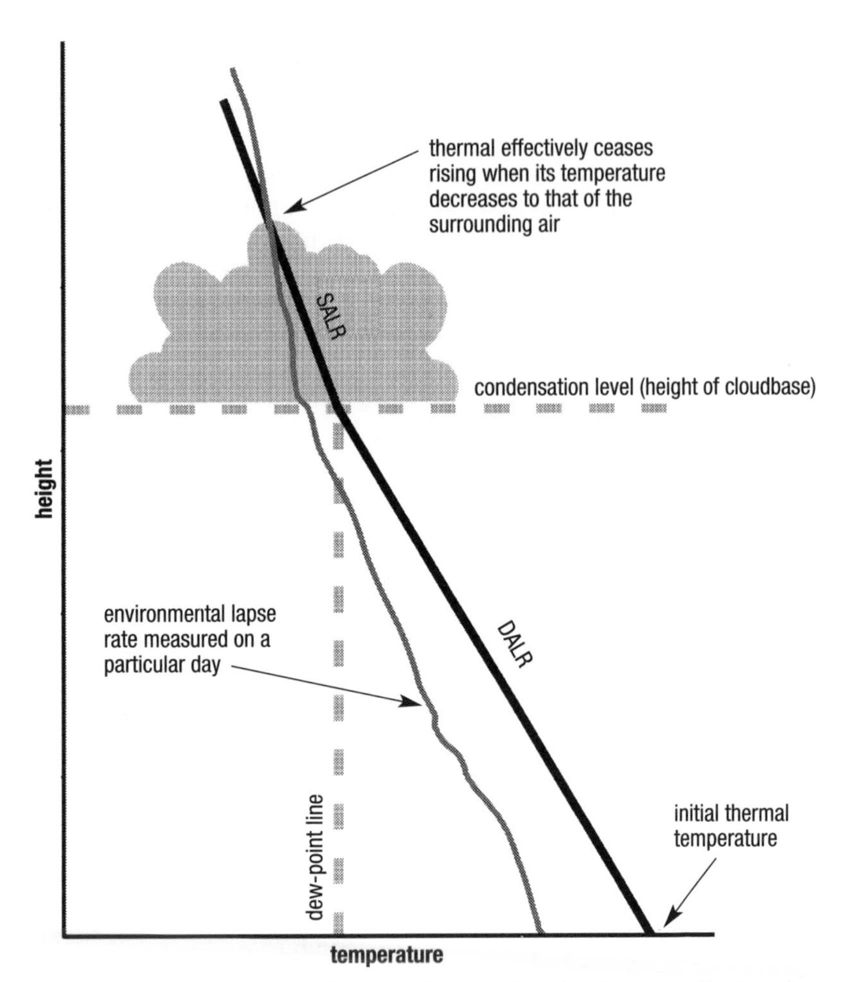

Figure 15.4 *A highly simplified tephigram showing factors affecting the progress of a typical thermal*

The height at which cloud – in this case cumulus cloud – forms depends on how much moisture the air is carrying as invisible water vapour. If the air is dry, the level at which cloud starts forming (cloudbase) will be higher than when the air is moist. This is because, as the air rises and cools, it becomes less and less able to carry the moisture as vapour, and this starts to condense out as droplets, which are visible as cloud. Obviously the drier the air, or the higher the temperature, the higher the thermal will be able to rise before any cloud forms.

The deciding factor on many cross-country flights is the altitude of the cloudbase. You can get a good idea of the prospective cloudbase height on a particular day by getting a weather report giving the dew point as well as the air temperature. Just do the following calculation:

[air temperature (°C) – dew point (°C)]° x 400 = cloudbase (feet)

Thermals become weak, or cease to form, when there is 'over-development' of the clouds, which means that they have spread out and cut off the sunlight heating the ground. On windier days the forming thermals are disturbed before they are ready to rise, or shredded on their way up.

Using thermals

If a glider is flying along a ridge where a thermal is rising, the ordinary slope-lift will be affected in a number of ways:

- It will be stronger within the confines of the thermal.
- It will modify the direction of the wind, because it is drawing in air from all around to replace that which has risen; this temporary alteration in direction can weaken the ordinary slope-lift to either side of the thermal.

If you unexpectedly fly into a thermal while ridge-soaring, you are likely to feel a surge or acceleration as you gain energy on entering the thermal, and a sinking feeling with loss of airspeed as you fly out of the other side of it. To get the best out of this lift, you should make a series of short beats back and forth so as to stay in it. If you are already well above the hill (and clear of other gliders), you should circle after heading out into the wind. If the wind is strong, it may be enough to just point into wind while poised in the strong lift. The easiest way to lose the lift will be to fall out of the back of it.

On a good day, thermals may pop up from the same source at intervals of 10 to 20 minutes; the interval may be shorter in light winds than in fresh. You can recognise their take-off, or their passage, by:

- dust rising from the ground
- gusts of wind blowing in towards the thermal source, which can be seen in the movements of leaves on trees
- changed direction of smoke.

On strong-wind days, thermals pass through the ridge-lift very fast, mixing with it and making life in the sky pretty rough. A lot of concentration is needed to distinguish good lift from gusts when flying into a passing bubble. On this type of day it is best to search for thermals further out from the ridge, where they will be less disorganised and easier to recognise. Use any height gained to work upwind towards good-looking clouds. In light winds it is easier to pick up thermals and gain enough height to set off. However, thermals low down can be tricky, particularly when they are strong but very small in diameter. On 'blue thermal' days they may exist in great profusion, but without clouds as indicators they can be difficult to find.

In thermals you should expect turbulence, which will be disconcerting when you first meet it, although in moderate thermals it usually feels worse than it actually is. The trick is to avoid over-controlling and 'fighting' the glider – allow it to ride the bumps while using the minimum effort to retain effective control.

When you do find lift, whether strong or weak, you need to work at centring in the core if you want to use it to the best advantage. Often the first indication of a nearby thermal is when the air roughens and the vario shows increased sink. This, hopefully, is followed by air that feels 'bubbly' or that gives you an upward surge, with a small increase in airspeed. One wing may be pushed up. You are now entering the thermal, and the quickest way to lose it is to turn or circle too soon – all that happens is that you immediately turn yourself out of it. Instead, wait a few seconds and then turn in what seems to be the best direction – towards the wing that was pushed up, or by using any other indicators, such as birds, or even instinct.

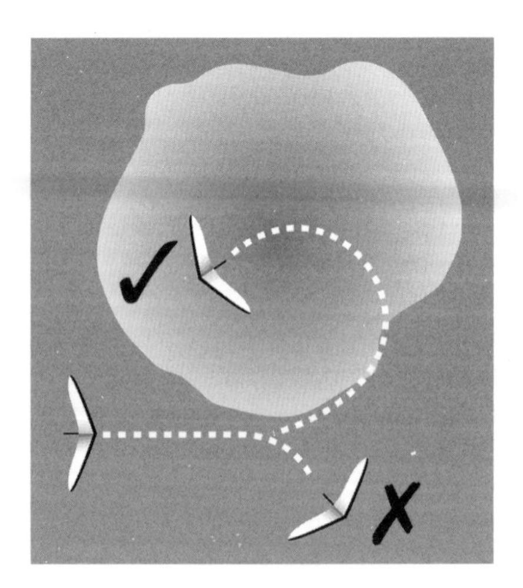

Figure 15.5 *If you fly into a thermal near its edge, you will lose it if you turn the wrong way. If a wing has been pushed up by the lift, push it down and turn towards it*

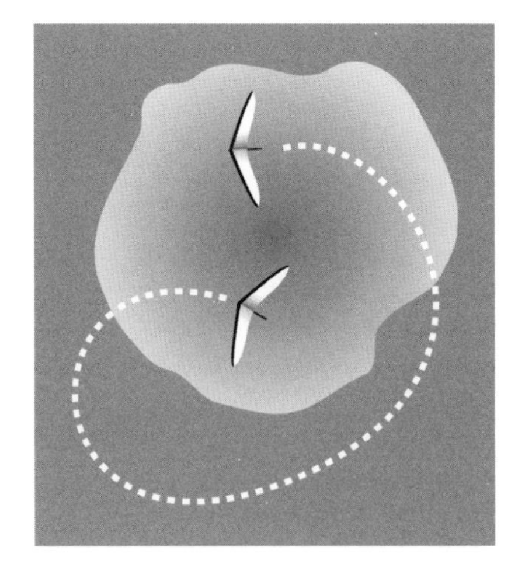

Figure 15.6 *As the glider surges upward on re-entering the lift, straighten up for 2-3 seconds and then circle in the same direction as before*

One method of centring in a thermal is to straighten up on good surges of lift for 2-3 seconds and then to tighten the circle as the lift starts to lessen. If the lift is strong, you can bank the glider quite steeply and make tight circles to stay in the core. But if the thermal is weak, then wider, smoother circles may be a more effective means of making the best use of the lift.

If the lift is erratic, it is usually sensible to continue to circle in the original direction, and carefully try to work yourself into the core, rather than making large changes in the circling pattern, or reversing direction. (This will usually lose you the thermal altogether.) It may help to note a landmark which is ahead when the lift is strongest, and next time round to straighten up for 1 or 2 seconds about 45 degrees before the landmark is ahead again. Then do a couple more steady circles to assess if there is any improvement, and if need be repeat the process. Try to visualise where the centre is in relation to you, and resolutely avoid wandering vaguely about in hope, even though you may be lucky occasionally.

> If you are soaring over a hilly or mountainous area, imagine the terrain has been coated in honey and then turned upside down. Where would the honey drip from? That's where the thermals will break away!

Cumulus clouds in an active state mark the position of the thermal, which will usually trail from a ground source upwind of the cloud. Cumulus shadows on the ground show the size of the cloud and the direction of the wind at cloud level. You can assess the wind-speed at this height by comparing the speed of, say, the leading edge of the shadow over the ground with that of cars or trains, or by timing it against some known or estimated distance. In general, the smaller and flatter the cumulus, the closer they will be together, and the taller they are, the further apart.

Figure 15.7 *Life-cycle of a cumulus cloud*

How to find a good soaring day in Britain

This can be a guide only, as the vagaries of the weather can sometimes frustrate even the professional forecasters and their computers.

- The second day following a cold front can give very good thermals in a moderate west to northwest wind.
- Pressure rising – but not too quickly.
- A ridge of high pressure will give fine flying weather with a veering, slackening wind and little cloud.
- Pressure not less than 1008mb or more than 1032mb. (Pressure that is too high can lead to inversions.)
- Anticyclonic weather, particularly in spring when the air is cold and the sun hot. This often occurs over southern Britain with a northeast wind.
- Sun high for many hours – so April to September.
- Spring and autumn – the sun is still powerful, and the air is quite cold.
- Wind speed not above 37kph (23mph) at 600m (2,000ft).

- Wind direction such that the air has been over land for some time. This produces drier air, so higher cloudbase and less chance of over-development.
- No overnight rain, so the ground is dry, giving good cloudbase height.
- Warm sectors, following the warm front, may produce reasonable soaring weather in summer, if the warm sector is wide with pressure rising in it. Winds south to west.

Wave

Ridge lift will rarely take you higher than twice the height of the hill you are soaring. Thermal lift will rarely take you above 1,800m (6,000ft) in the UK. Yet under the right conditions wave lift can easily take you to over 3,000m (10,000ft).

What is wave?

'Wave' is the name given to an organised pattern of vertical oscillations in the airflow that sometimes occurs downwind of a line of hills or mountains. As the sheet of air flows over the line of hills and descends the other side, it can – in certain atmospheric conditions – bounce back up again before descending again, producing a series of 'ripples' (or 'waves') downwind of the line of hills. In ideal conditions the wave amplifies the original disturbance, and the wave can extend to great heights – 12,000m (40,000ft) or more.

Wave is sometimes called 'lee wave', as it is found in the lee of the line of hills. It is also sometimes known as 'standing wave', as the 'waves' remain stationary relative to the ground – at least until the wind changes, when the system may collapse before reforming in a slightly different pattern.

Ideal weather for wave

The atmospheric conditions required for wave often occur in the outer region of areas of high pressure, or ahead of warm fronts, or in the warm sector of a low-pressure area. Given one of these situations, then the other requirements are:

- A wind speed of around 24kph (15mph) at hilltop height, steadily increasing with height.
- The wind blowing more or less at right angles to a ridge, and staying relatively constant in direction with height.

Smooth lens-shaped (or flying-saucer-shaped!) 'lenticular' clouds aligned at 90 degrees to the wind can provide a visual indication of the presence of wave. Sometimes these clouds will look like stacks of plates. Lenticular clouds appear stationary in the air, but in fact they are constantly forming at the leading edge and dissipating at the trailing edge.

Contacting wave

At low levels, wave is often broken and weak. If thermal activity is damped and patchy, and you fly into an extended area of weak lift, it is almost certainly wave. Slow down and try to maintain the same position over some feature on the ground by making small beats across the wind. Usually the initial contact with light wave will reveal the area of lift to be small – often smaller than a football field. The air will feel silky smooth, and your glider will feel very stable. Fly smoothly and sensitively, as the lift low down is often weak and elusive. As you gain height you will be able to explore by extending your beats to see if stronger lift is available. Strong wave is easy – you cannot help but go up! Lift in wave is usually less than 2.5m/s (500ft/min) but sometimes up to 5m/s (1,000ft/min) or more.

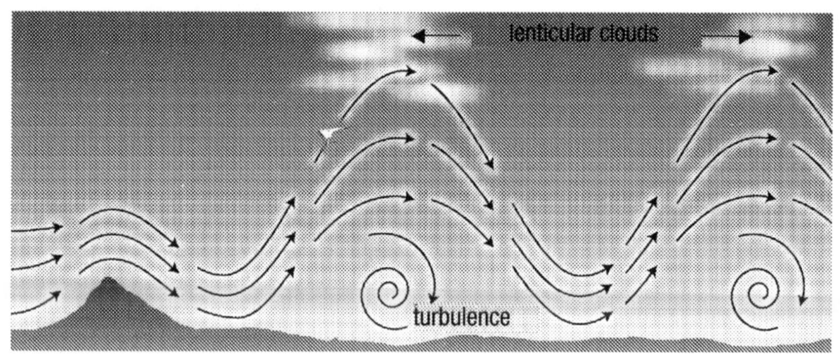

Figure 15.8 *Cross-section through a wave system*

Because of the higher performance of their craft, sailplane pilots are quite regularly able to exploit the delights of wave flying, often reaching 6,000m (20,000ft) or more and making long cross-country flights, soaring along wave bars and systems for hundreds of kilometres, sometimes above cloud. Listen out on gliding radio frequencies for sailplane pilots reporting contact with wave. Bear in mind that above 3,000m (10,000ft) hypoxia will almost certainly have some effect, especially over a length of time. Sailplane pilots will start using oxygen at this height. Going above 3,700m (12,000ft) without oxygen is foolhardy.

If you want to find the next wave peak or bar, it is sometimes best to fly at 90 degrees to the wind along the bar until the lift reduces. Then turn 135 degrees downwind until you are directly behind where you peaked in the first bar, a few miles downwind. You should find the lift of the next wave bar on the way, and you will have avoided the worst sink between the bars. If the wind is strong, turn into wind as soon as the lift reveals itself, and 'reverse' up the front of the next wave bar. The wavelengths of the wave systems flown by hang-glider pilots seem to vary from 1 to 5 kilometres (0.6-3 miles). Wavelengths can reach over 24km (15 miles), increasing with greater wind speeds.

Sometimes wave can be so powerful that it is hard to get down. The trick here is to move crosswind, upwind or downwind until out of the lifting region, before trying to descend.

Wave hazards

Turbulence

Although wave is usually nice and smooth when you are in the upgoing air, it can be very turbulent in between. If there are wave clouds around, and the wind speed on the hill varies by more than 24kph (15mph) in half an hour, then wave is probably working itself in and out of phase with the ridge lift – look out for turbulence.

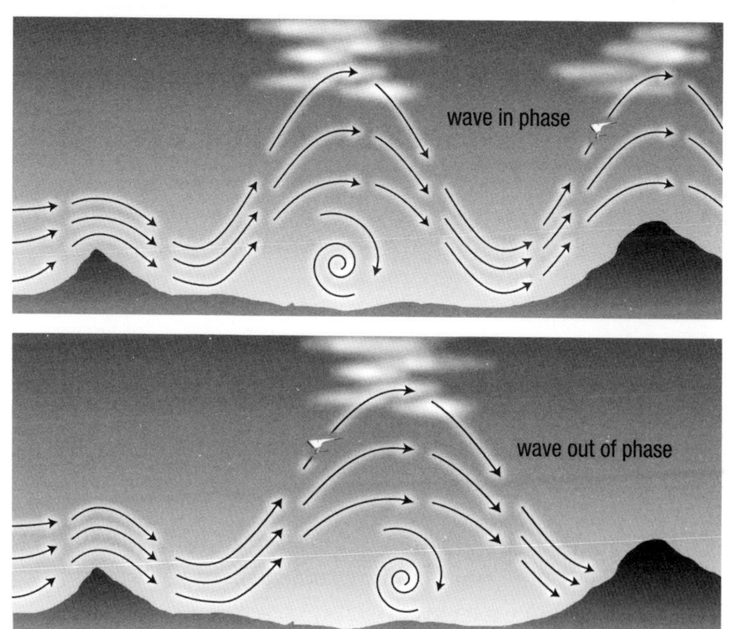

Figure 15.9 *Wave in and out of phase*

Wind speeds on the ground decrease under the lifting part of the wave and increase under the sinking part, so you may find that you end your wave flight landing in a very strong wind.

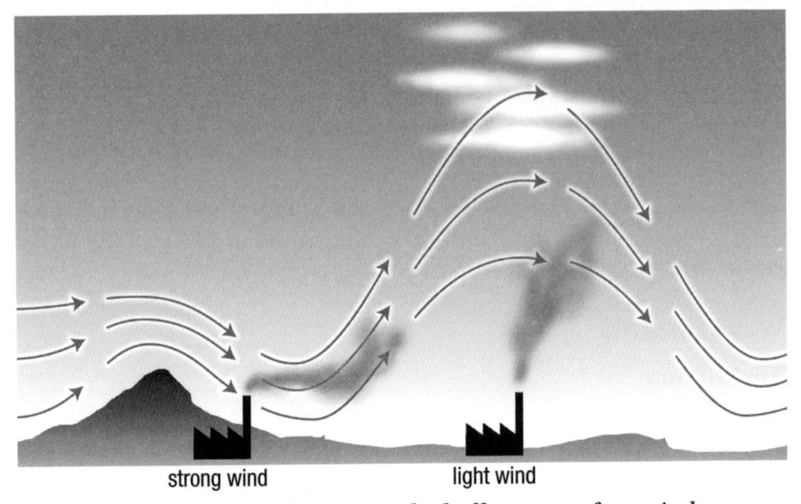

Figure 15.10 *Wave can have a marked effect on surface winds*

Wave clouds may suddenly form at varying levels in the wave system as air of slightly differing humidity and temperature moves through the wave. One minute you can be flying in clear air, the next above a cloud layer 600m (2000ft) thick which totally obscures the ground. It can really happen that quickly.

Gaps in the clouds will open and close quite suddenly, so be very careful if tempted to go up through a gap. Look for sunshine on the ground upwind and downwind: if there is little sun then this is one of the few gaps, and you could be in deep trouble if you go up and it closes beneath you! Forego the temptation – there will always be another day.

The most common – and easily observed – reason for the formation of clouds in wave conditions is the cooling of the rising air (due to its expansion in response to the reducing pressure) to below the temperature at which its moisture begins to condense. This normally occurs towards the top of the wave. The air levels off and begins the downward part of the cycle, descending – and warming – until the moisture evaporates again at lower levels. It is this phenomenon that gives wave clouds their characteristic lenticular shape and causes them to mark the crests of each successive wave.

Icing

Encountering the humid air within clouds at the temperatures to be found at altitude will almost certainly result in severe icing. This can seriously effect the glider's flying characteristics, even making the machine uncontrollable, so keep well clear.

Cross-country flying

Preparation is the key to success. Before flying, check the variometer batteries, and that you have the right maps. Make sure you have some money with you, and a drink and some sort of snack for after you land. If you've got a mobile phone, take that to use after landing to organise the retrieve. Make sure you've got your glider bag (or cross-country bag and harness bag for hang gliders) with you. Plan and mark your likely route, which will usually be downwind (see Chapter 24). If possible, check the soaring forecast on wind strength up to cloud level and the time thermals are likely to start and finish. Having done all this will leave your mind clear to think about the flight ahead.

Keep watching the clouds as you prepare for flight – this will give you a feel for the way the day is developing.

When you take off on the first flight of the morning you will soon feel if it is a good thermal day or not. The air should feel 'bubbly' or even a bit rough. Listen to your vario. If you have taken off early in the day (say 10 am), then you will possibly want to stay around the site for a while to allow the sky to improve. Usually the best part of the day is around 2pm. It is very frustrating to be on the ground five miles downwind at 11am, having taken a weak, unreliable early thermal, only to watch your friends fly over an hour or so later when conditions improve. While using the thermals around the site you should be monitoring the sky downwind, to see how it is developing. You should also get a feel for the type of thermals – some days they are quite big and gentle, some days they are quite small and punchy, and you have to circle quite tightly to centre in them.

Sooner or later you will find a nice strong core that isn't going to fizzle out on you on the way to cloudbase. This will coincide with a reasonable sky downwind. As you circle up in it (using all your best centring techniques), you will realise that you have drifted so far downwind of the site that getting back is impossible. So you are on your way!

Figure 15.11 *The nature of thermals changes throughout the day*

Which way to go?

As you circle up towards cloudbase, the temptation to zoom off downwind is almost irresistible. But patience is the name of the game – especially in UK conditions where you usually only have a few thousand feet with which to find your next source of lift. You are likely to be back on the ground very quickly if you haven't at least found an active cloud to aim for. Concentrate on getting more or less all the way to cloudbase with your first thermal. Break off the climb a few hundred feet below the cloud by flying off to one side, or upwind or downwind just a short distance. Then you can move back into the thermal as and when required. Sometimes good lift can be found under the same cloud for twenty minutes or so – and even if you can only find zero sink it is often better to drift downwind circling in this than to head off aimlessly in sink.

During this initial climb, check for good active growing clouds within easy reach (this is harder to do once you get near cloudbase). Only head off if a perfect building cumulus is clearly within very easy reach. Usually, if you have taken off from a UK hill site, the ground slopes back down behind the hill, so the air tends to sink, and thermals are depressed. The best height at which to cross this zone is cloudbase!

Once safely clear of the sink zone behind most hill sites, you can be a bit more adventurous. So look around, not only downwind but up to 45 degrees either side of your track for the nearest active cloud. (If there are none, and you are not in lift, then look in any direction for an active cloud within reach!) Now go for your chosen cumulus, trying to visualise the position of its thermal. As you near it you will probably find an increase in sink which you have to fly through if you wish to reach the lift, so increase speed a little and press on, trying to work out whether the core is to the right or left of you.

If you go for a cloud across wind, or even upwind, remember that your ability to reach the cumulus will be affected only by its air distance from you, regardless of the wind direction. The only difference in difficulty between reaching a cloud a mile upwind of you and reaching one a mile downwind of you is caused by the location of the thermal feeding the cloud. This will trail from the ground upwind of the clouds. If you head for the downwind cloud, you should run into the lift before you reach the cloud, whereas with the upwind cloud you will have to fly past the cloud before reaching the lift. (This effect is clearly greater on windier days, and makes more difference the further you are from cloudbase height.)

If you get too low to find thermals by positioning yourself beneath likely-looking clouds, it may be better to fly slightly downwind of possible thermal sources, such as villages, dry ploughed fields, quarries and disused airfields. Avoid shaded areas and damp areas! Concentrate only on finding lift and not on making distance. If you don't stay up you won't go anywhere at all.

Going cross-country with another glider increases your ability to search for lift. Between thermals, fly a couple of hundred yards apart. If you find lift first, climb in it and wait for the other glider to catch up.

Downwind, between thermals, use the audio on your variometer while looking for the next thermal. Keep your eyes peeled: indicators such as cumulus, other gliders, flocks of birds, and smoke from fires, are good markers.

Look where you are going. Some pilots don't. Keeping a proper lookout for other aircraft includes looking upwards while in a fast climb, as well as all around and behind. You are now among sailplanes, Cessnas, hot-air balloons, Tornados and the Red Arrows. See and be seen! (See the section on 'Safe flying in thermals' in Chapter 16.)

Watch that you do not get inadvertently swept up into cloud. 150m (500ft) below cloudbase may not be soon enough to leave. If cumulus are growing tall, let alone becoming cu-nimbs, keep clear. Break off any thermal climb if the variometer is reading fully up, at least 300m (1,000ft) below cloud. If cu-nimbs start brewing all over the sky, land as soon as you can.

Choosing a field

Eventually all good things come to an end, so at some stage you will have to find a suitable field to land in. From 600m (2,000ft) you will have a circle of perhaps 5km (3 miles) in which to select a field. This circle will, of course, be displaced downwind – usually the way you are going. At 600m (2,000ft) above ground level you should be keeping a good landing-area in mind; at 450m (1,500ft) you should be narrowing your choice to a few particular fields. By the time you are down to 300m (1000ft) you should be selecting the actual field. Do not rely on the altimeter to give you your precise height above the ground, as the land may be higher or lower than the altimeter datum you used. Just position yourself upwind of the field within easy gliding distance.

In choosing a field, consider the six Ss: size, shape, slope, surface, stock and surroundings. Choose a large field, and ensure that the shape gives you an ample into-wind path. Check for any slope before getting too close to the field (it is very hard to spot slope from above, much easier from an oblique angle). If you can see the slope from the air it will be quite steep: paragliders may be able to land across the slope but you will certainly have difficulty landing a hang glider in the field, unless you land up the slope. (If the wind is light this is the best option, if the only fields available have slopes.) As the ground tends to slope down towards water, remembering to 'land away from water' can be helpful.

Check the surface and stock – your field should be free from crops and clear of stock: animals are easily 'spooked' by sudden appearances from the sky.

Now concentrate on finding which way the wind is blowing; it is often surprisingly different from the direction you may have anticipated. Since it would be spectacular to land with a 30kph (20mph) tailwind, you should make an effort throughout any cross-country flight to monitor the wind direction. Reliable indicators include smoke, steam from cooling towers, ripples in tall crops or on the surface of lakes or reservoirs (the flat water at one end of the lake indicates the upwind end). Movement of cloud shadows over the ground will tell you the wind direction at cloud height: the surface direction is usually a few degrees back from this. When you are low your own drift over the ground may be noticeable, particularly when circling. It is also helpful after take-off to note the wind direction in relation to the sun. For example, 'I am into wind when the sun is off my left wing-tip'. The position of the sun is obviously only of limited use, particularly on a long flight, but it may be useful in confirming some other observation.

When you have determined the wind direction and decided the best landing approach, make another more detailed check of your surroundings for power or telephone lines near the field, or even embedded in the hedge over which you intend to fly. You are unlikely to spot the wires – so concentrate on trying to spot the line of poles. Look also for high trees on your chosen approach path.

When you are safely down, move your glider to the edge of the field and pack it away so that it does not appear to be a distress signal to other pilots passing your way. Then make for a telephone (or use your mobile phone) to arrange transport back and to inform others that you are safely down. Find the farmer, explain how you happen to be in his field and thank him.

Chapter 16: Flying with others

Mixing paragliders and hang gliders

When you learned to fly your glider at a school, you will have been used to having at most one or two other similar gliders in the air while you were flying. As you start flying in the club environment you'll almost certainly find yourself sharing the air with lots more of your fellow pilots, some on the same kind of craft as you and some on the other kind. You may also find the odd sailplane passing along the ridge, and radio-controlled slope-soaring gliders to add to the congestion!

Because of this it is absolutely essential that you maintain a constant lookout for other traffic. Always aim to give other traffic a wide berth: no other machine should ever get within three wing-spans of you when passing side to side, and potential head-on conflicts must be resolved while the aircraft are still well separated. You may drive nose-to-tail on the M25, but paragliders and hang gliders cannot brake to a stop like cars!

Key points that hang-glider pilots should know about paragliders

It is very difficult to spot the differences between intermediate paragliders and more advanced ones, so your best clue to the pilot's proficiency is the red streamer. If the pilot is a CP with less than 10 hours, then there should be a red ribbon attached to the seat or harness of the paraglider. If you see such a ribbon, stay well clear and avoid pressurising the pilot.

To help you predict what the paraglider pilot is about to do, look and see what he or she is doing with the controls. The primary method of control is by using the toggles or handles attached to the lines that go to the trailing edge of the wing. A quick look at the positions of the pilot's hands will indicate what the pilot is attempting to do, as the canopy will always turn towards the lower of the two hands. When both hands are lowered together it will slow down: when both hands are raised it will speed up. If you are above the paraglider, and cannot see the pilot's hands, the amount of pull-down on the trailing edge shows how much control is being used.

Paraglider pilots may also be seen using weightshift to augment their use of the steering controls. Leaning the body well over to the left or right helps produce a more efficient turn: if the pilot's body is leaning left, expect the paraglider to roll and turn left.

In stronger winds, paragliders are in danger of being blown back. This may be expected if the canopy is pointing directly into wind with the controls right up. The pilot now has no reserve of speed left, so avoid positioning yourself behind him. The only method of escape for the paraglider pilot in this situation is to use the speed bar/accelerator system. This bar is operated with the pilot's feet; tensioning it makes the canopy faster, but more prone to tuck.

Thermalling in the same thermal as one of the faster, more advanced paragliders can be accomplished without too much of a problem. The paraglider pilot will be reluctant to get too close to you, as the wake from your hang glider may cause a deflation. Canopies may also deflate when entering or leaving a powerful thermal, so it is advisable to make allowances for this.

Paragliders will usually top-land quite close to the front of the hill (where the canopy is in 'clean' air). It is therefore important that this area is kept clear whenever possible.

Finally, bear in mind that some inexperienced paraglider pilots do not always appreciate how much space their aircraft occupy – it can be hard to get used to the width of a wing which is several metres overhead – so always allow them a little extra space.

Key points that paraglider pilots should know about hang gliders

Again it is very difficult for the untrained eye to spot the differences between intermediate hang gliders and more advanced wings (unless they are the super-advanced 'topless' gliders with no top-rigging), so the red ribbon is the best means of identifying those pilots with less than 10 hours airtime. In this case the ribbon should be attached to the top of the hang glider's kingpost.

Hang gliders have a greater speed-range than paragliders, and their wings do not collapse. In the main the hang-glider pilot steers his craft by weightshift alone; look at the relative position of the pilot's body in the control frame – if it is in the middle the glider will fly straight ahead. If it is off to one side then the glider will turn towards that side.

The hang-glider pilot has one big advantage over you – he can dive, accelerating while doing so, and then make use of that speed to climb quickly and regain much of his original height. The pilot does this by pulling the bar in to dive, then pushing it out to climb. If you are off to one side, it is easy to see the pilot shifting position to initiate these manoeuvres, but it is not so easy to detect from behind.

Hang gliders leave quite strong wakes, so don't get too close if you want to avoid a possible canopy collapse.

One big problem facing hang-glider pilots is that once committed to the take-off it is almost impossible to abort without injury. Please make absolutely certain that you are not about to inflate your canopy in the path of a launching hang glider – remember that final check for clear airspace all round!

A hang glider on approach in light winds can fly in low from behind the ridge – the pilot will be aiming for the designated landing-area, so don't be tempted to take off from that area. If you need to fly through anywhere near the landing-zone, keep a sharp lookout for a hang glider coming in, as the pilot may have to abort the landing, overshoot, and then try to gain height in order to go round again.

In general a hang glider cannot be landed on a slope, so if the ridge lift starts to fail, the pilot will be desperate to gain the height needed for a top-landing if he is to avoid landing at the bottom – which on many sites effectively finishes his day. In this situation you can help the hang-glider pilot by landing and so giving him extra room. You can then launch again when the situation has resolved itself.

Model aircraft

Many hill sites are also used by radio-controlled model enthusiasts. These slope-soaring models range from 1-metre-span models of simple balsa and film construction, costing perhaps £100 and weighing 1 or 2kg, to 6- or 7-metre-span monsters built from composite materials, weighing 10kg and costing more than £1,000.

The operator of any type of model must have his concentration totally fixed on the model if he is to retain control. This results in a kind of tunnel-vision effect – other aircraft will only be seen when they are in close proximity to the model (or near the line of sight between the operator and his model). Allied to this is the fact that it is very difficult for the operator to know just how far away the model is: if a hang glider or paraglider does appear close to the model, the operator will find it difficult to judge whether they are on collision paths. Several years ago a hang glider pilot was killed following a collision with a model.

There is no safe way to fly together with models, so clubs have generally made arrangements with the local model clubs whereby one end of the ridge, or certain times of the day, or certain days of the week, are reserved for models.

It's good to talk!

Becoming familiar with potential problems, and seeking out and talking to other pilots on the hill (including the modellers), will undoubtedly make you a better and safer pilot. If there are problems, get along to the club night, discuss the problems openly and honestly, and try to agree sensible solutions.

Avoiding overcrowding and conflict

As you have by now no doubt realised, there are a limited number of sites from which we can fly, and on good days these can get busy. On bank holiday weekends with good weather they can become far more than busy, and it is essential for all pilots to act sensibly if everybody is to get a fair turn and accidents are to be avoided.

You should be particularly wary in light-wind conditions; everybody will be desperately scratching for lift, and the ridge face can become very crowded. The trick is to recognise quickly that it is going to become too busy for comfort, and organise a top-landing early. You can always fly again later.

In general:

- It is essential to be considerate to other pilots.
- All pilots must appreciate the flying behaviour of their own and other aircraft.
- When fast and slow aircraft share a site, it is vital that all pilots make themselves conversant with the operating procedures which may be in force on the day.
- In the interests of safety, any organised flying event or competition should have an appointed person in charge of operations.

On the ground:

- Areas for take-off and landing should be clearly established, and ad hoc take-offs and landings should be actively discouraged. If multiple landing and/or take-off areas are used, they should be arranged in such a way as to:
  - allow good communications

  - prevent flight paths from crossing each other.
- Overcrowding and site pressure can be relieved by:
  - limiting one's flying time and/or numbers in the air
  - launching in groups according to glider speed or pilot experience
  - all traffic conforming to a flying pattern. No single craft should 'hog the lift' or manoeuvre in such a way as to disturb an established pattern.

In the air:

- The airspace in front of the take-off area and that used for landing overshoots should be kept clear as far as possible. Traffic entering these zones should only do so in order to transit from one area to another.
- Pilots should slowly build up their experience of flying in busy airspace or airspace which contains aircraft with a marked difference in airspeed and manoeuvrability.
- Don't blame others for it being busy. You are part of the problem. Leave the area or land.
- Irrespective of the place, type of launch or aircraft involved, the use of anticipation and good airmanship is essential.

The single most important rule is to keep a sharp lookout, all around you.

Safe flying on the ridge

On the ground:

- If you are visiting another club's sites, make sure you contact them first (contact telephone numbers are printed in *Skywings*).
- Make sure that you know the site rules.
- Ask for advice from coaches or other pilots.
- Prepare your glider in a sensible place, away from the take-off, landing and overshoot areas.
- Move to the take-off area only when you are ready to launch. If you change your mind, move back out of the way.
- Do not launch if the sky is busy, especially if you are inexperienced.

In the air:

- Make all turns away from the ridge.
- Try to fit in with any soaring pattern that is established.
- Make sure you know all the anti-collision 'Rules of the Air' and how they apply to ridge-soaring. Make sure that you also know the appropriate conventions for ridge-soaring and that you fly in accordance with them. (See Chapter 23 for further details.)
- Understand that **the key to avoiding the risk of collision is anticipation:** small adjustments to your course when a conflict with another glider first starts to develop will avoid any need for last-minute extreme manoeuvres.
- Keep a constant lookout all around you.
- Maintain an adequate separation distance. You should be wary if a glider heading parallel to you or away from you gets closer than two wingspans between you sideways, or 100m (330ft) apart fore and aft. If a glider heading directly towards you approaches to within 200m (660ft), change your course after checking that it is safe to do so. If you are finding it hard to maintain these separation distances, land. You can always fly again later when it is less busy. (These separation figures are for guidance: in rougher air you may well need to increase them. In mellow evening conditions they may be excessive.) Do not confine your worries to gliders at your level: another glider below you can suddenly bob up 15m (50ft) or so as a stronger puff of lift comes through, so maintain adequate vertical separation too. Fly defensively – always assume that the other pilot has not seen you.
- If you find a thermal while ridge-soaring, be very careful about attempting to circle in it if there is any other traffic around. While it is generally accepted that a glider circling in a thermal has right of way over those joining it, this does not mean that you can drift back in a series of 360s through a ridge full of other gliders, expecting them to scatter out of your way. You are still equally responsible for maintaining separation! If you can't guarantee your ability to monitor separation while circling, **stop circling!** It is usually best to make short beats ('S'-turns) within the thermal until you are clear of any other traffic.

Back on the ground:

- After landing, move out of the landing-area quickly, keeping a good lookout for other gliders approaching in order to land.

Safe flying in thermals

The legal 'Rules of the Air' (see Chapter 23) still apply to gliders that are thermalling! However, as with ridge-soaring, there are certain conventions that have been developed to help minimise the chances of collision. These are all encapsulated in the points below, which closely follow those formulated by UK sailplane associations.

Joining a thermal:

- Gliders joining a thermal should give way to those gliders already established in it.
- All pilots should circle in the same direction as any gliders already established in the area of lift.
- If there are gliders thermalling in opposite directions, the joining glider should turn the same way as the nearest glider (least vertical separation).
- The entry to the turn should be planned so as to keep continuous visual contact with all other aircraft at or near the planned entry height.
- The approach should be flown at a tangent to the circle so that no aircraft already turning will be required to manoeuvre in order to avoid the joining aircraft.

Sharing a thermal:

- Pilots should adhere to the principle of 'see and be seen'.
- When at a similar level, never turn inside or point at or ahead of another aircraft unless you intend to overtake and can guarantee safe separation.
- Leave the thermal if, in your judgement, you cannot guarantee adequate separation.
- Look for other aircraft joining or converging in height.

Leaving a thermal:

- Look outside the turn and behind before straightening.
- Do not manoeuvre sharply unless clear of all other aircraft. None of the above absolves the pilot from the responsibility to take any necessary action to avoid a collision.

SECTION 4
INCIDENTS, ACCIDENTS AND EMERGENCIES

Chapter 17: Avoiding accidents

Flying skills shortfall

Inappropriate weather conditions

Equipment problems

Site factors

Third parties

Human factors

In general

Chapter 18: Emergencies in flight

Dealing with equipment emergencies

Landing in water

Landing in trees

Landing in power lines

Survival pack

Chapter 19: Dealing with incidents and accidents

Accident management

Reporting an accident or incident

Chapter 17: Avoiding accidents

One dictionary definition of accident is 'an unwelcome event happening by chance'. Defined in this way, the mishaps that paragliding and hang glider pilots have are invariably not accidents. The outcome is easily predictable from the undesirable circumstances that the pilot has put together, and the only role chance plays is that occasionally a pilot will 'get away with it'. That's the bad news. The good news is that making ourselves aware of the circumstances that lead to crashes makes it easier to avoid repeating them. 'Learn from the mistakes of others. You won't live long enough to make all of them yourself!'

The six factors listed below cover the causes of virtually all accidents and incidents reported by paraglider and hang-glider pilots:

- Flying skills shortfall
- Inappropriate weather conditions
- Equipment problems
- Site factors
- Third parties
- Human factors

Let's look at each of these in turn.

Flying skills shortfall

Inadequate training

A lack of skill can be caused by inadequate training. This can result in accidents such as mid-air collisions. Many pilots fly too close to one another, and fail to keep a good lookout. Perhaps they were never taught what an acceptable separation distance is, or how to keep a good lookout. Forgetting to clip in to your hang glider, or forgetting to fasten your paraglider leg/chest straps, might also be due to having never been taught a proper pre-flight checklist.

Inexperience

A lack of skill can also be due to inexperience. New pilots' skills are still developing, and it is easy for such pilots to get themselves into situations that they do not have the ability to deal with.

Lack of currency

If you do not fly frequently, your skills will become rusty – which means that you should fly with increased safety margins. All too often pilots come out after a winter lay-off expecting to fly as well as they did at the end of the previous season.

Inappropriate weather conditions

Too windy

The dangers of flying in winds that are too strong are well known: turbulence increases markedly, as does the risk of being blown back (especially if flying a paraglider). Choose a maximum wind-speed limit, and do not fly if the wind is stronger. For UK ridge-soaring 30kph (18mph) might be a top limit for an experienced paraglider pilot, while 40kph (25mph) might be the limit for an experienced hang-glider pilot.

Poor assessment of conditions

There is more to assessing the weather than just checking the wind speed. Carefully study the cloud types for indications of likely turbulence. Look for shower clouds approaching. Watch gliders already in the air.

Poor monitoring

Weather conditions will change while you are airborne. You must constantly update your assessment and land before any major deterioration.

Equipment problems

Over-advanced equipment

This is one of the most common factors in accidents! Pilots rush to buy a piece of advanced equipment that will scare them half to death (if it doesn't actually kill them), despite all advice to the contrary.

Design faults

Paragliding and hang gliding are still relatively small sports, and very small companies run by enthusiasts rather than engineers build much of the equipment. Some of their products are less than perfect: for example, it is possible to mis-rig most hang gliders. Many emergency parachutes are unintentionally deployed each year often because of some defect in the container closure system.

Lack of maintenance

All too often pilots ignore the maintenance schedules for their equipment. Paraglider line lengths are supposed to be checked every year, but rarely are. Wire breakages on hang gliders usually involve original wires still being used at three or four times the recommended replacement age.

Inept maintenance

Unfortunately many pilots will have go at doing some maintenance without understanding quite what they are doing, and so introduce more faults than they remove.

Site factors

Some sites and official landing fields seemed ideal in the early 1980s for the low-performance hang gliders then in use. But in truth some were always difficult and unforgiving to use, and with advances in glider performance, a number of these sites should be considered suitable for experts only. Read the advice in your club site-guide carefully, and then make your own assessment of suitability.

Third parties

Improperly briefed nose person or anchor person

There have been several accidents where a hang-glider nose person has failed to release the glider when he should, or has released when he shouldn't have, or has stood in the way of the pilot after release. There has even been a fatality where the nose person was knocked over a sheer edge.

Paragliding anchor persons can create the same sorts of problem if not properly briefed. Several accidents have involved canopies being launched in conditions that were too windy. The pilot uses an anchor person to assist, with the result that both of them are plucked into the air when the canopy is immediately lifted off. It was in just these circumstances that an anchor person was killed when he fell off from a considerable height: others have been hurt falling lesser distances. Work on the basis that if the wind is too strong for you to launch on your own, it is too strong to fly.

Human factors

Fatigue and stress

While flying is undoubtedly a great way of winding down, going flying when exhausted after several days of heavy shift work, or after a row with your partner, is not recommended. Nor is flying with low blood-sugar levels, or while affected by alcohol, drugs or medication. The CAA have published the following I'M SAFE checklist:

I Illness: any symptoms?

M Medication: does your family doctor know you are a pilot?

S Stress: any serious personal upsets?

A Alcohol or drugs?

F Fatigue: bad night's sleep?

E Eating: have you had enough to eat recently? Food is needed to maintain energy levels!

Attitude and over- or under-confidence

More experienced pilots often develop an over-relaxed, casual attitude to flight. They then fail to check their gear, or fail to prepare themselves properly for the next launch – and have an accident.

Showing off

A British hang-gliding champion broke his back when his well-known party piece of dive-bombing other pilots rigging on the hilltop finally (and inevitably) went wrong. He was by no means the first pilot to come to grief through showing off.

Competition fever

Normal, sensible, sane, level-headed club pilots enter inter-club competitions and get caught up in some sort of competition fever. Before long, they start making decisions that they would never normally take. Don't let this happen to you. If the conditions are such that you would not normally take off, then don't take off just because it is a competition. You will have enough to think about with all the other pressures involved in competition without adding marginal conditions to the list!

Dubious information

Unfortunately other pilots, coaches and instructors can sometimes give you doubtful information or advice. As a qualified pilot, the final decision is yours. If somebody else is advising you, make sure that they really understand your level of experience. (It is very easy for a coach with 500 hours to over-estimate the capabilities of a new Club Pilot with 2 hours.) Discuss any points that you are unsure about.

Over-optimism

Some pilots seem to fly on the basis of 'It'll be right'. An example of this is the pilot who took off from sea cliffs where there was no beach, to try to soar in light winds – and drowned when he landed in the sea. It is often the case that 'plan A' doesn't work out: that is why a 'plan B' is always required, along with a glimmering of a 'plan C'. Plan on the basis of 'it might go wrong' and be sure to have a way of dealing with that eventuality. Always keep a safe landing-place within easy reach!

Pride

A surprising number of mishaps seem to be due to a desire to avoid losing face in front of fellow pilots (for instance, by 'going down' when they've stayed up). This leads to desperate thermalling and ridge-soaring attempts at minimal heights, followed by disaster. Remember: 'Pride comes before a fall!'

Laziness

A similar number of mishaps occur because the pilot is desperate to avoid carrying his equipment any further than absolutely necessary. Landing safely in the middle of the tow field is infinitely preferable to crashing downwind at the launch-point. Landing safely in the bottom-landing field is infinitely preferable to crashing on top. Landing safely in the middle of a field is infinitely preferable to crashing into the power lines next to the gate.

In general

Most accidents occur when two or more unfavourable factors occur at the same time. You should never deliberately set up such a situation. Fly with a maximum of one new situation at a time: a new item of equipment, or a new site, or unfamiliar conditions. And exercise extreme caution. Remember that:

- One new thing may produce difficulties.
- Two new things at once is asking for trouble.
- Three new things at the same time, and you could be looking at your last problems ever!

Chapter 18: Emergencies in flight

However careful you or other pilots may be, things sometimes do not work out as expected. Part of being a competent pilot is that you know what to do in an emergency because you have thought about it beforehand. This chapter deals with only a few of the problems you might encounter and the actions you may need to take. You should also think carefully about what else could go wrong.

Dealing with equipment emergencies

Control-line failure (paraglider)

This sort of failure could only be the result of poor maintenance and Daily Inspection (DI) procedures. However, if it does ever happen to you it is worth knowing that most paragliders can be steered by gentle use of the rear risers.

Harness zip stuck (hang glider)

If you ever find yourself with your flying suit jamming the harness zip so that you cannot get your legs out for landing, bear in mind that most zips are Velcroed in. It is therefore possible to kick or unpeel the zip to free your legs.

If you don't have the time or height for such antics, concentrate on flying a perfect circuit with a perfect into-wind prone landing. With wheels on it won't hurt at all, and even without wheels you should get away with it if you really hold off the landing (and let go as the glider touches down!). Either way it will be better than joining the ranks of pilots who have hit the ground, out of control, heading downwind or crosswind while trying to fly one-handed, concentrating on the minor problem of getting their legs out while ignoring the main priority of flying the machine!

Landing in water

The sad reality is that landing a hang glider or paraglider in water will almost always result in the pilot drowning. The only exceptions are prearranged arrivals into calm, warm water close to manned safety boats, as seen at SIV courses and hang-gliding aerobatics competitions, although there have been some close calls even in these circumstances.

An unplanned arrival in winter into a heavy swell off the British coast, dressed in full flying gear and with nobody on hand to effect immediate rescue, is going to be fatal. How good a swimmer you are is of absolutely no importance, as nobody can swim in a hang-gliding harness or wrapped in paraglider lines. **Never fly out of range of a safe landing-area! Ever!** Crashing downwind on a beach might be survivable – **going into the water is not.**

If, despite these clear warnings, you still somehow find yourself heading for the water, the following tips may be of benefit.

Landing in water (hang glider)

The main problem you face is getting unclipped from your glider and getting out of your harness. Most pilots have enough problem getting themselves clipped out when on dry land – imagine the difficulties when you are floating or underwater, disorientated and blinded, and with your breath taken away by the shock of the cold water.

Therefore you should pre-plan how to unclip, having regard to the peculiarities of your own equipment. Get rid of your gloves early. From then on you might try to find the karabiner and unclip; or use your webbing cutter to slash the hang-loops; or cut your way free of your harness. (With some pod harness types it is possible to cut or undo the leg straps, and then to slip off the shoulder straps to escape through the top of the harness.)

If you do manage to get out from under the glider, and if the glider is floating, then stay with it and await rescue.

Landing in water (paraglider)

The main reason that paraglider pilots rarely survive a water landing is that they become entangled with the canopy and its lines. So the priority is to get clear of your equipment. Do not be tempted to hang onto it, especially if you have come down in the sea, where there may be waves.

To prepare for the landing, remove your gloves, sit back in the harness and loosen your leg and chest straps. If you are using quick-release buckles, these can be released fully just before splash-down.

Try to land downwind, allowing the canopy to over-fly away from you. **Do not flare,** as this may cause the canopy to land on you. Keep everything tucked in, as in the PLF position: the water may not be as deep as you think. For the same reason **do not jump** from your harness, as it is extremely difficult to judge your height above the water in this situation.

Having landed, release yourself from your harness if necessary, and then swim away. Now you just have the problem of swimming fully dressed, with boots on, in the cold sea, to deal with.

You do not have to be out of your depth to drown. There have been several shallow-water deaths caused simply because of entanglement with the equipment or where the undertow catching the canopy has pulled the pilot from the beach into the water.

Landing in trees

The biggest danger with landing in a tree is that of falling back out of the tree. If a tree landing is inevitable, aim for the middle and plant yourself firmly in it.

To prepare for the tree landing, adopt the PLF position but with your legs crossed, arms tucked in tight and hands over your face. This will help protect the more sensitive parts of your body – including the bits with arteries. Either flare into the top (if above it) or, if heading into the side of it make sure you are heading for the centre of the tree before you cover your face. The aim is to fly in relatively quickly to get past the outer branches, so that you can grab onto something more substantial. If you flare, the chances are that you will fall down the outside of the tree and hit the ground, risking serious injury.

Once safely in the tree, grab a big branch and hold on. Do not attempt to climb down, but wait for help.

Landing in power lines

Do not hit power lines! Even more so than with trees, there is a grave danger of falling to the ground, with very serious consequences. Beyond that, there is the obvious danger of electrocution and burns.

If you end up dangling but alive, then sit tight and keep very still. It may still be a long drop to the ground. Wait for the emergency services. **Do not allow rescuers to come within 100 metres (300ft)** – the ground may be live if any cables have fallen. Do not assume that the power is off until the engineers from the electricity supply company turn up and confirm the situation. Most circuit-breakers have automatic circuits that cut back in after a delay to try to blast fallen branches from the line!

If you end up on the ground and find you are still alive, then walk carefully away, taking very small steps if there is any chance of a live cable touching the ground. That minimises the potential and reduces risk of electrocution. **Do not touch your equipment.** It may still be live and potentially lethal. Call the emergency services.

Survival pack

For all the situations mentioned in this chapter it would be handy to carry a survival pack that includes a bridle knife, a whistle, dental floss (useful if you're in a tree for passing down to your rescuers so they can attach a proper rope), pencil and paper.

Chapter 19: Dealing with incidents and accidents

Unfortunately pilots do sometimes have mishaps resulting in injury (i.e. accidents), and it is important for all the pilots on the site to act sensibly and calmly so as to ensure the best possible outcome for the injured person. Incidents also occur from time to time. An incident is an occurrence associated with the operation of an aircraft in which safety has been compromised, though no accident actually occurred. In both cases it is important that the required steps are taken to notify the correct authorities so that the appropriate level of investigation can be carried out to help prevent future occurrences.

Accident management

Most often there will be a coach or an instructor on the site, and they will take charge of the situation. If no such person is present, then someone, preferably an experienced pilot, must take charge. Having a single person in charge prevents confusion and enables the problem to be tackled quickly. It also prevents multiple calls to the emergency services.

You can expect the person in charge to check for any danger to would-be rescuers, and then to request volunteers to help with a variety of tasks. These will include administering first aid, and contacting the emergency services and ensuring that they are directed to the site. If a rescue helicopter is likely to be sent, then the 'All land' signal (a large 'H') needs to be set out to get other pilots out of the sky.

Dealing with serious accidents

If the accident is of a serious nature (i.e. a serious or fatal injury has occurred), then somebody should be deputised to help any later investigation by recording the scene, using a camera, notepad and pencil, video, or whatever means is available. (This can be extremely unpleasant, but is essential to the investigation process.) The aircraft must not be moved except to free trapped persons or animals or to avoid danger to the public. The names and addresses of all witnesses should be obtained, and ideally they should be asked to write down what they saw there and then, before talking to other people clouds their recollection.

Reporting an accident or incident

It is a legal requirement that any accident involving an aircraft ('boarded with the intention of flight') must be reported to the police and the Air Accident Investigation Branch (AAIB) of the Department of Environment, Transport and the Regions by the quickest available means. The AAIB and BHPA have an agreement that the BHPA will investigate hang gliding and paragliding accidents, so your legal duty is fulfilled by informing the police and the BHPA by the quickest available means. By reporting it to the BHPA you also satisfy the Association's requirements and those of the insurers.

In serious cases the BHPA technical staff must be informed immediately. (Serious cases include unusual equipment failures as well as accidents resulting in serious injury.) Contact telephone numbers are published in *Skywings* and are given on the BHPA office answerphone.

The BHPA accident-reporting system is a vital link in the chain of accident prevention. Without faithful reporting of accidents and incidents, we would lack the essential information needed to discover the causes of accidents, to identify trends, and to take action to put things right, nor would it be possible to continue to improve the safety record. It is up to every pilot to report any accident which he or she is involved in – or has witnessed – and every incident that might have led to an accident. This is especially true of airworthiness problems.

Incident Report Form

The BHPA has a single form – the Incident Report Form (IRF) – that covers all types of accident or incident, and it is widely circulated to members and to clubs. If you fill in a form, or help another pilot to do so, please complete it as thoroughly as possible, as a great deal can often be learned from what may at the time appear to be an unimportant detail. In all cases an IRF should be sent in within 48 hours. Never assume that someone else will send one in. It is much better that the same accident is reported several times than not at all. Don't let the lack of an official form prevent you from reporting. Notes on plain paper are much better than nothing.

SECTION 5
FLIGHT THEORY AND PERFORMANCE

Chapter 20: Lift, drag and the balance of forces

Lift

Drag

The balance of forces

Chapter 21: Stability and control

Pitch

Roll

Yaw

Chapter 22: Performance

Sink rate

Glide ratio (l/d ratio)

Polar curve

Ballast

Chapter 20: Lift, drag and the balance of forces

Lift

Wings and things

For any aircraft to fly, it must produce enough upward force to support the weight of the machine and its pilot. A wing, such as a paraglider's or hang glider's, generates this force when it is moved through the air at a slight angle. The speed of movement through the air is termed airspeed, while the slight angle to the airflow is called the angle of attack.

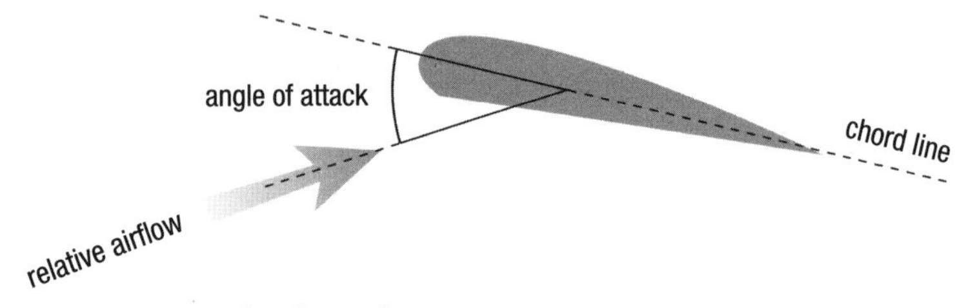

Figure 20.1 *Angle of attack*

Airspeed

After take-off, a glider maintains its airspeed by flying on a descending path through the air, using gravity to propel it, just like a cyclist or skier descending a hill.

Figure 20.2 *Propulsion due to gravity*

If you choose a steep flight path (controls 'up' on a paraglider, bar 'in' on a hang glider) then, just like the bicycle on the steep hill, you will progress more quickly. Conversely, if you flatten the glide path, then, like the bicycle on a very gentle gradient, you will progress quite slowly.

Any attempt to angle the flight path upward (on an unpowered machine) will result in a rapid loss of airspeed, followed by a stall. (When gaining height in wave, thermals or ridge lift, the glider is still actually flying on a descending flight path through the air. The 'trick' is that it is being flown in a mass of air that is rising faster than the glider is sinking – giving a net gain of height. Rising-air lift has nothing to do with aerodynamic lift created by a wing: make sure you never confuse the two concepts – they are quite separate!)

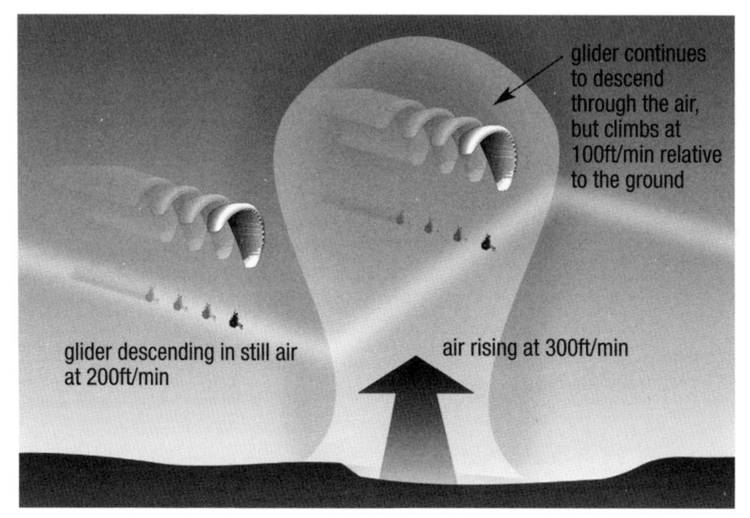

Figure 20.3 *Gliders climb by remaining in rising-air lift*

The wing section

Any more or less flat surface, held at a slight positive angle to an airflow, will produce an upward reaction: this is because the air pressure is slightly increased below the wing and slightly decreased above it. This upward force (known as the resultant or **total reaction**) can be broken down into those elements acting at 90 degrees to the airflow (upwards), which we call **lift**, and those elements acting at 180 degrees to the airflow (opposite), which we call **drag**.

A crude flat surface is not very useful as an aerofoil section; it will create lift, but the angle at which it is held to the airflow – the angle of attack – is very critical. Its efficiency (expressed as its **l/d ratio** – the amount of lift it produces compared with the amount of drag produced) drops off rapidly if the angle of attack is varied a few degrees above or below the optimum.

The curved single-surface aerofoil shape (as used on training hang gliders) is more efficient, and much less critical in respect of angle of attack, while extended tear-drop-shaped sections (as used on advanced hang gliders) provide an even greater level of efficiency over a wide range of angles of attack.

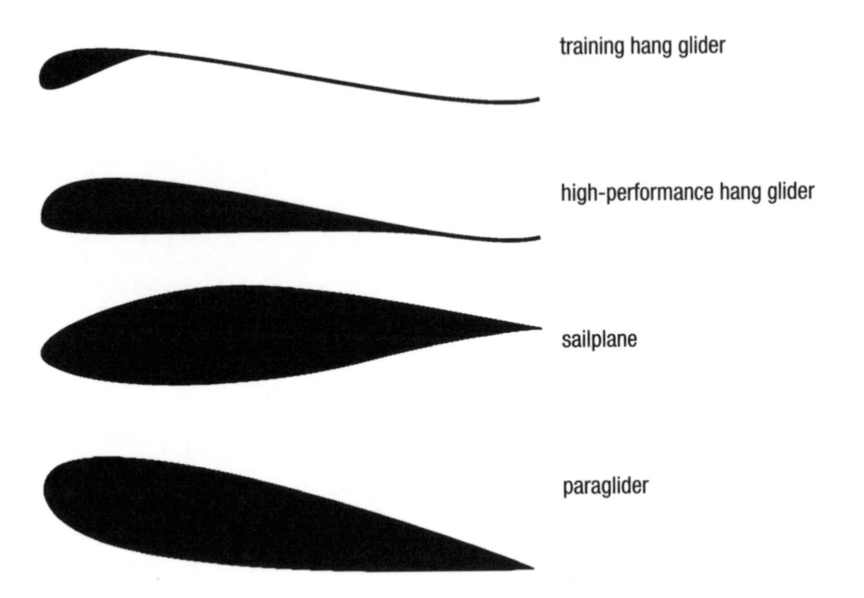

Figure 20.4 *Gliding aerofoils*

All fixed-wing aircraft, from sailplanes to Jumbo jets, use variations of this shape, optimised for their particular application. Paragliders also use this shape, with the 'missing' portion at the nose being effectively replaced by a dam of air.

How an aerofoil works

When air is passed through a constriction (e.g. a venturi tube), its velocity is increased and its pressure reduced. (This phenomenon was first recorded by the physicist Bernoulli, and is usually referred to as 'Bernoulli's theorem'.) The upper surface of an aerofoil-section wing acts as a one-sided constriction, with the result that the airflow over it experiences an increase in velocity and a decrease in pressure. At the same time the lower surface of the wing is slowing the air down, and therefore increasing its pressure. These two effects combine to produce a force which attempts to move the wing upward.

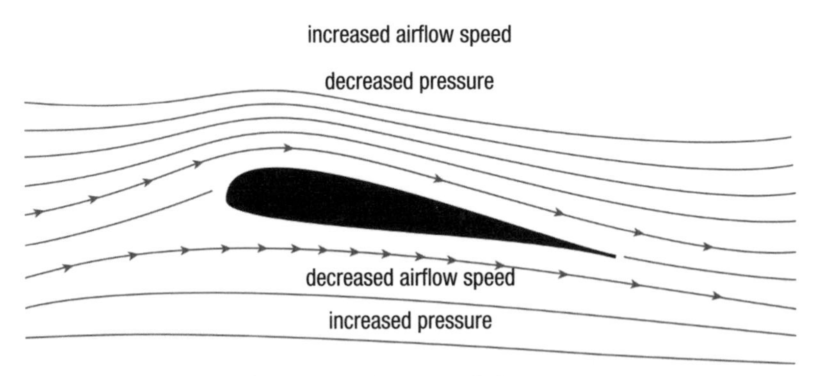

Figure 20.5 *The airflow around an aerofoil creates a pressure difference*

Centre of pressure

Various pressure differences are created all around a wing when it is generating lift. The forces that these pressure differences generate, and their distribution, will change as the angle of attack is varied. (This has significant effects on the aircraft's stability, which are explained later.) All the pressure-generated forces around a wing can be added together and represented as a single force acting through a point called the **'centre of pressure'.**

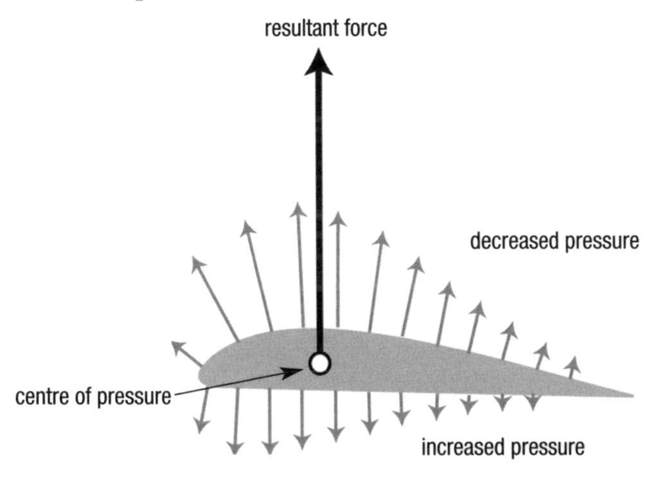

Figure 20.6 *The combined forces act through the centre of pressure*

The concept of the centre of pressure is very similar to that of the centre of gravity, in which all the weight forces acting on a body are added together and considered as a single force acting through a single point.

Drag

Drag is present as soon as anything tries to move through the air, because air is a fluid with considerable substance. This is not particularly noticeable when you go out walking on a calm day, but it becomes very obvious when you try walking against a strong wind. The drag generated by an aircraft can be conveniently grouped under two headings: **parasitic drag** and **induced drag**.

Parasitic drag

This is the name given to all the drag generated by the act of moving the aircraft through the air. Parasitic drag is mainly made up of:

- **form drag** – generated when the blunt shape of the glider, pilot, wires etc. is moved through the air
- **skin-friction drag**, which is the name given to the drag force caused by the air's tendency to 'stick' to the exposed surfaces.

Parasitic drag increases with the square of the airspeed – if the airspeed is doubled the parasitic drag is four times as great. A modern sailplane provides a good example of the aircraft designer's attempts to minimise parasitic drag, with the smooth streamlined shape minimising form drag and the smooth polished surfaces minimising skin friction.

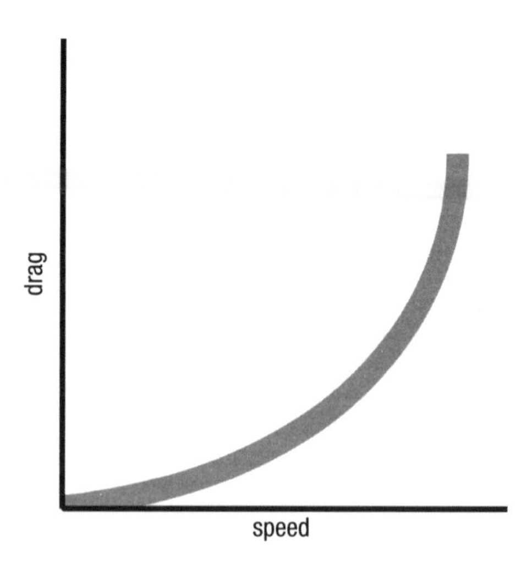

Figure 20.7 *Parasitic drag increases with speed*

Induced drag

Induced drag is an inevitable by-product of the generation of lift by a wing, and so is much harder to reduce than parasitic drag! At the wing's trailing edge, the somewhat divergent paths of the lower-pressure flow above the wing and the higher-pressure flow below the wing come together and spin off vortices, which migrate towards the wing-tip. Here they combine with the air flowing around the wing-tip from the higher pressure underneath to the lower pressure above the wing, so forming large wingtip vortices.

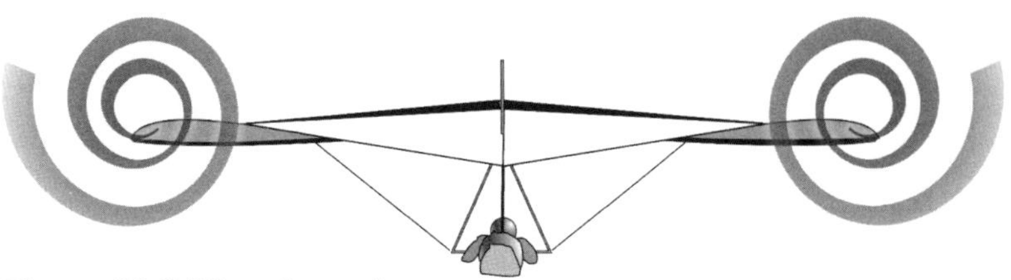

Figure 20.8 *Wing-tip vortices*

These tip vortices result in a substantial downwash behind the wing, and this actually modifies the net airflow around the wing. The result of this is that lift (acting at 90 degrees to the airflow) is angled back further from the direction of flight. This angling back introduces a drag vector.

Induced drag can be minimised by flying in 'ground effect', where the wing is a very small distance from the ground, and so the downwash behind the wing cannot occur. The net airflow direction therefore remains unmodified, and, as there is now reduced induced drag, the glide angle is flattened. Hang gliders sometimes encounter this phenomenon when 'holding off' during a light-wind landing – though at this stage of flight the pilot would usually rather have less efficiency from his wing!

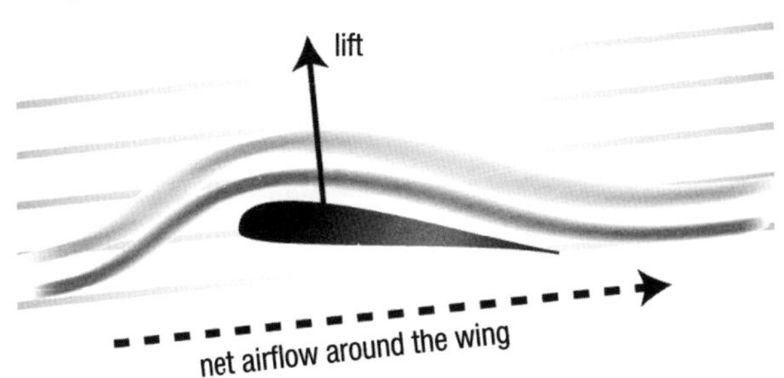

Figure 20.9 *Hypothetical wing with no downwash*

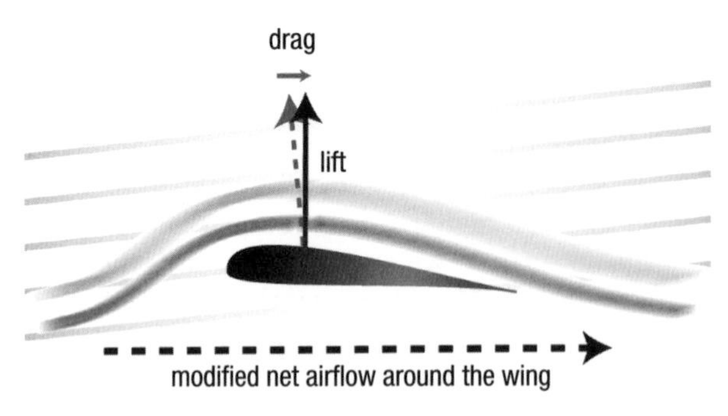

Figure 20.10 *Real wing with downwash*

On big jets wing-tip vortices produce the dreaded wake turbulence which can up-end a small aircraft following even as much as several miles behind it. This vortex turbulence is worst when the aeroplane is being flown slowly (high angle of attack), as when coming into land. As the aircraft increases speed (lower angle of attack), so the vortex turbulence – and the induced drag – reduces.

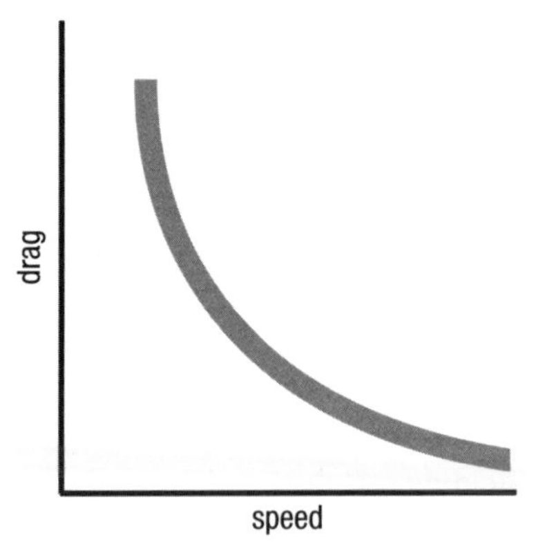

Figure 20.11 *Induced drag decreases with speed*

Long, thin wings (i.e. wings with a high aspect-ratio) have the smallest induced-drag penalty, which is why sailplanes are configured this way.

Total drag

The total drag of an aircraft is the sum of both the parasitic and the induced drag. As the pilot you have a dilemma, because as you increase speed the parasitic drag becomes worse, and as you reduce speed the induced drag worsens. But by putting both together, you find that there is one speed (one angle of attack) at which the drag will be least – in the example shown in Figure 20.12 this speed is indicated by a dashed line.

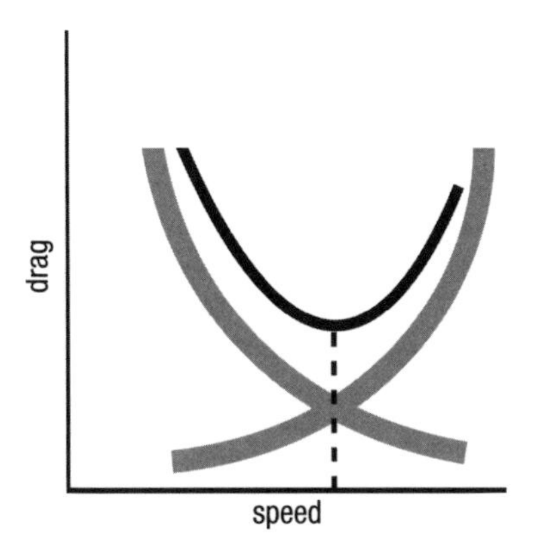

Figure 20.12 *Total drag is the sum of parasitic and induced drag*

The balance of forces

It was stated earlier that for any aircraft to fly it must produce enough upward force to support the weight of the machine and its pilot. Logic tells us that these two forces must be exactly equal, otherwise the glider would accelerate faster and faster vertically in the direction of the greater force.

So when a hang glider or paraglider is in steady flight, gliding smoothly along a chosen flight path, we know that the downward force (the weight of the pilot, glider, harness etc.) is being exactly balanced by an equal and opposite upward force, which is being generated by the wing. This force generated by the wing is called the **total reaction** or resultant.

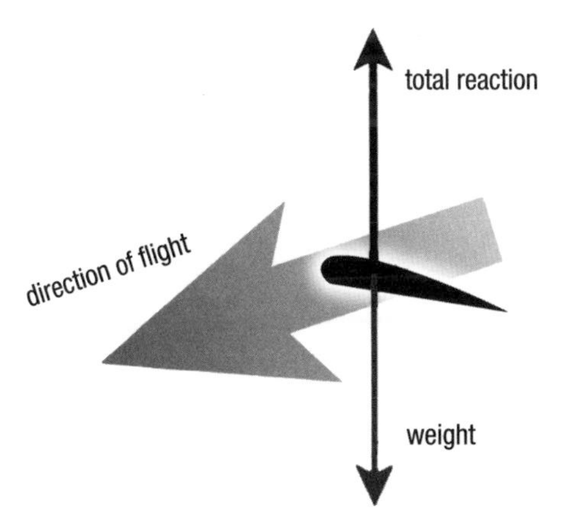

Figure 20.13 *Total reaction*

As mentioned earlier, this total reaction can be broken down into those elements acting at 90 degrees to the direction of flight (upwards), which we call lift, and those elements acting at 180 degrees to the direction of flight (opposite), which we call drag.

In steady gliding flight the three forces on the glider – lift, drag and weight – will balance (i.e. each force is balanced out by the other two), so that that are no accelerations in any direction.

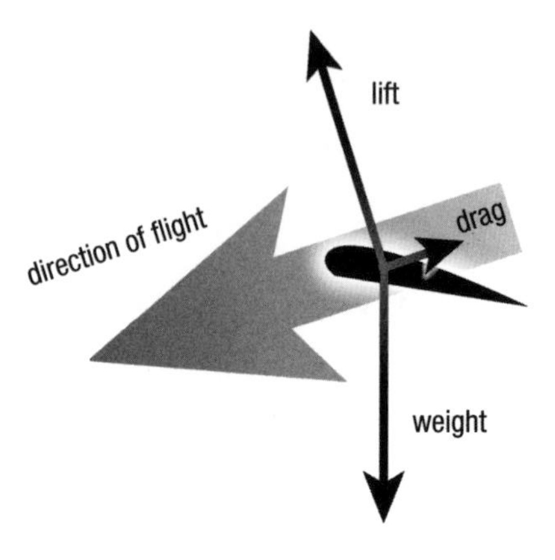

Figure 20.14 *Balanced forces*

Chapter 21: Stability and control

For any aeroplane to be safe to fly, it must have a certain amount of stability. Stability is the tendency of the aircraft to settle down in normal trimmed flight, and to restore itself to normal trimmed flight after a small disturbance (perhaps caused by turbulence or by the pilot using the controls). Although every aircraft needs enough stability to make it safe and pleasant to fly, if it is given too much it will be difficult (or 'heavy') to control. This means that the pilot will not be able easily to make use of the machine's full performance. So the designer has his work cut out in balancing these often competing demands.

In this section the discussion of hang-glider control is confined to explaining the workings of weightshift control in traditional tailless flexwing designs. The various rigid-wing and semi-rigid-wing hang gliders use a wide variety of conventional control methods, and their operation can be looked up in any good aerodynamics textbook.

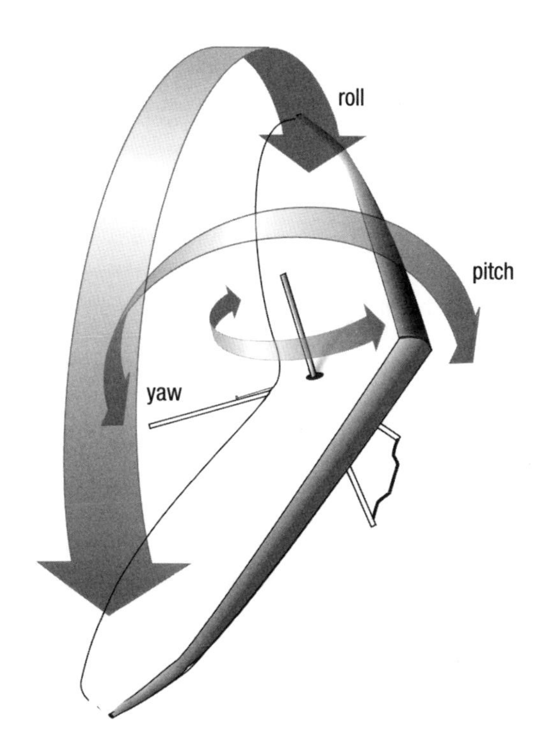

Figure 21.1 *The three axes of movement: pitch, roll and yaw*

Pitch

Control

Paragliders have very limited pitch control, as the angle of attack is set by the lengths of the suspension lines. However, when both controls are applied together, the trailing edge of the wing is deflected downward; besides increasing drag, this effectively raises the angle of attack of the aerofoil, increasing lift. With no control applied, the wing is at its fastest (lowest) angle of attack. With the controls applied fully, the wing is at its slowest (highest) angle of attack. (Speed bars and trim tabs also work as secondary pitch controls, by actually altering the wing's angle of incidence.)

Temporary dynamic pitch-control effects also arise due to the pilot's weight being located a long way beneath the wing: if the wing is slowed by the sudden application of the controls the pilot will tend to swing forward, which in turn further raises the wing's angle of attack.

A **hang glider** is controlled in pitch by the pilot moving his weight fore and aft. 'Pushing out' on the control bar raises the glider's nose, by reconfiguring the glider with a more rearward centre of gravity. 'Pulling in' on the control bar lowers the glider's nose, by reconfiguring the glider with a more forward centre of gravity.

Stability

A conventional wing section is unstable. When its angle of attack is increased, the centre of pressure moves forward, so creating a moment that acts to raise the angle of attack further. Similarly, when the angle of attack is decreased, the centre of pressure moves rearward, creating a nose-down moment. The designer of any aircraft has to find a way of counteracting this tendency.

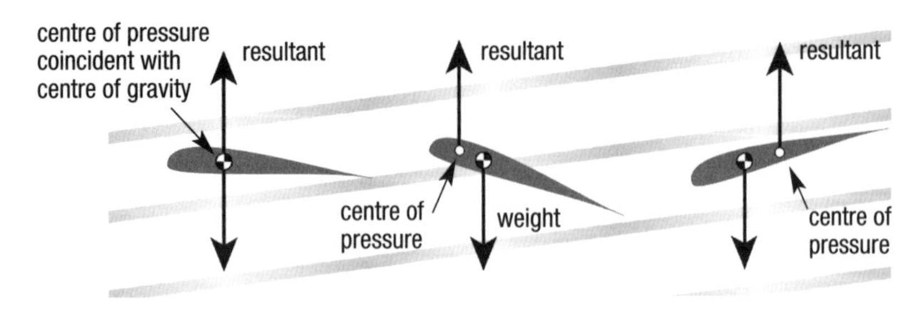

Figure 21.2 *The position of the centre of pressure changes with the angle of attack*

A conventional aeroplane has a tailplane (or, as the Americans call it, a 'stabilizer') to provide stability in pitch. As the angle of attack of the wing is increased, so producing the unwelcome forward movement of the centre of pressure, the tailplane's angle to the airflow is also increased. It now creates increased lift which raises the aircraft's tail, so restoring the wing to the trimmed angle of attack. A similar process works when the aircraft suffers a nose-down disturbance: in this case the amount of lift produced by the tailplane is reduced (it may even create a downward force), which restores the aircraft to trimmed flight.

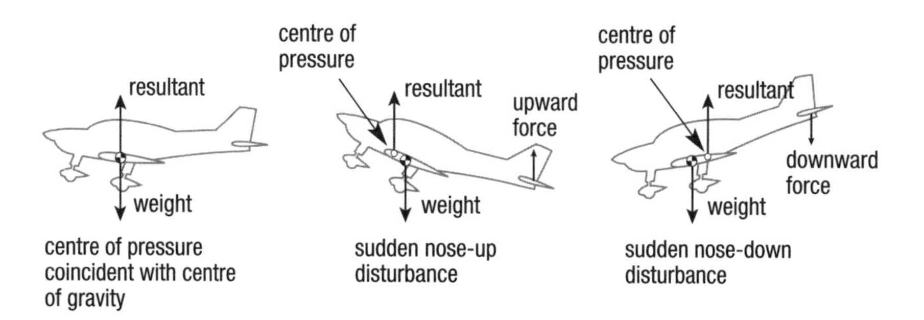

Figure 21.3 *Pitch stability on a conventional aircraft*

Hang gliders and paragliders are (generally) tailless aircraft, so alternative methods of providing pitch stability have to be found.

With **paragliders,** pendulum stabilising forces are used. By having the mass of the pilot suspended a considerable distance below the wing, the moments generated by movement of the centre of pressure are generally counteracted by the large restoring moments created by the displaced weight. This mechanism is effective for ensuring recovery from most minor disturbances. If a more severe nose-down disturbance occurs, then a very dynamic situation – possibly involving canopy deflations – may exist.

Stability in pitch (both small and large disturbances) is one of the areas explored by the paraglider certification schemes, to check that the designers have arrived at acceptable characteristics.

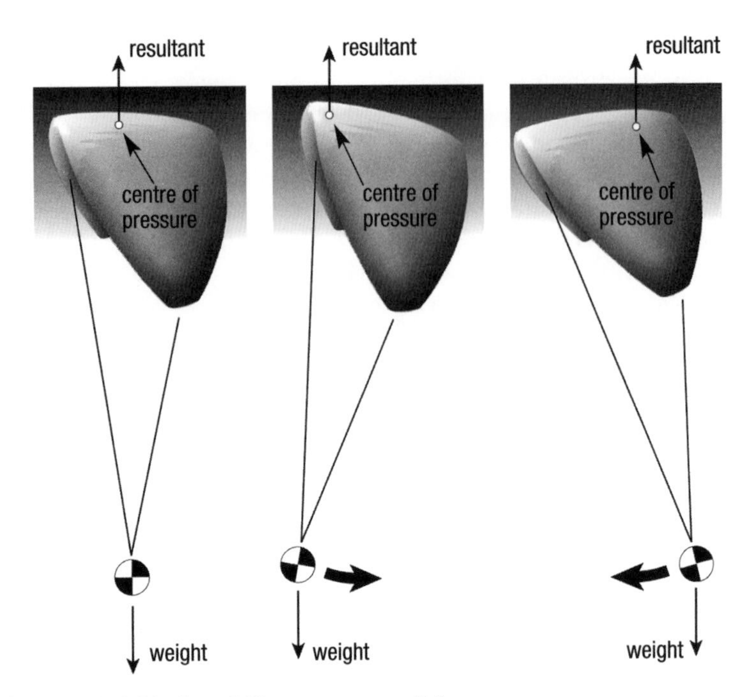

Figure 21.4 *Pitch stability on a paraglider*

With **hang gliders**, pendulum forces are also present, but they are only small as the pilot is not very far below the wing, and on their own they are incapable of ensuring adequate stability. So hang gliders use a combination of devices to keep them the right way up.

The principal mechanism is the use of washout and sweepback to effectively create two tail surfaces. Washout is twist built into the wing, so that the angle of attack at the tips is less than in the centre of the wing. Sweepback puts the wing-tips well behind the centre of gravity of the aircraft.

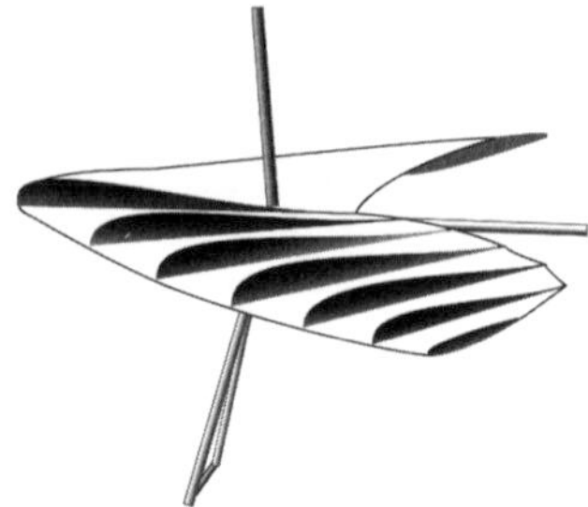

Figure 21.5 *Washout and sweepback are important components of hang-glider stability*

When washout and sweepback are combined, then as the glider's nose is raised and lowered the centre of the wing and the wing-tips contribute differing amounts towards the total lift in such a way as to promote pitch stability. (In effect the wing-tips act like the tail surfaces on a conventional aircraft.) For instance, when the glider's nose is lowered, the centre of the wing creates proportionally more lift than the wing-tips – which will now be at a very low angle of attack – so the nose tends to rise. Conversely, when the glider's nose is raised towards the stall, the wing-tips become increasingly efficient, so creating a strong nose-down pitching moment.

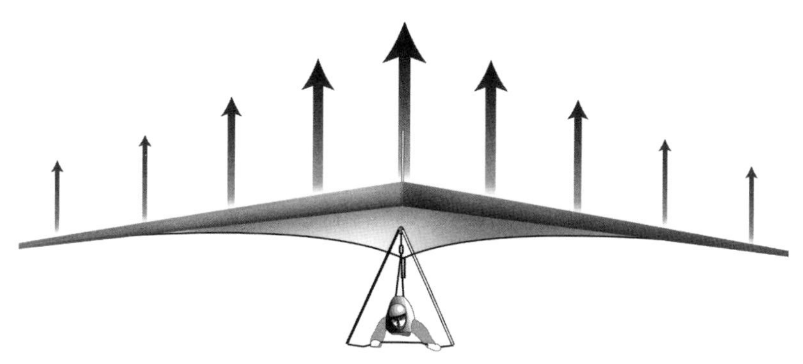

Figure 21.6 *The glider is flying slowly, and the whole wing is producing lift*

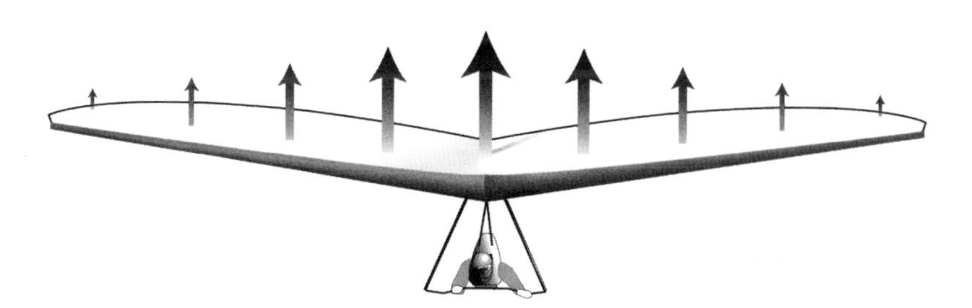

Figure 21.7 *When the glider is flown fast, washout results in the tips producing less lift*

For the angles of attack experienced in normal flight, these two factors (washout and sweepback) play a very significant part in pitch stability. However, on their own they are not sufficient to make a hang glider safe: designers therefore use tip-rods (also known by a variety of other names – see Glossary) and reflex to provide additional stability.

Tip-rods function as follows: if the nose of the glider gets tipped to a very low angle of attack, then the tips need to create a downward force to help push the nose back up. An unsupported area of sail at the tip cannot create a downward force, but by fitting tip-rods the sail is held up at the tip and will create a downward force at low and negative angles of attack.

Reflex is the name given to aerofoil sections which curve upwards at the trailing edge. These sections are more stable (but less efficient) than more normal wing sections: at low angles of attack the air flowing around the curve at the rear of the section creates a downward force which pushes the rear down – and the nose up.

Figure 21.8 *Reflex aerofoil*

Most hang gliders also use luff-lines, which hold the trailing edge up when the rest of the sail moves down during flight at low angles of attack. This automatically converts the aerofoil section into a reflexed shape when extra stability is needed.

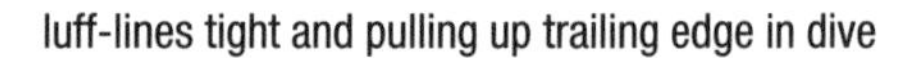

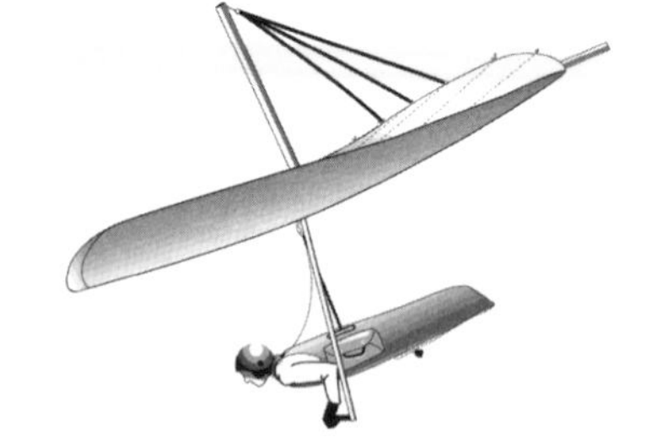

Figure 21.9 *Luff-lines in action*

On 'topless' hang gliders (which have no kingpost) there are no luff-lines. Instead, internal washout struts are used, often in conjunction with a transverse batten. These work along with the standard tip-rods to limit the downward movement of the sail in the outboard portions of the wing.

When you are flying a stable hang glider, you will, or should, find increasing resistance to your efforts the more you try to dive, and when you release pressure on the control bar the aircraft will, or should, want to return to normal (or trim) speed. (Trim speed is the speed at which the glider is trimmed to fly with no pilot effort – it is possible to fly 'hands off ' at this speed.) **WARNING: Vehicle testing is the only way of checking that a glider design is stable across the full range of angles of attack that may be encountered in service.**

Once again, do not fiddle about with any part of your glider that could possibly effect its stability: the description of pitch stability given above explains how it all works when the designer has got it just right. The angle of the tip-rods, the lengths of the luff-lines, the flexibility of the batten ends, the shape of the battens – all these features and more are precisely adjusted to create a safe glider, and any alteration to any feature can make a good glider dangerous. You should ensure that you maintain your glider meticulously and regularly check features such as the trailing-edge height and the batten shape (your glider's user manual will explain how to do this).

Roll

Control

A **paraglider** cannot usually be directly controlled in roll, although when it is fitted with a weightshift harness some roll control can be exerted. Yaw (see below) is the primary initiator of directional control.

A **hang glider** is controlled in roll by a process that starts with the pilot's lateral weightshift. This results in the wing flexing, effectively raising the trailing edge on the loaded semi-span (so reducing the angle of attack) and lowering the trailing edge on the unloaded semi-span (so increasing the angle of attack). The resulting differential lift results in roll.

Stability

Paraglider roll stability is again achieved by the pendulum effects of having the pilot's centre of gravity located a long way beneath the wing.

The usual way of obtaining adequate roll stability in **conventional aircraft** is to set the wings at a slight dihedral angle. 'Dihedral' means that the wing-tips are slightly raised above the level of the centre section, giving the wing a slight 'V' shape when viewed from the front. If the aircraft is displaced in roll, say by a gust, it will sideslip. Due to the dihedral angle, the lower wing will meet the airflow at a slightly higher angle of attack than the raised wing, and the resulting lift imbalance will tend to roll the aircraft back to level flight.

Swept wings are usually very stable in roll, and as a consequence most modern **hang gliders** are designed with a small amount of anhedral angle – an inverted 'V' shape when viewed from the front – to ensure satisfactory roll control.

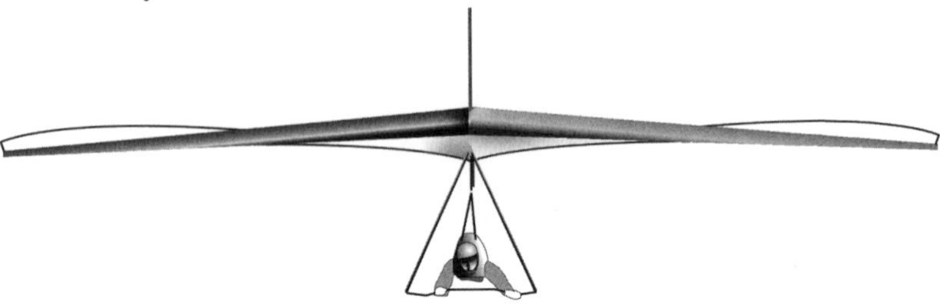

Figure 21.10 *Performance hang glider, showing the leading edges with a slight anhedral angle*

Yaw

Control

A **paraglider** is directly controlled in yaw: when the pilot applies the control on one side, the trailing edge of the wing is deflected downward. Because the control lines are attached to the very rear of the fabric wing, a very sharp pulled-down 'lip' is formed. This 'lip' significantly increases drag, causing the glider to yaw. The result of this yaw is that the outer wing has higher relative airspeed and so creates more lift than the inner one. This produces the roll needed for a balanced turn. (The effect of the pilot being swung to the outside of the turn also helps in this.)

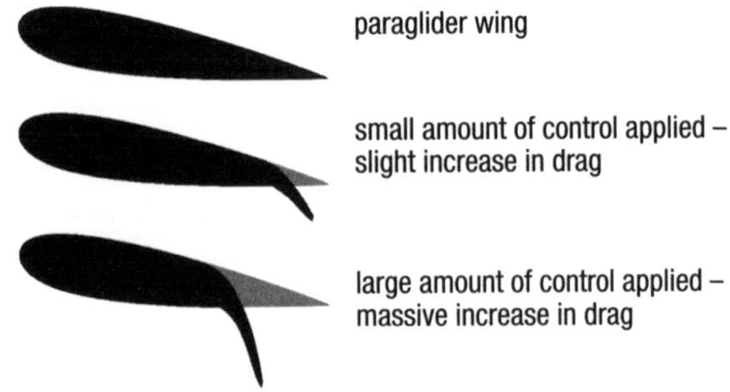

Figure 21.11 *The operation of paraglider controls*

A **hang glider** cannot be directly controlled in yaw. (The yaw needed as part of a balanced turn is generated by sideslip following roll.)

Stability

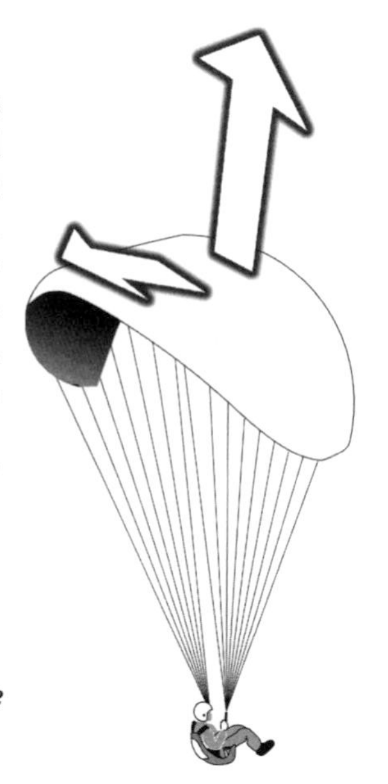

With a paraglider aerofoil, the centre of lift is situated at around the 15-20 percent chord position. The wing's centre of drag is located at approximately the middle of the wing: i.e. the 50 percent chord position – significantly rearward of the centre of lift. The drag force acts at 180 degrees to the direction of travel. If you imagine the wing supported from this 15-20 percent chord position, with the pilot's weight suspended below, it is easy to see how the drag force pulling rearward from the 50 percent chord position will act to keep the paraglider correctly aligned in flight.

Figure 21.12 *The centre of drag is behind the centre of lift: this stabilises the glider in yaw*

Many hang gliders have a vertical keel pocket at the rear of the centre section. This acts like the vertical fin at the rear of the fuselage on conventional aircraft, providing directional stability through the generation of a side-force if the aircraft is yawed. However, modern high-performance hang-glider designs manage without a vertical keel pocket, relying instead on the restoring forces created by sweepback: if a swept wing is yawed, then unequal drag forces are created by the two semi-spans, with the result that the glider yaws back into balance.

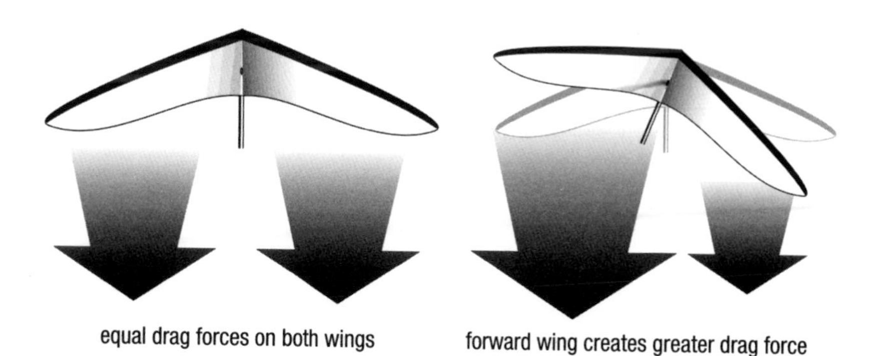

Figure 21.13 *Hang-glider yaw stability*

Chapter 22: Performance

The performance of any glider is considered in terms of sink rate and glide ratio – and the pilot wants them both to be good.

Sink rate

As the glider flies along in steady air, it will be sinking down towards the ground. The minimum-sink rate is presently of the order of 1.05m/s (210ft/min) for a good paraglider, 0.90m/s (180ft/min) for a good hang glider. The sink rate will vary according to the speed at which the glider is flown, owing to the way total drag changes with airspeed.

Glide ratio (l/d ratio)

Most of the time you want to fly as far as you can from any given height. If, for example, you can fly 1,000m (3,300ft) distance from a height of 100m (330ft), your glide ratio is 10:1. If you fly a distance of 500m (1,650ft) from the same height, your glide ratio would be only 5:1. The best hang gliders have a glide ratio of over 12:1, which in cross-country terms means that from a height of 1 km (3,300ft) you would arrive on the ground 12km (7.5 miles) away, given totally still air. The best paragliders are not far behind this performance, with glide ratios of around 8:1.

Polar curve

A polar curve is a simple graphical representation of a glider's performance. Measurements are taken of a glider's sink rate as it is flown at various speeds in smooth air, and these are then plotted on a graph.

The polar curve for this imaginary glider shows that the best sink rate is obtained at an airspeed of 32kph (20mph). If the speed is increased to 61kph (38mph), the sink rate increases to 2.2m/s (440ft/min). Note also what happens if you fly slower. At 24kph (15mph) the sink rate has increased dramatically. Slow down further, and the glider stalls.

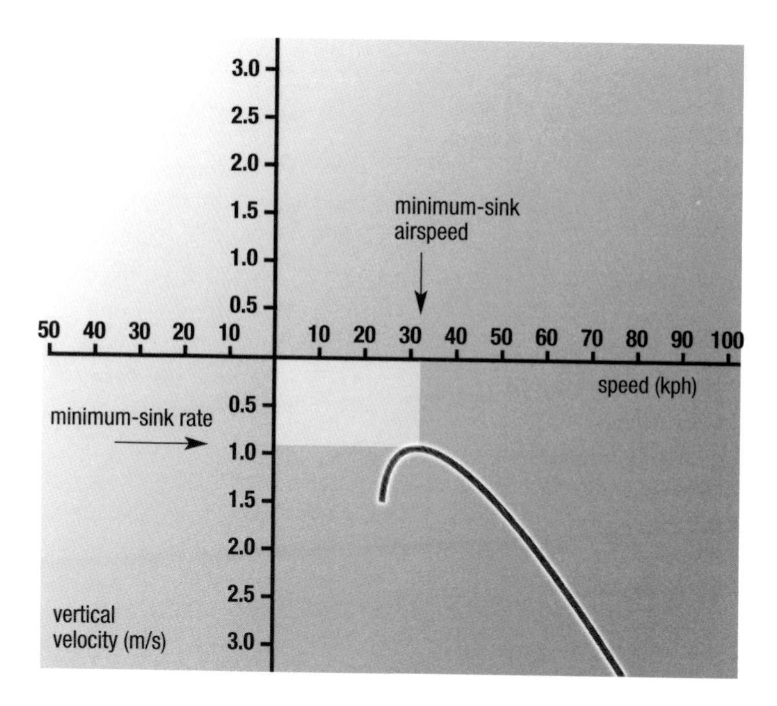

Figure 22.1 *Determining the minimum-sink airspeed and rate using the glider's polar curve*

From this polar curve we can also establish the minimum-sink rate of this glider – which is approximately 0.9m/s (180ft/min) at 32kph (20mph).

By taking a straight line from the origin to touch the curve at a tangent, we can use the polar curve to discover the airspeed to fly for the best glide ratio. In this case it is 40kph (25mph). At this speed the sink rate is approximately 1.1m/s (220ft/min), which gives a best glide ratio of 10:1.

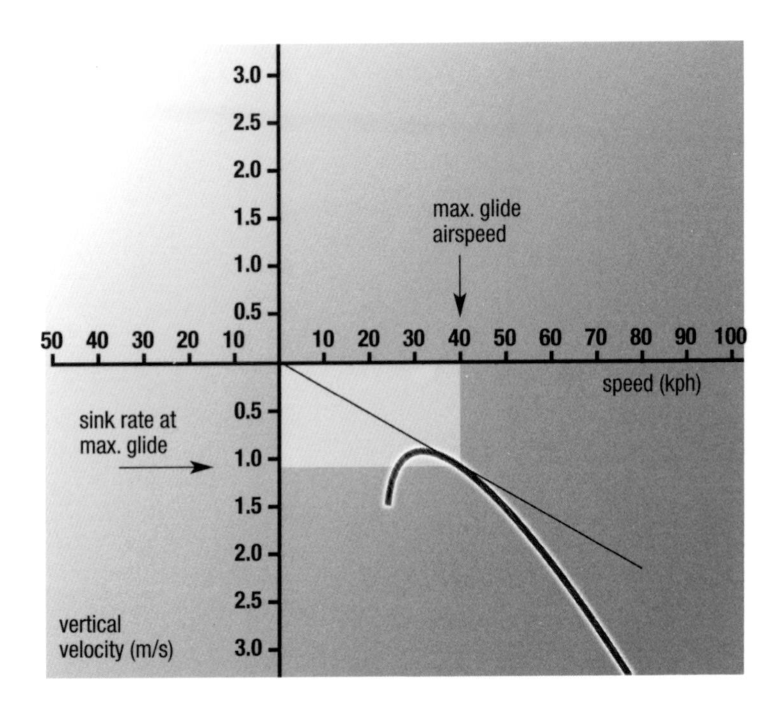

Figure 22.2 *Maximum glide performance*

In real life you may want to fly at a less efficient speed, in terms of your glider's performance, in order to achieve a specific objective. For example, there is no future in flying at minimum-sink speed in a strong down-current, as you may reach the ground before you have got clear of the sink. In such cases it is much more sensible to increase speed and quickly get out of the sinking air. The height sacrificed by flying faster than the best-glide speed will be much less than the height that would have been lost by your flying in the sinking air for a longer period.

By displacing the origin upward (on the y-axis) by the magnitude of the sink, the polar curve can be used to find the speed to fly for best distance. With our imaginary glider, and air sinking at 1.5m/s (300ft/min), this speed would be approximately 60kph (37mph), and the glider would be descending at 3.7m/s (740ft/min).

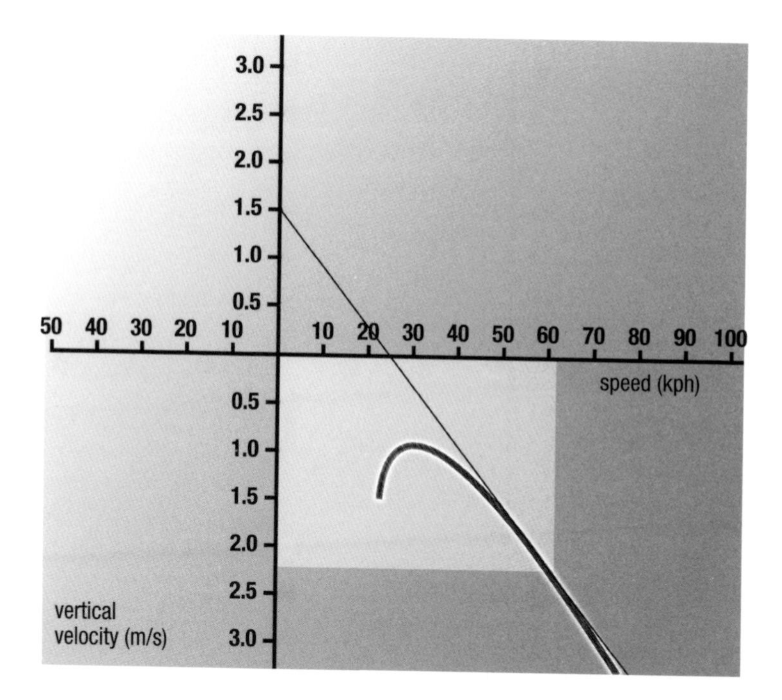

Figure 22.3 *Speed to fly for best distance in air sinking at 1.5m/s*

Nor is there any future in flying at 30kph (20mph) against a 30kph headwind if the goal field is a kilometre upwind. Increase your speed to 70kph (43mph), and you'll be there in one and a half minutes – and although it will cost you nearly 250m (800ft) of height, proceeding as you were would have cost you all your height without reaching the goal.

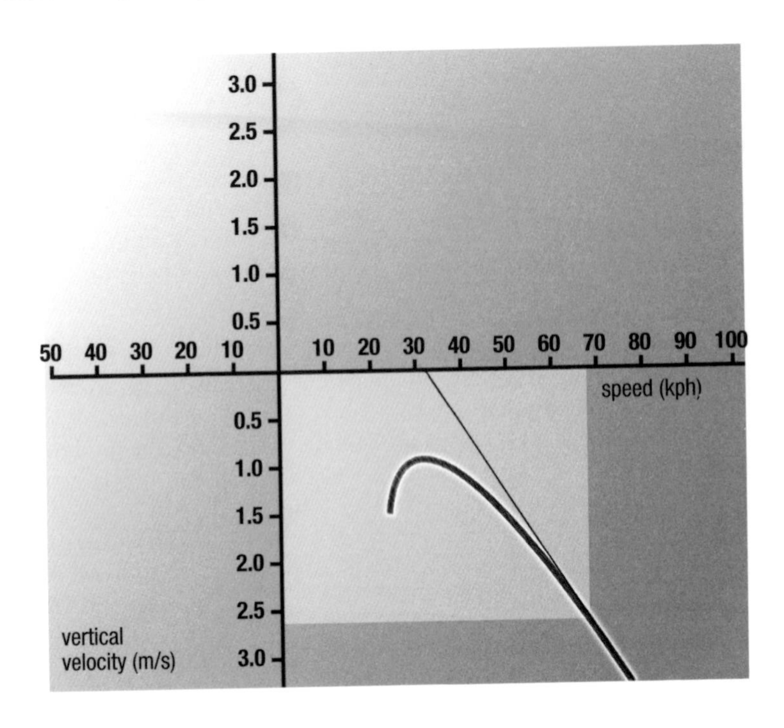

Figure 22.4 *Speed to fly for best distance against a 30kph headwind*

By displacing the origin to the left of zero on the x-axis, the tailwind case can be explored, and the lifting-air case can be examined by displacing the origin below zero on the y-axis. It is also possible to combine two factors, so for instance you can work out the best speed to fly to cover the ground when faced with sinking air and a headwind.

From playing around with a polar graph, you will discover some 'golden rules' for efficient cross-country flying. Fly slowly in lift; fly faster in sink; fly fast if you want to penetrate a headwind, fly slowly in a tailwind.

Ballast

Pilot weight will also affect performance. Sailplane pilots often carry water ballast in their machines. This has the effect of moving the polar curve down and to the right. The maximum glide ratio will remain unchanged, but will be achieved at a higher speed, so enabling higher cross-country speeds and giving better penetration. The minimum-sink rate does suffer, but if that becomes important the pilot dumps the ballast.

Some paraglider and hang-glider pilots also use ballast. In theory they should enjoy the same benefits as the sailplane pilots. With ballast the pilot will be able to move around the sky faster, but should the lift weaken he can dump the ballast (fine dry sand or water) and use the minimum-sink rate to the best advantage. When flying cross-country in strong thermal conditions the ballasted pilot will climb fractionally more slowly in the thermal, but will be able to fly faster without loss of performance to reach the next one.

But this is in theory. It is not clear that these theoretical benefits are always fully realised in practice. Flexible wings deform when carrying heavier loads, and – in some cases at least – the performance loss caused by these changes to the wing-shape are greater than any benefits to be gained from the use of ballast.

In any case, the usable weight range of the glider is decided by the manufacturer on the basis of many inter-related factors, including handling, stability and structural strength. You should never operate outside the certified weight range.

SECTION 6
AIRLAW, AIRSPACE AND OTHER LEGALITIES

Chapter 23: Air law

Introduction

The Air Navigation Order

Rules of the Air Regulations

Chapter 24: Airspace

Introduction

Types of airspace

The aeronautical chart

Using an altimeter

Chapter 23: Air law

Introduction

While the subject of air law may seem a bit daunting at first glance, it needn't be. Nearly all air law is about being sensible. Any right-minded person would agree that flying an aircraft while incapacitated through drugs or alcohol is not a good idea: perhaps it is not a great surprise to find that it is also illegal. Any good pilot would agree that an aircraft should be inspected before flight: it is also a legal requirement. Ninety-nine percent of air law falls into this 'be sensible' category.

Scope

All of the following information applies to hang gliders and paragliders, which includes Self Propelled Hang Gliders (foot launched powered hang gliders and powered paragliders).

The sources

The Air Navigation Order (ANO) forms the basis of the UK's air law and airspace legislation. This document contains more than 120 Articles of law covering airworthiness, operation of aircraft, documentation, licensing and so on. It also includes a number of Schedules (appendices) which provide supplementary detail.

Supporting the ANO are the **Rules of the Air Regulations** (looked at next) and the **Civil Aviation (Investigation of Accidents) Regulations** (see the section on 'Reporting an accident or incident' in Chapter 18). There is one further important document: **the UK Aeronautical Information Publication (AIP)**. This details airspace regulations, hazards and so on (these are explored in Chapter 24).

The Air Navigation Order

Many of the Articles contained in the ANO do not apply to gliders. Summarised below are those that clearly do, and are most relevant to normal paragliding, hang-gliding and parascending operations. (Where appropriate, additional information is included.)

Pre-flight actions

The pilot must satisfy himself that the aircraft is fit for flight and checked, that any passengers have been briefed and that the flight can be safely made. (This includes checking weather conditions and forecasts, and accessing up-to-date airspace information.)

Radios

For a pilot legally to operate a radio from a hang glider or paraglider, he must comply with the law in three areas:

- The radio transmitter must be of a **type approved** by the CAA.
- The glider operator or owner must have a **station licence** for that radio. These can be obtained by writing to: Radio Licensing Section, Directorate of Airspace Policy, K6 Gate 6, CAA House, 45-59 Kingsway, London WC2B 6TE, by telephoning: 020 7453 6555, by e-mailing: radio.licensing@dap.caa.co.uk, or from their web site at www.caa.co.uk (search for 'hang glider').
- The pilot must either possess **a Flight Radiotelephony Operator's (R/T) licence** or must only use the following frequencies:
  - 118.675MHz. This is a dedicated paragliding and hang gliding frequency which can be used anywhere in the UK FIR, up to and including 5000ft AMSL.
  - 129.9MHz, 129.95MHz, 130.1MHz, 130.125MHz and 130.4MHz. These are sport-aviation frequencies, and their users include parachutists, balloon pilots and sailplane pilots.
  - The International Distress Frequency, 121.5MHz. This frequency can be used to alert the emergency services. Among the station licence conditions is the requirement that operators must exercise strict radio discipline and that the procedures must be based on those set out in the CAA publication CAP 413.

Dropping persons or articles

Articles shall not be dropped or be permitted to drop from an aircraft in flight, except for the purpose of saving life, ballast in the form of fine sand or water, or (at an aerodrome) tow ropes.

Imperilling safety

Persons must not endanger the safety of an aircraft or cause an aircraft to endanger any persons or property.

Drunkenness

Persons must not fly while under the influence of drugs or alcohol.

Exhibitions of flying

Display flying is tightly regulated: pilots must have a CAA Display Authorisation, and each display and item must be vetted by the CAA.

Inadvertent entering of a Restricted or Prohibited Area

If a pilot inadvertently enters such an area then he must, unless otherwise instructed, leave the area as quickly as possible and not descend over the area.

Winch/tow-launching

It is illegal to winch or tow to an altitude greater than 60 metres above ground level (AGL) – or at all within an aerodrome traffic zone (ATZ) – unless permitted by a current specific CAA Tow Site Permission.

Public transport and aerial work

The law attempts to draw a clear distinction between private (recreational) flying and commercial (moneymaking) flying. In order to fly commercially (public transport or aerial work), very closely defined levels of pilot qualification, operator organisation and aircraft airworthiness must be met. These are not available for hang-glider and paraglider operators!

To help deal with 'grey areas' which emerged as people tried to find ways around the law, the CAA introduced the term 'valuable consideration'. The CAA's short definition of valuable consideration is 'a consideration which is of more than a nominal nature'. If valuable consideration is accepted as part of a flight, then that flight is commercial, and therefore subject to all the rules and regulations applicable to commercial flying. However, in order to allow some normal aspects of recreational flying to continue, the CAA have defined a few special cases where valuable consideration may be exchanged in connection with a flight, without the need for special licences and paperwork:

- Receiving reimbursement of costs directly related to a competition flight is allowed, as is receiving a prize of less than £500 per contest.
- If a pilot is taking part in a display, then receiving reimbursement of the costs directly related to the flight is permitted – but remember that there are a whole host of other regulations relating to display flying.

- The direct costs of a flight may be paid for by or on behalf of the pilot's employer, provided neither the pilot nor any passenger are legally, contractually or otherwise obliged to fly.
- When dual-flying, only qualified instructors may be paid, and only then to instruct fellow-members of their club when flying aircraft owned or operated by the club.

In addition to the above conditions, payment to anyone other than the aircraft's pilot or owner is only acceptable if the only beneficiary of the valuable consideration is a registered charity and the flight is completed in accordance with a specific CAA written permission.

The holder of a PPL (Aeroplanes) may tow a glider using an aircraft owned or operated by a club of which the tug pilot and all those carried in the glider are members. The tug pilot may not receive payment for these services (but the club may charge the glider pilot for the launch).

You will be flying illegally if you accept any 'valuable consideration' for any flight other than under these conditions shown above.

Other Articles

Other Articles that may be relevant in certain circumstances cover the law relating to **'Aircraft Towing Gliders'** (covered in the BHPA Technical Manual), **'Dropping People'** (CAA permissions required except in an emergency) and the **'Method of Carriage of Persons'** (only in purpose-designed seating etc).

Rules of the Air Regulations

The Rules of the Air Regulations concentrate on the practicalities of safely operating an aircraft. These are summarised below with specific regard to gliders (encompassing sailplanes, hang gliders and para-gliders).

Low flying

Gliders must not fly over congested areas below a height that would allow them to land clear of the area and without danger to people or property, or less than 1,000ft above the highest fixed object within 600 metres, whichever is the higher. (A congested area means any area that is substantially used for residential, industrial, commercial or recreational purposes.)

An aircraft may not fly over an open-air assembly of more than a thousand people below 1,000 feet or enough height to enable it to land clear, whichever is the higher. Nor may it take-off or land within 1,000 metres of such an assembly.

An aircraft must not fly closer than 500ft to any person, vessel, vehicle or structure. This provision does not apply to an aircraft taking off or landing, flying low for the purpose of dropping tow ropes, or to gliders that are ridge-soaring.

Right-hand traffic

An aircraft flying within sight of the ground and following a road, railway, canal, coast or other line feature must keep that feature on its left (except where otherwise instructed by ATC).

(Hang gliders and paragliders rarely follow line features, but pilots should remain aware when crossing line features that other aerial traffic may be doing so.)

Choice of VFR or IFR

There are two sets of rules under which an aircraft may fly: the Visual Flight Rules (VFR) or the Instrument Flight Rules (IFR).

Which set of rules you must fly under depends on the Meteorological Conditions and the class of airspace you are flying in. If you are in one of the few classes of controlled airspace that gliders may enter, then you must fly in Visual Meteorological Conditions. Visual Meteorological Conditions means that you are no closer than the set distance clear of cloud (horizontally and vertically) and can see for at least the minimum set distance forward (flight visibility). (See page 231-2 in Chapter 24 for details.)

Outside controlled airspace, by day, you may fly in Visual Meteorological Conditions (VMC) or in Instrument Meteorological Conditions (IMC) as you choose. If you do not maintain the minimum distances for VMC (because the weather is deteriorating or you are flying rather closer to a cloud) then you are automatically in Instrument Meteorological Conditions.

If your flight (outside controlled airspace, by day) is in VMC, then you may choose to conduct your flight in accordance with either the Instrument Flight Rules or the Visual Flight Rules. If on the other hand you fly in IMC, then there is no choice: you **must** operate in accordance with the Instrument Flight Rules.

Rules 33 and 34 are the Instrument Flight Rules that apply to aircraft flying under IFR outside controlled airspace. Rule 33 is a minimum height rule, and forbids flying at less than 1,000ft above the highest obstacle within 5 nautical miles except as necessary for taking off or landing, and except when flying at or below 3,000ft AMSL, clear of cloud and in sight of the surface. Rule 34 is only applicable to aircraft above 3,000ft AMSL cruising in level flight. (Rule 34 prescribes set altitudes for given headings; gliders are constantly ascending and descending, so this does not apply.)

(The foregoing is the legal position. While it is clear that in many situations hang gliders and paragliders could legally fly in cloud, the fact remains that this would be extremely foolhardy. Maintaining control without visual reference to the horizon is virtually impossible, as is avoiding other traffic and keeping track of your position. Exploit the freedom to fly right up to just below cloudbase if you wish – but leave it at that.)

Night flying

An aircraft flying at night shall be flown in accordance with Instrument Flight Rules. 'Night' means the time from half an hour after sunset to half an hour before sunrise (both times inclusive), sunrise and sunset being determined at surface level. At night, lights must be carried in accordance with the Air Navigation Order.

Rules for avoiding aerial collisions

The prime rule is the first one!

- It is the pilot's responsibility to take all possible measures to avoid a collision with any other aircraft.
- An aircraft shall not be flown so close to another aircraft as to create a danger of collision.
- No formation flying is permitted unless all the pilots have agreed.
- When required by these Rules to give way, an aircraft shall avoid passing over, under or ahead of another unless well clear.
- An aircraft that has right of way under these Rules shall maintain its course and speed.

Converging

Other than in the cases of approaching head-on and overtaking:

- A powered aircraft shall give way to airships, gliders and balloons.
- An airship shall give way to gliders and balloons.

- A glider shall give way to balloons.
- When two aircraft of the same classification converge at approximately the same altitude, the one with the other on its right shall give way.

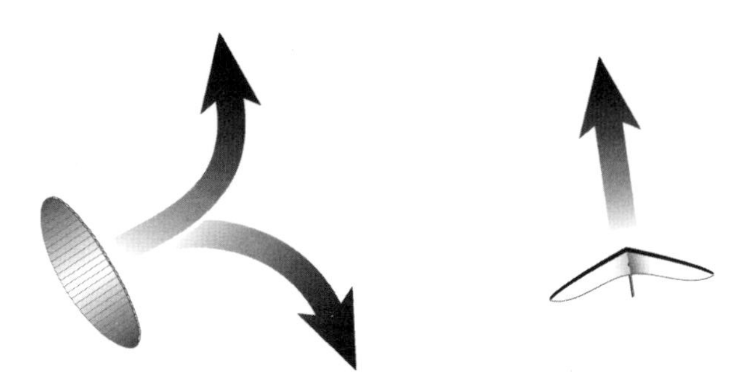

Figure 23.1 *Converging courses (gliders and distances not to scale)*

When approaching head-on

When approaching approximately head-on with a risk of collision, both aircraft shall alter course to the right.

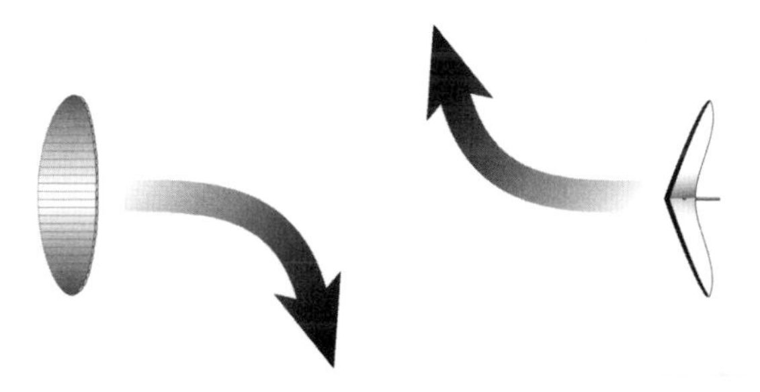

Figure 23.2 *Approaching head-on (gliders and distances not to scale)*

(This rule is modified slightly by UK ridge-soaring conventions: when ridge-soaring, if two gliders are flying towards each other at similar height, the pilot with the ridge on the left should move out so that the other has room to maintain course without having to turn into or over the ridge.)

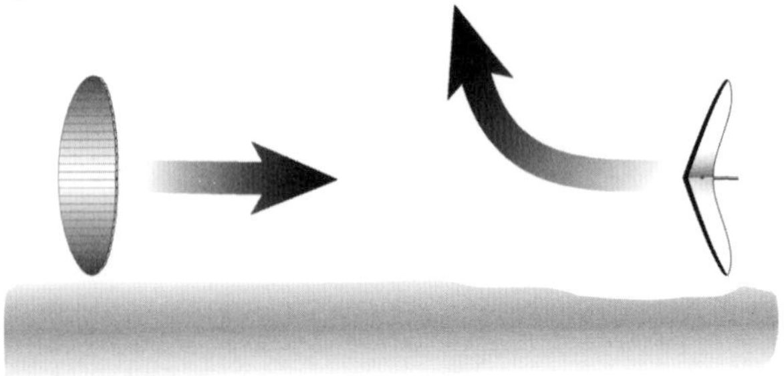

Figure 23.3 *Approaching head-on when ridge-soaring (gliders and distances not to scale)*

Overtaking

When overtaking another aircraft, you must give way to it and alter course to the right to overtake. In the UK a glider may overtake another glider to either the left or the right.

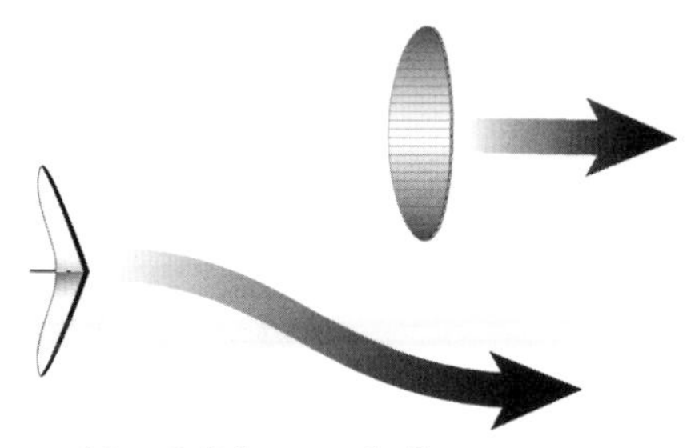

Figure 23.4 *Overtaking (gliders and distances not to scale)*

(This rule is modified slightly by UK ridge-soaring conventions: when ridge-soaring, overtaking should be done on the hill side, so that the overtaken glider remains free to make a normal turn, away from the hill. Beware – in other countries different rules or protocols apply.)

Flight near aerodromes

Part of the official definition of an aerodrome is: 'Any area of land or water designed, equipped, set apart or commonly used for affording facilities for the landing and departure of aircraft…' Therefore it can be claimed that all our sites are aerodromes, just as Heathrow is!

When flying in the vicinity of any aircraft's take-off or landing sites you must keep clear or conform to any established pattern, making all turns to the left unless ground signals indicate otherwise.

(Although this is how the Rule is written, it is rare for ground signals to be used at our sites, and because of the constraints of location and weather any turn pattern may not be to the left. However, there may be an established pattern which you need to be clear about before you launch. If in doubt, ask.)

Landings

- An aircraft landing or on final approach has right of way over all other aircraft in the air or on the ground.
- The lowest aircraft of any on an approach to land has right of way, provided it does not cut in front of or overtake any aircraft on final approach.
- When landing, you should leave clear on the left any glider that is landing, has landed or is about to take off. (This Rule may have to be modified to suit the site.)
- After landing, you must clear the landing area as soon as possible.

Chapter 24: Airspace

Introduction

Every cubic inch of sky above the UK is within a block of airspace that has a formal designation, and for which there are rules governing who or what can fly in it and under what circumstances. Thankfully, a sizeable chunk of this airspace is Class G, where we can fly more or less unimpeded, but an awful lot of UK airspace is no-go territory for hang gliders and paragliders. You need to know which is which...

Types of airspace

The term 'glider' is used in this chapter to include all paragliders and hang gliders.

ICAO airspace classification

The UK uses the system of international airspace classification developed by the International Civil Aviation Organisation (ICAO) whereby the status of a piece of airspace is denoted by a letter that is shown on all aeronautical charts. It is this letter that determines the rules applying to it. Airspace Classes A, B, C, D and E are all forms of **controlled** airspace, while airspace Classes F and G are uncontrolled.

Controlled airspace comes in various shapes and sizes: aeronautical charts depict the horizontal boundaries accurately and state the vertical dimensions.

Class A Controlled Airspace

This airspace is effectively closed to gliders. (Exceptionally, gliders may cross sections of Class A airspace by virtue of a Letter of Agreement which will have very detailed procedures which must be followed.)

Class B Controlled Airspace

No UK airspace currently falls into this category.

Class C Controlled Airspace

The entire airspace over the UK above FL 195 is Class C airspace.

(It is expected that it will be possible to temporarily activate a few specified areas for glider flights using a special procedure.)

Class D Controlled Airspace

For gliders to enter and transit Class D Controlled Airspace, an ATC clearance is required. This usually involves using radio to:

- Contact the ATC unit and pass details of the aircraft's position, level and proposed track.
- Obtain entry clearance.
- Listen out on the relevant frequency while in that airspace.
- Comply with ATC instructions.

Class E Controlled Airspace

Gliders may fly in Class E airspace without ATC clearance, subject to maintaining VMC. In this situation VMC is defined as:

- Below 3,000ft AMSL: minimum flight visibility of 5km, clear of cloud, in sight of the surface.
- Above 3,000ft AMSL: minimum flight visibility of 5km, 1,500m horizontally clear of cloud and 1,000ft vertically clear of cloud.

You must still comply with the rules governing other airspace with specific restrictions (e.g. ATZs) that may exist within the Class E airspace.

Local agreements

Letters of agreement between local clubs and the nearby airport can make airspace more or less restrictive than previously described. The local club will have details of any such agreements.

Class F Airspace (Advisory Airspace)

An advisory route (ADR) is a route used by airline-type traffic, but without the full protection of an airway. Although depicted only as a centreline on UK aeronautical charts, it is nominally 10 nautical miles wide. Gliders may cross Class F airspace without restriction, but caution should be exercised.

In this class of airspace, VMC for aircraft flying at hang-glider and paraglider speeds is defined as:

- below 3,000ft AMSL: in sight of the surface, clear of cloud, minimum flight visibility of 1500m
- 3,000ft AMSL to FL100: 1,500m horizontally clear of cloud, 1,000ft vertically clear of cloud, minimum flight visibility of 5km
- above FL100: 1,500m horizontally clear of cloud, 1,000ft vertically clear of cloud, minimum flight visibility of 8km

But bear in mind the fact that you may choose to fly in IMC (see Chapter 23).

Class G Airspace

This term is given to the 'open' FIR (Flight Information Region), the uncontrolled airspace not subject to any of the above classifications.

The VMC criteria in this class of airspace are identical to those for Class F above, as is the freedom to choose to fly in IMC.

Other types of airspace

Even within 'uncontrolled' Class G airspace there are various non-ICAO types of airspace that have entry restrictions or requirements, some of which are described below.

Aerodrome Traffic Zone (ATZ)

Aerodromes with an ATZ have it shown on the charts, except where they are already inside controlled airspace (in which case they still have one but it is not shown). An ATZ consists of the airspace from the surface to a height of 2,000ft above the level of the aerodrome, bounded by a circle of either 2 nautical miles or 2.5 nautical miles radius, depending on the length of the main runway. (The horizontal dimensions are drawn accurately on the aeronautical chart.) The aerodrome's altitude is printed alongside the symbol. Gliders, including hang gliders and paragliders, are not allowed in active ATZs without having been given permission by the ATC unit.

At airfields without an ATZ, pilots should conform to the traffic pattern or keep clear of the circuit airspace, and should observe the normal rules of good airmanship.

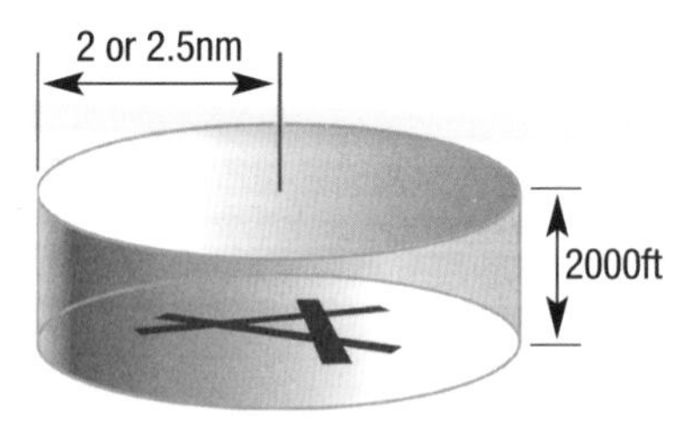

Figure 24.1 *Aerodrome Traffic Zone*

Military Aerodrome Traffic Zone (MATZ)

These typically consist of the airspace from the surface to a height of 3,000ft above the aerodrome's altitude (which is printed alongside the symbol, as with ATZs), bounded by a circle of radius 5 nautical miles from the aerodrome's reference point – plus a projecting stub aligned with the principal runway 5 nautical miles long and 4 nautical miles wide – between 1,000ft and 3,000ft above the aerodrome's altitude. They look like a pan with a very oversized handle; indeed, the stub is sometimes called the pan-handle. Some MATZs have no stub, or have two or more stubs, or form part of a combined MATZ (CMATZ). Again, the aeronautical charts clearly show their horizontal dimensions.

The rules applicable to entering an MATZ are not compulsory for civil aircraft, but there are two very important things to consider: every MATZ contains an ATZ (which you cannot enter without permission), and an MATZ is usually a very busy bit of sky, especially during the week.

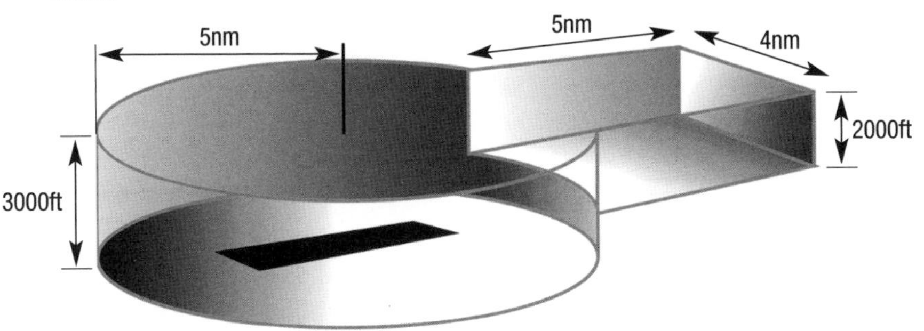

Figure 24.2 *Military Aerodrome Traffic Zone (ATZ not shown)*

Royal Flights

Temporary controlled airspace (CAS-T) is established for short periods of time (usually a matter of hours) to protect flights in fixed wing aircraft by some Royal family members and V.V.I.P's, whenever they operate outside of existing Class A / C airspace. Gliders are not allowed to enter CAS-T airspace at any time. A Royal Low Level Corridor (RLLC) is established for Royal helicopter flights. Civilian pilots flying near the route should keep a good look out and maintain adequate separation from the Royal aircraft.

Information on Royal Flights is available daily on Freephone 0500 3548021 and on the Web at www.ais.org.uk.

Danger Areas

A Danger Area is exactly that: an area where there is an activity that is dangerous to aircraft. Not all of them have by-laws prohibiting entry – but they are all best left well alone unless you are certain that they are inactive. They usually extend from the surface upwards. On the charts they are identified with a 'D' number, e.g. D306/5. The first part is the serial number of the Danger Area, and the final figure (or figures) is the altitude in thousands of feet that it goes up to. The charts also differentiate between those Danger Areas that have published hours of activity (which may be varied by NOTAM) and those that are only activated by NOTAM.

Prohibited and Restricted Areas

As with Danger Areas, the number on the chart after the 'P' or 'R' number indicates the altitude to which the area extends, usually from the surface. The names Prohibited and Restricted are self-explanatory, referring to areas that are established to protect places or activities that are potentially very hazardous or have security implications. Prohibited areas are exactly that: details of the rules governing specific Restricted Areas can be found in *En-Route 5.1*, a section of the AIP (which is a very expensive publication). In the absence of accurate information to the contrary, all Restricted Areas should be avoided. Temporary Restricted Airspace (RA[T]) is set up from time to time, and this is notified on Freefone 0500 354802 and on the Web at www.ais.org.uk daily.

Areas of Intense Aerial Activity (AIAAs)

These areas contain a large amount of civil and/or military aircraft activity. Paragliders and hang gliders are allowed to enter these areas, but should keep an even better lookout than normal (if that's possible!).

High Intensity Radio Transmission Areas (HIRTAs)

Again this is self-explanatory: the transmissions may cook either you or your instruments – or both – from the inside out!

Other warnings

These include a variety of things, including areas where free-fall parachuting takes place. Collecting a parachutist wouldn't do you or him any good!

Other symbols

On the ICAO chart you will see a lot of other symbols. Obviously navigation aids such as TACANs, NDBs, VORs and DMEs do not matter to us, but we should avoid non-ATZ airfields, microlight, gliding and parascending sites unless visiting by prior arrangement.

Summary

A simple summary could be 'if in doubt, keep out', but if in doubt you should not be considering cross-country flying at all. If you have not passed your BHPA Pilot exam (and therefore have not had your understanding of air law and airspace proven) you should not fly cross-country. Even for non-cross-country flying at your local site, you should know the local airspace requirements.

Air-misses (Airprox)

Any pilot who considers his or her flight safety to have been compromised by the proximity of another aircraft may file an Airprox. The United Kingdom Airprox Board investigates all such reports in order to ascertain what lessons can be learned for the future. (They have no remit to take punitive action or to apportion blame.)

If a BHPA member wishes to file an Airprox, the procedure should ideally be as follows:

1 Inform the BHPA Airspace Officer (should this not be possible, do not delay the initial telephone report; this would reduce the likelihood of being able to trace the other aircraft involved).

2 Initial Report – call the Aeronautical Information Section (M) on 01895 426153 or 01895 426716/426718, who will start tracing procedures and inform the UK Airprox Board.

3 Confirmation Report – follow up within seven days with a completed report form CA1094. (Forms are available from the BHPA Office on request.)

4 Complete a BHPA Incident Report form (see Chapter 19).

If you are in any doubt or have any questions, please contact the BHPA Airspace Officer or any of the BHPA technical staff. Note that Airprox reports cover conflicts with both military and civilian aircraft.

References

The information in this chapter is only a brief synopsis of the airspace rules as they affect glider pilots, and is believed to be accurate at the time of writing. In case of doubt, the authoritative primary sources should be consulted. These are:

- the Air Navigation Order
- the Rules of the Air Regulations
- the UK Aeronautical Information Publication.

Pilots requiring clarification on airspace rules should contact the BHPA Airspace Officer, whose telephone number is always given in *Skywings* magazine.

The aeronautical chart

From the foregoing explanation of UK airspace, it should now be abundantly clear that you must have an up-to-date aeronautical chart if you intend making any sort of cross-country flight.

Types of chart

Charts are available in two scales: 1:250,000 and 1:500,000, and come plastic-laminated. The laminated finish allows you to draw on the map with a chinagraph pencil or washable felt-tip pen and then wipe it clean afterwards.

ICAO aeronautical charts

Scale 1:500,000 (United Kingdom)

These charts (known as 'half mil.' charts) show all airspace below FL195. Half mil. charts are the best ones to use for long-distance cross-country flights, simply because you can fly a lot further without going off the edge of the map! If you travel around the country a lot you will only need three charts: Scotland, Orkney and Shetland; Northern England and Northern Ireland; and Southern England and Wales. Airspace above FL195 is not shown.

Topographical air charts

Scale: 1:250,000 (United Kingdom)

These charts (known as 'quarter mil.') only show airspace that has a lower limit below 5,000ft AMSL or Flight Level 55, and so are of limited use if your flight goes above that altitude – unless you are prepared to buy the half mil. and add the extra detail yourself. These charts (with the added information!) are better for local flying and for triangle, out-and-return or short cross-country flights, and also for giving retrieve information, but if you travel around the country you will need more charts to cover the required area (seven for the UK).

Keeping charts up to date

Airspace is regularly changed as civil airports grow, military aerodromes are abandoned, airways are raised or lowered and other changes occur. The CAA replaces charts as required, and this can be as often as within twelve months of the previous issue. You should therefore check at least annually to make sure you are using the most up-to-date issue. But even with an up-to-date chart, the information is only valid on the day of issue! In order to keep your chart fully up to date between new editions, it is necessary to consult the Aeronautical Information Publication (AIP) and NOTAMs (Notices to Airmen) that the CAA issues and amend your chart as necessary. Ideally your Club should have access to NOTAMs. Don't forget to read the Airspace Update column in *Skywings*.

It should be remembered that all these charts contain long-term information only and there is nothing about those Royal Flights or Red Arrows displays that we must avoid. (See the section on 'Flight planning with respect to other air users' in Chapter 1.)

The CAA list all airspace changes that will be incorporated into the next chart issue, on a map by map basis, on their website. Go to **www.caa.co.uk** and follow the links to Airspace Policy and Aeronautical Charts.

Where to get them?

You can obtain these charts from a number of different sources, some of which advertise in *Skywings*. When ordering, you should always check which edition you will be sent. You can also order them from the CAA's main chart agent: CAA Chart Sales, tel. 0161 499 0013, fax. 0161 499 0298. They take credit cards, so it is possible to order by telephone.

Using a chart

It's difficult to read and understand airspace dimensions and rules, work out where you are and where you are heading, and centre in a thermal all at the same time – so planning a cross-country in advance will always make the flight easier. A list of abbreviations used in ICAO charts can be found in the Appendices on page 292.

Navigation techniques are the same whichever scale of chart or type of map you decide to use. Take the time to sit down with the charts or whatever maps you choose to use, and draw on them the line of your proposed track, whether it is a downwind cross-country, a triangle or an out-and-return.

First look for any airspace along your route that you must avoid (the reference block at the bottom of the chart explains what each symbol represents) and highlight the boundaries in an obvious way (e.g. a bright red line). Redraw your track if necessary – although you may be able to continue your flight underneath some airspace that you are not allowed into. If this is the case, besides the boundaries mark the altitude that you must keep below, and remember to set your altimeter properly. (If you get near to the local airway base height it is wiser to leave, as many light-aeroplane pilots find it convenient to follow airways just under their base height.) Flying **over** airspace that you are not allowed in is pushing your luck; gravity has a way of cutting short your flight when you least want it to!

Secondly, look for airspace which you can enter, but where you must obey certain rules. Are you prepared and able to fly by those rules? If not, then mark them as areas to avoid; if you are able and prepared then mark those boundaries in a different but still obvious way (e.g. a line of bright red dashes) – learn the relevant rules and fly by them.

Thirdly look for landmarks that you can use to check your position in flight: recognisable road junctions, isolated large towns, railway junctions and disused airfields are just some examples (remember, woods and forests can change, and objects like radio masts are virtually invisible from above!). Highlighting a landmark every five to ten miles along the track should be enough.

Finally, when folding your map to put it into your map-holder, make sure that your take-off site is positioned near the bottom of the visible bit and that your intended track runs up the map away from you and in the direction of flight. It is much easier to follow like that: landmarks that appear on the right of your drawn track-line will appear on the right as you fly.

If on a flight you run out of map, you have run out of information; sooner or later you will also run out of luck, and so you should land and not put others' lives and our sport at risk by irresponsibility.

Using an altimeter

Aeronautical charts show vertical limits expressed using a variety of terms such as 'ALT' and 'FL' or 'Flight Level'. Part of learning how to use a chart involves understanding what these terms mean, and learning how to use your altimeter correctly.

Atmospheric pressure reduces with increased height, by approximately 1 millibar (mb) per 10m (30ft) at lower levels. Altimeters are effectively pressure-measuring devices that display this reduced pressure as height in feet. In order for these devices to be used to judge height relative to blocks of airspace and other aircraft, agreed altimeter-setting datums have to be used. These allow for the fact that atmospheric pressure also changes as weather systems move across the country, and that some airfields are sited on hills and others in the lowlands. Three standard altimeter-setting datums are used: QFE, QNH and Flight Level – these are detailed below. Aircraft altimeters have a sub-scale and knob to change the pressure setting, allowing them to use any of these three datum bases.

QFE

QFE is the pressure setting that results in the altimeter showing zero on a particular airfield. If you are going to remain flying around the airfield, then the altimeter will provide accurate **height** information. If you choose to fly to another airfield, then when you get there you will need to get (by radio) the current QFE setting at that field to enable you to reset your altimeter to give the accurate **height** above that particular airfield.

QNH

When flying between airfields, pilots set their altimeters to the current pressure reading at mean sea level. This is given the code QNH, and vertical distance measurements using this datum are known as **altitudes**. The country is divided into altimeter setting regions (shown on air charts as ASRs), and within each region the regional QNH value (updated hourly) is available from ATC and advised routinely to pilots whenever they contact ATC for instructions. This ensures that all pilots in that area are operating with the same pressure information, so making it possible for them to rely on their altimeters when judging safe terrain clearance and vertical separation from other aircraft.

Flight Levels

Aircraft cruising well above the terrain and crossing many regions and countries would constantly have to change altimeter settings to each regional QNH value. Since at cruising levels accurate separation from other aircraft is the prime consideration, it is safer and easier for all aircraft to use a standardised pressure setting. The International Standard Atmosphere (ISA) sea-level pressure setting of 1013.2mb is used. (On any given day this could be above or below the actual pressure at sea-level.) The vertical position measured on an altimeter set to this datum is referred to as a **Flight Level**. FL95 thus means 9,500ft above the level at which the pressure is 1013.2mb. Below the Transition Altitude, aircraft pilots alter their altimeters to give an altitude reading (QNH) rather than a Flight Level reading. Except around airports, where it may be increased, the Transition Altitude in the UK is 3,000ft.

Hang gliders and paragliders

If just flying locally (e.g. ridge-soaring) where there are no airspace restrictions, most pilots will use QFE, zeroing their altimeters at take-off or at the intended landing-point.

If you are planning to fly cross-country, you will need to set your altimeter to QNH. One way to do this is to accurately determine your altitude from an OS map before launch and adjust the altimeter to that indication. This (local QNH) setting will enable you to avoid controlled airspace where the lower levels are defined by altitudes. When the lower levels of controlled airspace are defined by Flight Levels, your altimeter will need to be set to 1013.2mb to determine your proximity to the controlled airspace. Most modern altimeters have the ability to be switched to such a setting – it is sometimes (incorrectly) labelled QNE.

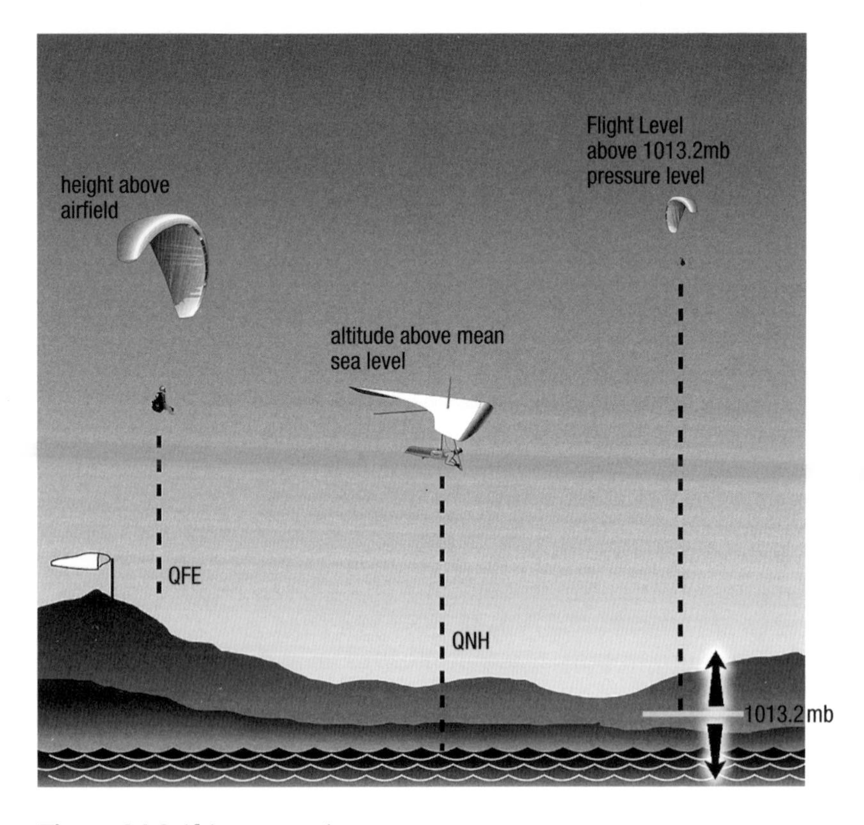

Figure 24.3 *Altimeter settings*

SECTION 7
WEATHER, FORECASTS AND FLYING CONDITIONS

Chapter 25: The weather

What makes it?

Airmasses and their weather

Frontal systems

Low-pressure systems (depressions)

High-pressure systems (anticyclones)

Clouds

Chapter 26: Getting and using a forecast

Getting a forecast

Using the forecast

Chapter 27: Flying conditions

Measuring wind strength and direction on a hill

Turbulence

Wind gradient

Anabatic and katabatic flow

Sea breezes and sea-breeze fronts

Chapter 25: The weather

What makes it?

The energy that drives our weather originates 150 million kilometres (93 million miles) away in the Sun. Incoming solar radiation warms the Earth's surface, which in turn heats the air and sets up air currents.

The portion of the Earth's surface most perpendicular to the Sun's rays receives the most intense incoming solar radiation. This means that equatorial regions receive more heat than the poles. The air warmed at the equatorial regions tends to rise and flow towards the poles, while cold air from the poles slides along the surface to replace it. But the Earth is covered with large areas – such as oceans and deserts – that warm up and cool down at different rates, and these set up other airflows that complicate that basic model. And all the time the Earth is rotating and dragging the atmosphere around after it, which further confuses matters. But basically it all starts with the Sun!

The phenomena we call weather – pressure systems, wind, precipitation, cloud etc. – all occur in the very thin lower layer of the Earth's atmosphere, called the **troposphere**. This layer is about 17km (55,000ft) thick at the equator, about 9km (30,000ft) deep at the poles. Within this layer, temperature generally decreases with height.

Airmasses and their weather

The weather associated with a body of air or 'airmass' is largely determined by the characteristics of the area where the airmass originated, and by the surfaces it travelled over on its way to us. For example, an airmass that originated in the tropics and arrived at the UK via the Atlantic is likely to be warm and moist, while one that originated in the Arctic and arrived via northern Europe is likely to be cold and dry. The following list outlines the various airmasses that affect the UK and gives an idea of the flying possibilities associated with them; they are shown in Figure 25.1.

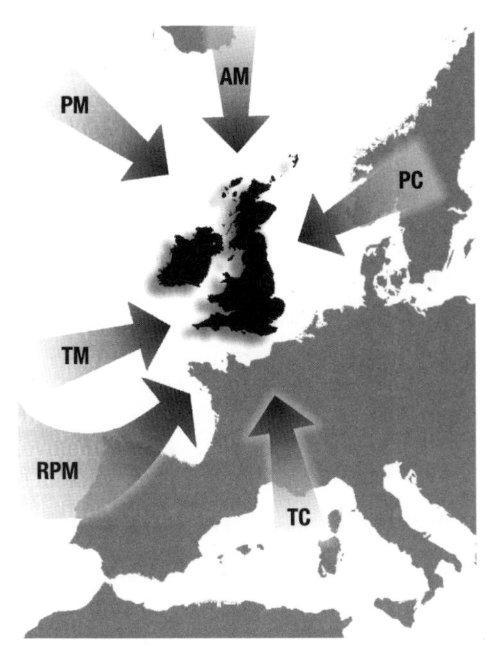

Figure 25.1 *Airmasses that affect the UK*

Tropical maritime (TM)

Winter flying is relatively warm, but you must dodge possible low cloud and rain. In the lee of the mountains of west Wales and the Pennines, conditions can be generally good and ideal for novices. Summer flying can be variable; again, the best conditions are likely to be in the lee of western hills.

Tropical continental (TC)

This airmass generally only reaches the UK in summertime. When the airmass first arrives, conditions can be very thermic with high cloudbases. As pressure builds, inversions are quick to form, reducing visibility and limiting the height that thermals can reach. Established TC air can be very rough in the afternoon.

Polar continental (PC)

As PC is a predominantly winter airmass, flying conditions are very cold indeed. This airmass can give pleasant sunny ridge-soaring or wave-flying in the west, and in the east coastal flying with sea thermals is possible if you can avoid the snow.

Polar maritime (PM)

This common airmass (second only to TM) can provide good thermal flying. Depending on the time of year and the moisture content, cloudbase is often between 1,200 and 1,500 metres (4,000-5,000ft) – a little lower on the hills. Thermals can be very strong, producing a lot of turbulence; not as rough as TC air, however.

Returning polar maritime (RPM)

The RPM airmass produces damp, overcast weather, with a possibility of complete stratus cover – generally poor flying conditions.

Arctic maritime (AM)

If you are a keen, skilled cross-country pilot, then book a day off. Spend the evening preparing your gear and studying the air maps. Arrive on site early, double-check your gear, and then wait for the cumulus to start popping! (Less experienced pilots may find these conditions rather too lively!)

This is the classic cross-country airmass, most common in spring. The air is cold, clear and unstable, giving rise to fair-weather cumulus, booming thermals and a high cloudbase. There is little chance of over-development, as the air is relatively dry. This airmass can bring heavy wintry showers to north- and east-facing coasts of Scotland and northeast England, but these don't penetrate far inland, leaving the air fresh, clear and dry.

Frontal systems

When two dissimilar air masses meet, they tend to collide rather than mix, with one air mass (the warmer, less dense air) being forced upwards by the other. These collisions are the cause of most of our clouds, rain and variations in wind direction, although the intensity of the resulting weather depends on the amount of dissimilarity between the colliding airmasses. Sometimes very severe weather can result, while at other times some cloud and light rain is all that occurs.

The meteorologists term these 'collision zones' fronts. Fronts come in three main forms: cold, warm and occluded. The weather patterns associated with each type are quite different.

Warm fronts

This is the name given to a front where a warm air mass is advancing into a region of cooler air. The warm air tends to slide over the top of the cooler air for several hundred miles. (The slope of the transition between warm and cold air is between 1:50 and 1:400.) As the front approaches, thin high cloud and a solar halo are often seen. Gradually the cloud lowers and thickens until the rain belt arrives, perhaps 150-300 km (100-200 miles) ahead of the front. The rain is usually persistent drizzle that lasts for some hours. Warm fronts tend to move quite slowly – in general their speed does not exceed about 24kph (15mph).

Behind the front the rain lightens or ceases, but it remains cloudy. Generally it is noticeably warmer and more settled, and the winds will veer (change direction clockwise), usually by around 60 degrees.

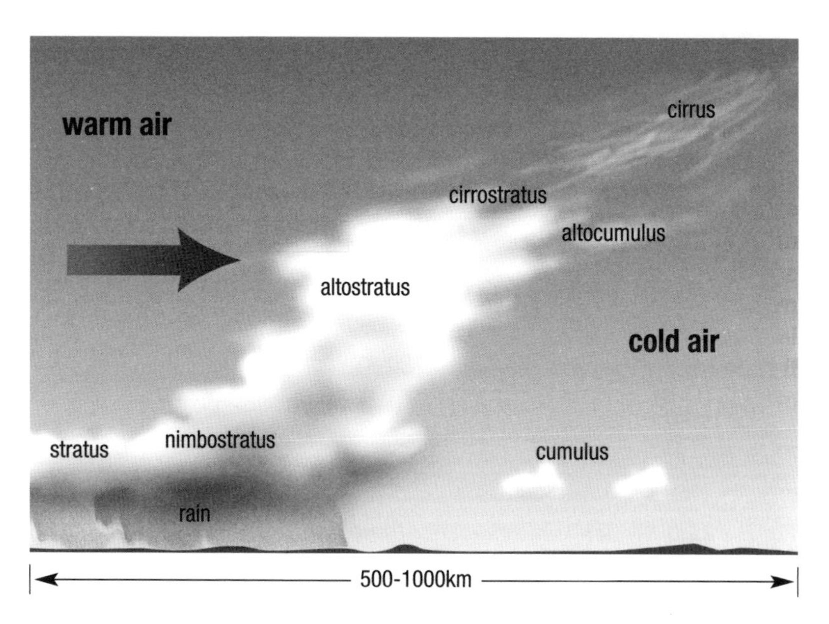

Figure 25.2 *Section through a warm front*

Cold fronts

When a mass of cold air encroaches on a body of warm air, a cold front occurs. The cold air tries to push under the warm air, acting as a wedge. The slope of this wedge is quite steep, about 1:30 to 1:100.

Cold fronts are quite complicated, depending not only on the temperature differences but also on the relative stabilities of the air masses. They can consequently range from very active, inducing severe weather, to quite gentle, producing hardly any rainfall, although a narrow band of heavy rain is quite usual. The cloud and rain is caused by the uplift of the warm air. Cold fronts move quite quickly, at up to 32kph (20mph), and strong updraughts may be encountered 150km or more (100 miles) ahead of a front.

As the front passes it will become noticeably colder and the wind will veer, typically by around 90 degrees. After the passage of a cold front, it is usually cooler, brighter and showery, and the air is often turbulent. These conditions are generally very good for cross-country thermal flying.

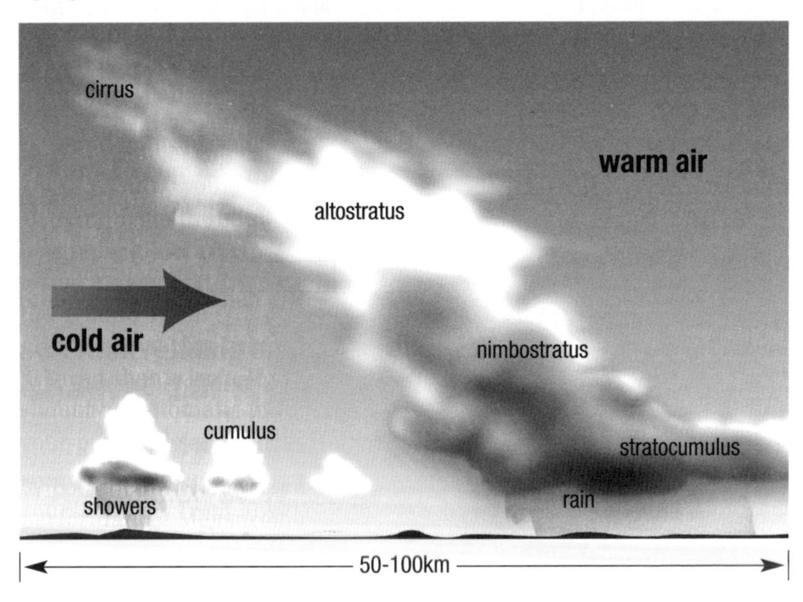

Figure 25.3 *Section through a cold front*

Occlusions

Because cold fronts move faster than warm fronts, they eventually catch them up and form an occluded front or occlusion. The occlusion can have some of the characteristics of a warm front or a cold front, but generally on a much milder scale.

Occlusions are generally slow-moving, and represent the final stages in the decay of a frontal system. The weather produced by an occlusion can range from that of the two frontal types to prolonged periods of rain.

Low-pressure systems (depressions)

Weather – that is, mainly wind and rain – comes **with low-pressure systems**. In an area of low pressure the air is generally rising: as it rises it cools, hence the cloud and rain. Because of this upward flow, at the surface air is drawn in towards the centre of the low, but owing to the effects of the Earth's rotation, it takes a spiral path. At high levels the air flows out from the low – towards high pressure where it sinks back down. This outward flow at high levels in the low-pressure area is greater than the low level inward flow: this prevents the low from quickly filling.

In Figure 25.4 you can see a stage in the development of a typical low. A mass of cold dense air from the Arctic has converged with a warm, moist tropical airmass. At the transition zone between the two air masses – the polar front – a small wave (or kink) forms: at one side the warm air is flowing up over the cold air (a warm front), while at the other the cold air is swinging around and undercutting the warm air (a cold front). The kink progresses into a deep inverted 'V' shape, and the whole system then starts to spin up (anti-clockwise in the northern hemisphere), as the cold front swings around and closes on the warm front. This continues to force the warm air higher, resulting in more cloud and rain, and further reduces the pressure at the surface, resulting in more wind. This huge vortex then typically moves north-eastwards in the prevailing flow around the northern hemisphere, to bring cloud, wind and rain to the UK!

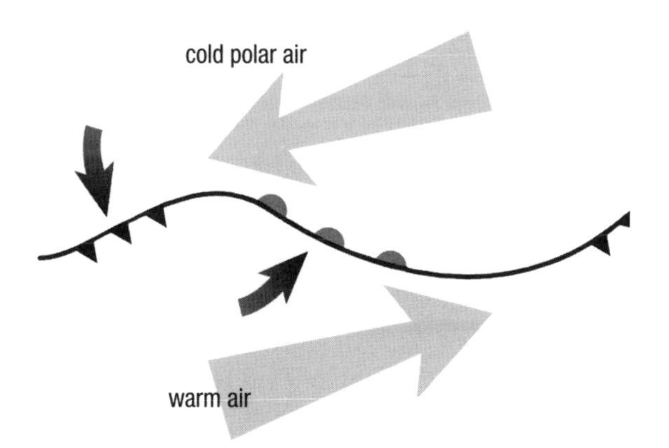

Figure 25.4 *Early stages of a forming depression*

High-pressure systems (anticyclones)

A high-pressure system is a huge area of slowly descending air. This area could be as big as the whole of Europe.

High-pressure systems reduce the possibility of upward movement of air, bringing settled weather and light winds. It is not unusual for inversions to occur (an inversion exists when the air temperature increases with height). If there is a large area subject to an inversion in summer, the atmosphere becomes hazy, because dust, pollen, smoke and other pollutants cannot escape upwards to be dispersed.

In winter, high-pressure systems bring cold, clear frosty nights as the ground radiates heat straight out into space because of the lack of cloud cover. During the day it is often clear and crisp with brilliant blue skies (although fog becomes a danger if the high persists for more than a day or two).

In the depths of winter and the height of summer a 'blocking high' may form over Europe which prevents the low-pressure systems coming across the Atlantic from reaching the UK. Then the weather gets 'stuck', and we may experience either long periods of hot, sunny weather in summer or extremely low temperatures in winter.

Clouds

The amount of moisture that the air can carry as water vapour depends on its temperature. If warm air containing some moisture is cooled below its dew point, the moisture will condense into small droplets and form a cloud. If the process is allowed to continue and the correct conditions prevail, the cloud droplets will amalgamate until they are too large to remain in suspension in the cloud – and they will then fall as rain.

One of the simplest ways to cool air below its dew point is to force it upwards. A stream of air flowing over flat ground will be forced upwards if it encounters a hill. If the hill is large enough, the moisture in the airstream will condense, and so-called **'orographic'** cloud will form on the hilltop. Orographic rain can result.

A bubble of air rising after being heated by 'hot spots' on the ground may cool sufficiently to pass its dew point and form **convection** clouds. These clouds have a distinct puffy form with flat bases, often described as looking like a heap of cotton wool, and are consequently called by the Latin for heap: **cumulus**. These clouds mark the tops of thermals, and indicate good, if somewhat bumpy, flying conditions.

Sometimes the atmosphere is sufficiently unstable for large heap clouds with towering dark tops to develop. These are called **cumulonimbus** clouds (*nimbus* is the Latin for rain-cloud). These clouds are colloquially referred to as 'cu-nimbs'. If large enough, they produce thunderstorms. They also indicate dangerously strong lift and severe turbulence.

General lifting of masses of air can cause widespread areas of cloud. Layer, or **stratus**, cloud is a boringly familiar sight to all of us in Britain. If it is well developed, the thickness of the layer makes the cloud appear darker, and rain is likely. In this state the cloud is called **nimbostratus**.

At very high levels, the water droplets freeze and form rather prettier clouds. The thin, wispy 'mare's tail' or **cirrus** clouds often seen high in a clear blue sky are an example of this type (*cirrus* means 'curl of hair' in Latin). These clouds are formed at altitudes of 5-13 km (3-8 miles) in our latitudes. Their distinctive hooked shape is due to the strong winds at these high altitudes. Ice particles that fall to lower levels are left behind and form the hook. As they fall to still lower levels they evaporate away.

Chapter 26: Getting and using a forecast

Getting a forecast

Pilots use forecasts to help them decide whether or not to make the journey to the flying site. But never forget that a forecast can be wrong. Look out of your window, and check to see which way the clouds are moving and how fast they are moving. If there's half a chance that it will be flyable, go and have a look. The only certainty is that you will never fly sitting at home!

Obtaining a weather forecast is relatively simple, though there are a variety of sources, depending on the technology you have at your disposal.

Television and radio

Perhaps the easiest and most obvious forecasts to find are the television forecasts that follow the news. These forecasts tend to vary in quality, though they all originate from the Met. Office in Bracknell. Probably the best are the BBC forecasts following the evening and late evening news.

The radio can also be a good source of weather forecasts. The BBC Radio 4 weather forecasts are among the most comprehensive, although there are also some good forecasts from local radio stations. Some, such as Swansea Sound, also include gliding and sailing forecasts.

Newspapers

Most of the better-quality newspapers have good forecasts that also include a basic pressure map. The pressure maps are useful, as they let you follow the weather over a period of time, enabling you to practise your own forecasting. But remember that these maps will have been prepared some time in the evening of the day before you see them, so they are not up-to-the-minute.

MetFax

If you have a fax machine, then MetFax (from the Met. Office) provides a variety of aviation weather-forecast services. This information is updated regularly, and is as accurate as you can get. The downside is the cost, currently 75p per minute.

Information on all the MetFax services available can be obtained from the Met. Office customer centre on 0870 900 0100 fax 0870 900 5050

Internet

The Internet is another good source of weather forecasts, if you know where to look. There is a vast amount of weather information on the Web, though much of it is of negligible value to the glider pilot. The BHPA Web site (www.bhpa.co.uk) has some good weather links, as do some of the paragliding and hang-gliding school sites. Also, check out the following sites – but be aware that, as with everything on the Internet, the situation changes rapidly:

Basic forecasts

www.metoffice.gov.uk/weather/uk/uk_forecast_weather.html

www.bbc.co.uk/weather/ukweather/

www.onlineweather.com

www.wunderground.com/global/UK.html

More in-depth forecasts

www.itadvice.co.uk/weatherjack/STARS.htm

www.itadvice.co.uk/weatherjack/wx.htm

www.xcweather.co.uk/

www.metcheck.com/V40/UK/FREE/synoptic.asp

The Met. Office web site (www.met-office.gov.uk) contains all the information provided by MetFax and more. The only problem is that you have to pay a subscription fee. There is a handy booklet that you can download from the site:
www.metoffice.gov.uk/aviation/services/getmet.pdf

Wendy Windblows

A very popular option is the 'Wendy Windblows' system. This is a network of computerised weather stations, set up by a long-time hang-glider pilot, that gives detailed and frequently updated reports on the actual weather (wind strength and direction, changes, cloud cover etc.) at an increasing number of flying sites around the UK. The system may be accessed either by telephone or via the Internet, but it is a subscription service and you must pay the annual fee (currently £46) for a personal code.

Alternatively, you can access the information without paying a subscription on a series of telephone numbers that cost 50p per call.

For more information contact Rod Buck on 0800 358 0405 or at www.wendywindblows.com.

Using the forecast

Having obtained your forecast, the next step is using the information to your advantage. This is obviously straightforward if you have got your forecast from a television forecast, though not so obvious if you have a surface-pressure chart from the Internet or from MetFax.

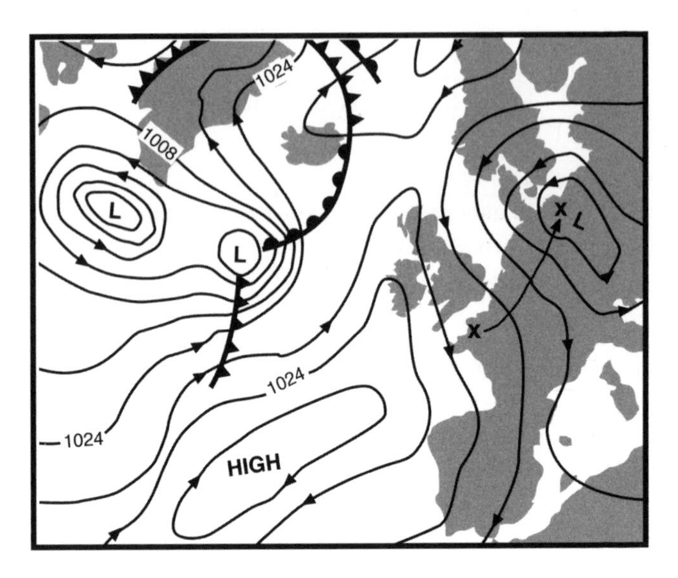

Figure 26.1 *A typical surface-pressure chart*

User's guide to surface-pressure charts

The surface-pressure charts (often colloquially referred to as 'synoptic charts') commonly available in the UK are produced in the Central Forecasting Office of the Met. Office in Bracknell. These charts show more detail than usually seen in newspapers or on television forecasts, and are intended to aid the forecaster to follow the development of pressure systems and fronts.

The charts fall into two categories:

- the **analysis chart,** indicated by the letters ASXX, which shows the current surface pressures (at the time of issue)
- the **forecast charts,** indicated by the letters FSXX, which show what is expected. They are available for 24, 48, 72 or 96 hours ahead.

The main features shown on a surface-pressure chart are as follows:

Isobars

These are lines joining areas of equal mean sea-level atmospheric pressure. The units used for pressure are millibars (mb), and the isobars are usually drawn at 4mb intervals. The pressure values may only be marked every 16mb and are often shortened to the last two digits of the number.

Areas of low and high pressure (depressions and anticyclones)

The isobars tend to form definite patterns, two of which are the most important. When the isobars form a series of closely spaced, more or less concentric, roughly circular patterns (rather like the contours of a hill on an OS map), with pressure reducing towards the centre, then this indicates a **depression** or **low**. These are denoted by an **L**. An **X** indicates the point of the lowest pressure. The track of a low over the preceding 24 hours (solid line) or less (dashed line) is sometimes shown, and the earlier lowest-pressure position is shown by a smaller **x**, alongside which is the date, time and pressure. This enables the forecaster to follow the evolution of a system.

When the isobars form a similar but more widely spaced pattern, and with the pressure increasing towards the centre, this indicates an **anticyclone** or **high**. These are marked with an **H**. An **X** marks the point of highest pressure, and an arrow indicates movement of the high since the date, time and pressure shown by the small **x**.

The major highs, lows and fronts are given another identifying letter to enable the forecaster to follow changes in pressure systems from one chart to the next. Sometimes arrowheads are provided on the isobars to indicate the direction of the wind flow. Winds in the lower layers of the atmosphere – at around 600m (2,000ft) – blow roughly parallel to the isobars: **clockwise around highs** and **anticlockwise around lows**. Surface winds tend to blow slightly across the isobars: in towards low pressure and out from high pressure. The closer the isobars, the stronger the wind.

Fronts

- **Warm fronts** These are represented by a line with semi-circles spaced along it, the semi-circles facing the direction the front is moving in. The line is drawn at approximately the point where the front meets the ground, so the main rain-band extends in front of that position, and the cloud is even further in front.

- **Cold fronts** These are represented by a line with triangles spaced along it. Again the triangles face the direction the front is moving, and again the line is drawn at approximately the point where the front meets the ground. The rain-band (usually quite narrow) will be along or just behind the line.
- **Occluded fronts** A line with alternate semicircles and triangles is used to signify these.

Other symbols

There are a number of other symbols that may sometimes appear on a surface-pressure chart. Among these are:

- Trough lines are seen both on the analysis and on the forecast charts. These are shown as a black line like a front but without triangles or semi-circles. Trough lines indicate regions where air is ascending, sometimes giving rain along the line.
- Hurricanes and tropical storms may occasionally be seen at lower latitudes. These are marked by a § symbol and usually show the name allocated to them.

Chapter 27: Flying conditions

Measuring wind strength and direction on a hill

It is vital that you accurately check the wind strength and direction before flying. On a paraglider the difference between nice ridge-soaring conditions and being blown backward over the hilltop can be of the order of 8kph (5mph). Inspired guessing can be easily confounded, especially by temperature: the wind always seems stronger when it's cold.

To aid you in making a reliable assessment, you can buy a hand-held wind-strength meter. These are reasonably accurate, and as you become familiar with a certain meter you will soon begin to relate its readings to the actual flying conditions experienced, and so will very quickly be able to use it to help you judge whether the wind conditions are within your limits.

The problem with wind-strength meters is that they can only measure the wind close to the hill. They are therefore very susceptible to localised effects. It is worth thinking through the possible airflow pattern around your site, and measuring the wind strength at other points along the ridge if there is any doubt.

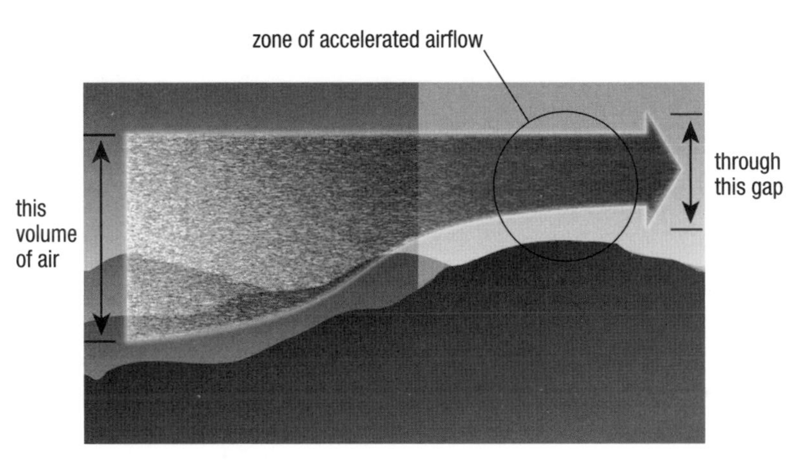

Figure 27.1 *Zone of accelerated airflow*

Figure 27.1 shows the zone of accelerated airflow – often erroneously called the compression zone – over the top of a hill. (The air pressure will actually be **reduced** in this region, just as it is over the upper surface of a wing in flight.)

There is a similar problem with establishing the true wind direction on certain sites, especially if they are bowl-shaped. A strategically placed windsock that inflates at a known velocity is a useful tool, but it is worth remembering that the windsock will only demonstrate what is happening in its immediate vicinity. Figure 27.2 shows a typical situation where a pilot observing only one windsock could become confused if he or she had not taken into account the shape of the site.

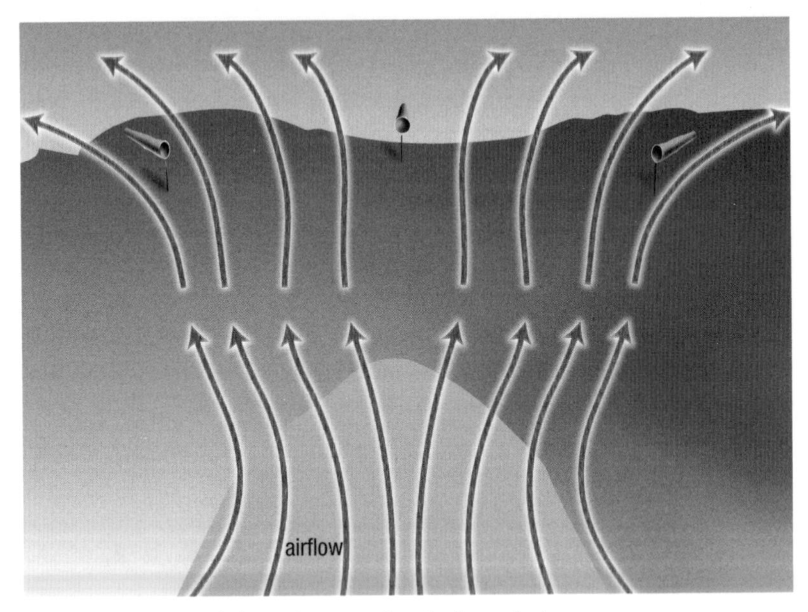

Figure 27.2 *Wind direction at a bowl-shaped site*

Besides the wind strength you must check for gustiness, and you should monitor the general weather.

Turbulence

Turbulence is a swirling motion imparted to the air by some external disturbing force – and it can have very unwelcome effects upon low-mass aircraft such as hang gliders and paragliders.

When air flows around a smooth streamlined shape it will follow the shape. Sharp edges and sudden changes in shape will tend to produce turbulence.

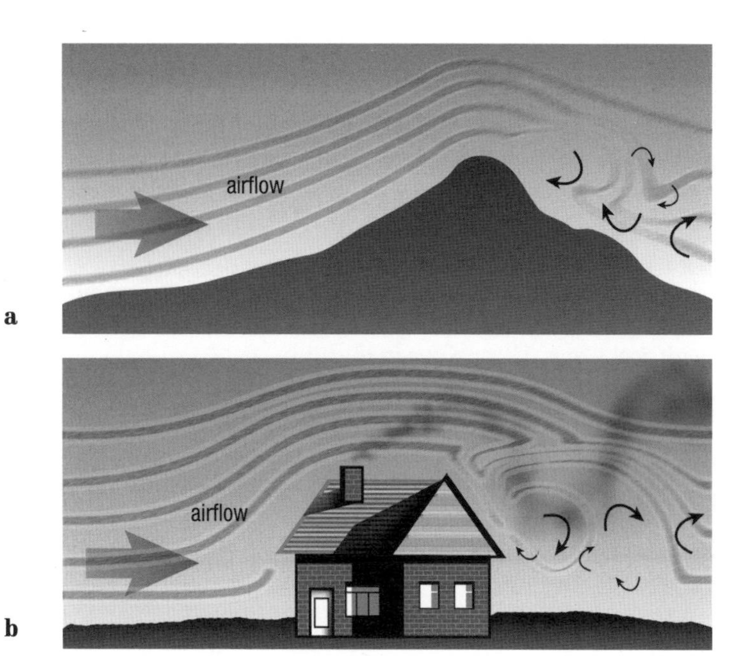

Figure 27.3 *Sources of turbulence*

In Figure 27.3 (b) you can see air encountering a very unstreamlined building. Eddies are produced, because the shape is too angular for the air to flow smoothly around it. Standing eddies can form: they do not change position, and because they spin around on the spot they are often referred to as rotors. When soaring near sharp-edged cliffs or spine-backed ridges, you should be very careful not to drift back. You should also avoid flying in the lee of trees and buildings.

Turbulence will also be found around thermals and other forms of wind shear, such as in a wind gradient.

Wind gradient

Air flowing across the ground is slowed down by contact with the surface and with crops, hedges, trees, buildings and so on. Because air is slightly 'sticky' (viscous), the layer of air just above the slowed layer is also slowed to a lesser extent. This effect carries on until eventually the true wind speed is found at some distance from the ground. On tow fields, pilots often find that the very gentle surface breeze is a strong blow at 300m (1,000ft). This situation is most common on relatively stable days when thermal currents are not vertically mixing the atmosphere.

You must guard against wind gradient when landing on a windy day, as the glider may suddenly lose airspeed as it descends into slower-moving air. Similarly, when soaring close to a ridge it is possible for the general airflow to tend to roll the glider towards the hill. In both cases you should fly with extra airspeed.

Anabatic and katabatic flow

As we have seen, air is heated by contact with the ground. In hilly and mountainous areas the sun warms the faces of the slopes, especially those with rocky tops. This results in the air in contact with these slopes being warmed, and starting to rise, flowing up the face of the slope. This is called **anabatic flow**. This effect is most apparent in quiet situations in hot weather, such as summer anticyclones, and is strongest in the early afternoon on rocky scree slopes directly facing the sun. While not strong enough on their own to provide ridge-soaring conditions, anabatic flow often encourages and entrains thermals. In valleys, both sides can experience anabatic flow, while in the middle of the valley the unheated air (now colder and heavier than the air nearer the slopes) sinks down. (A tip for flying in hilly or mountainous areas is to remember that 'valleys suck'!)

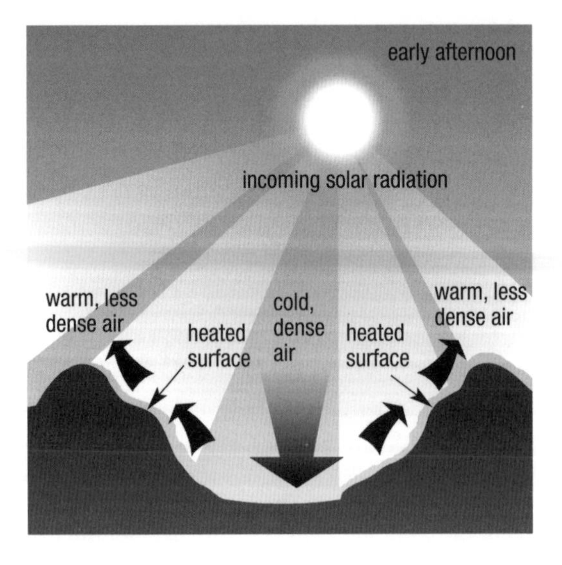

Figure 27.4 *Anabatic flow*

Towards the evening a reverse effect is common. The hill slopes radiate the heat away quite rapidly, and the air in contact with the slopes cools rapidly too. It becomes denser, and starts to flow down the slope. This is known as a **katabatic flow**. In valleys, this influx of cold dense air undercuts the warmer air in the valley bottom, forcing it to rise in the centre of the valley. This can provide wonderful smooth early-evening flying conditions – pilots refer to this phenomenon as 'magic lift', 'restitution lift' or the evening 'glass off'.

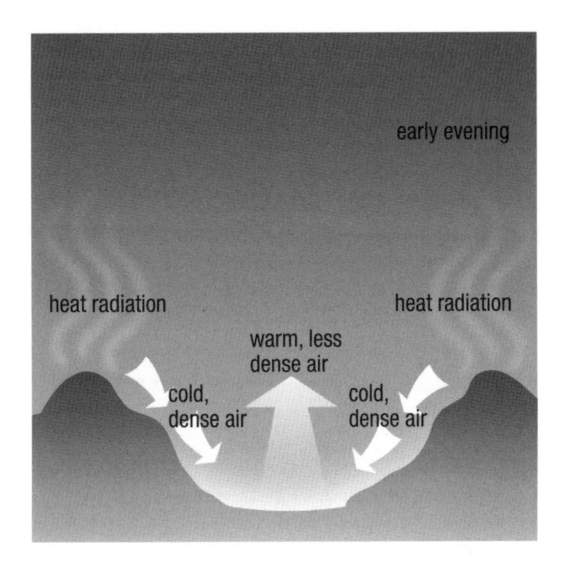

Figure 27.5 *Katabatic flow*

Valley winds

In mountainous areas, the anabatic (or katabatic) flows mentioned above can result in vast quantities of air being in motion. This can lead to strong winds blowing in the interlinking valleys, especially where the valleys are narrow and the flow is accelerated by the venturi effect. These valley winds are usually strongest just a few hundred feet above the valley floor.

If you land in the valley bottom in mid-afternoon, when the anabatic flow (and hence the valley winds) are at their strongest, you can easily be caught out as you descend from nil-wind buoyant conditions higher up into winds as strong as 32kph (20mph) in the valley bottom.

Sea breezes and sea-breeze fronts

On sunny summer days, the air over the land is heated and tends to rise, with thermals playing a major role. This leads to reduced air pressure near the surface. The sea warms much more slowly, so the air over the sea surface remains cold and heavy. On light-wind days this sea air is drawn into the low-pressure zone, creating an onshore flow known as a sea breeze. Usually this flow is strongest in the early afternoon, when the convection over the land is at its maximum.

Quite often the sea air pushing inland forms a mini cold front, wedging in underneath the warm air and forcing it to rise. This is called a sea-breeze front. It can usually be recognised as a broken line of especially vigorous cumulus clouds lying parallel to the coast, with no (or very little) cumulus on the seaward side. You will often see ragged 'curtain' clouds apparently hanging underneath these cumulus clouds.

Such a sea-breeze front progresses inland as the day goes on, and – depending on the terrain – can regularly push inland 15km (10 miles) or so, and sometimes as far as 50 or 60km (30 to 40 miles) before collapsing towards evening. (Sea-breeze fronts tend not to climb over hills, but make good progress across plains and up valleys.)

The most active sea-breeze fronts occur when the prevailing weather systems are causing a light offshore wind. The collision of this flow with the sea-breeze flow causes a convergence-line effect. On less active days, the sea-breeze front may simply be marked by an obvious change in visibility.

Sea breezes pose a hazard to unwary pilots finishing cross-country flights near the coast. Very often the surface wind at the coast in the afternoon of a thermic day will be light onshore, irrespective of the fact that most of the flight will have been conducted in wind from some other direction.

Sea breezes can also spoil soaring conditions at sites a few miles from the coast. A good morning's ridge-soaring can suddenly end as the cold sea air arrives and the wind swings off the hill.

On the positive side, sea-breeze fronts can present wonderful thermal soaring opportunities. The trick is to fly along the line of the front, climbing in the stronger cores. Do not fly through the front into the sea air, as it will be lifeless and you will have a head wind if you try to fly on towards the coast. If you inadvertently drop into this air, you need to fly back inland to regain the front edge of the front – which can be difficult, as you will be in sinking air and your glide ratio may only be a bit shallower than the slope of the front!

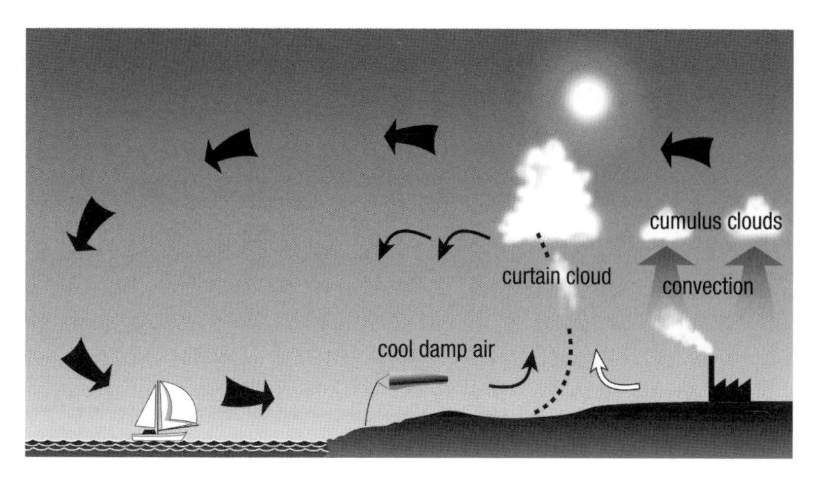

Figure 27.6 *Sea breeze effect*

SECTION 8
WHERE TO NOW?

Chapter 28: Flying abroad

For many pilots, the lure of 'guaranteed' good weather provides a powerful incentive to head off abroad in search of some airtime. For most this will mean journeying to the mountains of mainland Europe. Here many sites offer top-to-bottoms of at least 1,000m (3,300ft), cable cars that whisk you back up to the take-off area (or tarmac roads to the top), good weather, well-organised launch and landing-sites, easy thermalling, spectacular scenery and good cross-country flying potential. Sounds like paradise – and it can be, but make sure that for you it doesn't become a fool's paradise!

On a good summer's afternoon in the mountains you can find conditions that have got the better of some of the best pilots in the world. Incredibly strong thermals and even stronger sink, violent wind-shears, howling valley winds in the valley floor, tricky nil-wind take-offs, small landing fields with no leeway for overshooting or undershooting… it's all waiting to trip up the unwary pilot who doesn't understand the mountain environment. And it is certain that a few hours (or tens of hours) ridge-soaring in the UK do not give you the knowledge you need to understand the mountain environment.

So how should you go about it? The key point is to make sure that for your first time in the mountains you are guided by an instructor or coach who really is familiar with the area you are heading for, knows the local rules and regulations, and is in tune with the needs of a low-airtime pilot new to the mountains. Many trips are organised by British schools and clubs to various parts of mainland Europe, and there are even a few British run establishments based there. Check their credentials, and then sign on with one of these. In no time you'll be flying high and safely, with a good understanding of new and different conditions.

Listed below are some further essential points about the mountain-flying environment; you should understand them fully before venturing forth.

Weather

The most turbulent conditions are usually found between midday and 3pm, when the sun is kicking off powerful thermals. Calmer conditions during the early morning and the late afternoon and evening will provide excellent flying for the less experienced mountain pilot.

Mountains and winds

Sun-baked, steep-sided valleys will often send off strong thermals. As the thermals rise, replacement air is drawn in from lower land. This can set up valley winds so strong that they are not safe to land in, especially in areas with narrow and deep valleys. Do not fly into deep, narrow valleys in the afternoon on a hot summer's day! (In areas with wide valleys, the valley winds are usually much lighter in strength and rarely create the same problems.)

Wind in the mountains is dangerous. The sort of wind strengths regularly used for ridge-soaring in the UK would be incredibly dangerous in a mountain-flying area, where every mountain is in the lee of another one. Any substantial prevailing wind can create very serious rotor conditions which are not always detectable by the untrained eye.

Most often the wind felt at take-off in the mountains is the anabatic flow – air being drawn up the face of the mountain directly into the clouds sitting on the top. Think about it: a vertical flow of 24-32kph (15-20mph) is something like 9m/s (1800ft/min) lift at take-off, with all the turbulence to be expected from such a flow that has rolled its way up the mountain face. And then think about the valley winds below – for all that air going up is being replaced by air drawn in from somewhere, accelerating down narrow valleys.

Cumulonimbus dangers

Keep a very careful eye on conditions, both before and during your flight. The growth of a big cumulus into a cumulonimbus is difficult to spot from underneath. Cumulonimbus clouds develop suddenly, and often creep up from behind (from the other side of the mountain). If mountains – or your failure to monitor the conditions – prevent you from seeing what's around, the first indication of danger may be a large smooth area of lift – sometimes quite strong. If you are slow in making your escape, you will probably be sucked up into the cloud, with the odds heavily stacked against your survival.

The dangers most usually associated with cumulonimbus flying – severe icing of the glider, hypothermia for the pilot, and turbulence – may turn out to be insignificant compared with the (usually final) shock of finding that the cloud is full of rock. Cumulonimbus clouds usually lower their bases while maturing, and mountains can become clagged-in when earlier they were clear!

Even if you do recognise the danger, and manage to escape the lift without being sucked into the cloud, you still have the problem of the gust front. Cumulonimbus clouds usually have associated gust fronts, which can be many miles ahead of the cloud. In an instant the gentle wind in your landing-field can be turned into a gale, with very little hope of your making a safe landing.

The message is, if you see the clouds brewing up as though they could turn nasty**, land immediately.**

Flying skills

Before you go, make sure that you are proficient at nil-wind (alpine) launches and at setting up sensible landing approaches so that you land exactly where you intend. If not, make sure that your instructor takes you somewhere benign where you can put some effort into brushing up these skills.

Check the landing-areas and the launch-site. Talk to the pilots from the local school or local club, and learn as much as you can about local conditions and dangers. Listen to the locals – if they are not flying, find out why!

Be certain that you understand where the tricky areas might be, depending on the time of day and the weather conditions on the day.

As with all flying, always stay within easy reach of a safe landing-area. All your height can soon disappear if you are fighting a valley wind that you didn't allow for.

Collision avoidance

In many countries there is little emphasis placed on teaching the Rules of the Air to new pilots, so very few pilots know them or stick to them. There are also subtle differences from country to country, concerning conventions such as which side to overtake on if ridge-soaring. Bearing this in mind, you should fly particularly defensively, and never rely on the other pilot doing the right thing. Bear in mind the first rule of collision avoidance, which is that it is your responsibility as a pilot to take any action necessary to avoid a collision. Try to fly according to the Rules, but fall back on Rule Number One very quickly if a conflict of flight paths seems to be developing.

Things do sometimes go wrong. Make sure that you have medical repatriation insurance that covers your flying risks. The bill for a helicopter rescue from an alpine mountainside is guaranteed to bring tears to your eyes.

Take your IPPI card with you (see panel). In some countries these are now mandatory.

Don't let this chapter scare you off the big stuff: the intention is to make prospective mountain-pilots think about where, when, and how to safely enjoy what is undoubtedly some of the best flying in the world. Flying for hours in pure thermic conditions, circling up with the eagles and topping out above snow-capped peaks in the clear blue is a marvellous, indescribable feeling. Once you have experienced mountain-flying in these incredible environments, ridge-soaring will never be the same again!

The IPPI Card

The International Pilot Proficiency Identification card is a neat, internationally recognised means of certifying your pilot proficiency, and so helping to prove your competence when visiting foreign sites. It uses an internationally agreed common pilot-rating format: the **Safe Pro** system (for hang-glider pilots) and the **Para Pro** system (for paraglider pilots). An IPPI card can be purchased from the BHPA Office: this will be issued with the 'pro' level that matches your pilot rating under the BHPA scheme.

Chapter 29: Competitions and cross-country tables

Many pilots find that their abilities improve most when their flying has a goal. The tasks in the pilot-rating scheme provide a series of goals to help new pilots develop their flying skills, but it is usually not long before they are adding their own goals to the list. Usually these start with 'I'm going to stay up for thirty minutes' or 'I'm going to fly right to the wood at the end of the ridge', or 'I'm going to land right on the target'. Before long these develop into 'I'm going to get higher than Fred', and then 'I am going to try to get to the top of the stack'.

Competitions are a natural extension of this process, and taking part in some level of competition is usually a guaranteed method of improving your abilities. Once you are thoroughly conversant with handling your glider in a variety of weather conditions, and confident (and practised) at landing out in strange fields, find out when your next club competition is being held, and put in your entry! Competing is an exciting way to learn more about flying, meet other pilots, fly new sites – and have some fun!

All hang-gliding and paragliding competitions are open to both male and female pilots. Many women pilots are active in British competition flying and compete on equal terms with male pilots – it's one of the very few sports where this is the case.

Competitive flying in the UK takes two principal forms: the cross-country tables, and pre-arranged competition events.

Cross-country tables

The cross-country tables (one for paragliders, another for hang gliders) are for pilots to send in details of their cross-country flights to a co-ordinator, who publishes a running total in *Skywings*. At the end of the year the pilot with the highest total distance from his or her best five flights is declared the winner. These tables are also used to select pilots to join the British Paragliding Championship and the equivalent British Hang Gliding Championship. These are both series of higher-level competition events that (over the course of the year) decide who is to be the British Paragliding Champion and the British Hang Gliding Champion. They are also used to select teams to represent Britain in international competitions.

Competitions

In competition events, the pilots who have entered meet in an area for a number of days and fly set tasks (usually one per day) against each other, in the same air, from the same site.

Some competitions are club-level events, but they extend through national championships to international and world-level events.

Accuracy competitions

In parascending accuracy competitions, the pilots are tow-launched, and the task is always to fly their canopies down onto the target. A team of judges keenly watches the final seconds and records the pilot's distance from the 10-cm centre of the target. Quite incredible levels of precision are achieved and maintained over several rounds.

Hang-gliding and paragliding competitions

Most clubs will take part in local or inter-club competitions from time to time. Competitions at this level are usually two-day (weekend) events, and are ideal for getting a taste of competition in a friendly environment.

In advanced-level competitions, you will need good thermalling skills, the ability to navigate well, to assess and exploit the weather, and to fly at speed – and a competitive nature. You will also need physical stamina (tasks can last for many hours, and competitions for several days) and mental skills to deal with the pressure. Lastly you will need an eye for detail: if the rules say that your GPS track-log download from the previous day has to be with the scorer by 9am, and yours isn't, then you will not get any points even if you made the best flight. (At inter-club competitions things are not usually taken quite as seriously as this!)

Tasks

The tasks are set to take into account the weather conditions on the day and the skill-level of the participating pilots. The better the conditions, the longer and more technical the task.

A popular task in inter-club competitions is **Open Distance**, where pilots try to fly as far as possible from the take-off site in any direction they choose (normally downwind). Occasionally such tasks are set along an axis (a particular direction) or via a turnpoint for safety or airspace reasons.

In more advanced competitions, the most frequently set task is **a Race**

to Goal. Here the pilots race each other to a designated goal (landing-place), often via several turnpoints. The turnpoints are usually obvious features on the ground such as distinctively shaped buildings, bridges or radio antennae, and the pilots have to clearly overfly these features to allow their GPS to record that they have rounded them correctly. The goal-field will include a marked line that has to be crossed, and the pilots' finish times are noted. (Sometimes the 'race section' is just part of the course, between two of the turnpoints, in which case the timing is entirely taken from each pilot's GPS track-log evidence.)

Task starts

There are various types of start for cross-country speed tasks. These include:

The **simultaneous start from the ground**, where the clock starts running the moment the launch 'window' is opened.

The **simultaneous start in the air (air start)** uses a marker (the 'start gate') which is unfurled at a pre-determined time, and the pilots (already airborne) record this before setting off on the course.

Individual start from the ground Once the launch 'window' is opened, each pilot launches when it suits him or her. If the task is timed, then each pilot's launch time is recorded, although this sort of start is more often used for tasks where there are no points awarded for speed.

Individual start in the air Here the pilot uses his GPS track-log to record passing the start gate in the air, at a time he or she chooses. A similar GPS verification at the end of a race section or at the finish line confirms the pilot's time for the race.

Scoring systems

There are various systems used in advanced competitions, but most give points for position (i.e. pilot ranking in the task), distance, and time taken (for the race sections). Complicated mathematics then usually comes into play to try to make the maximum score awarded reflect the difficulty of the task, and to prevent the odd pilot who gets lucky on one day (when the rest of the field go down) getting an unassailable lead.

Equipment

The first thing you need to start your competition career is an easy handling glider that you are totally confident on. Don't rush out to buy a glider that will have you permanently flying in fear of the thing: a confident pilot on a lesser machine will always outfly a nervous one on a 'hotter ship'.

An emergency parachute is obligatory in most competitions, as is an up-to-date airspace chart. In more advanced competitions a reliable and easy-to-use GPS is necessary for turnpoint verification, and most competitors nowadays regard a GPS as essential, especially for racing to unknown goal-fields.

Competing requires good preparation and organisation. Basic things like a pencil and notepad with which to record briefing information can make all the difference. If you are taking off at the right time and place, unflustered, with all your equipment working properly, and the task fully understood – then at least you are in with a chance. Missed briefings, flat vario batteries, incorrectly-entered turn-point co-ordinates – all will have you beaten before skill in the air even gets a look-in.

Have a go!

Flying with others in the same air, all attempting the same task, provides massive learning opportunities. You will never cease to be amazed by how well pilots can do on days when you wouldn't normally attempt to leave the hill. Usually at the morning briefing the previous day's winner tells how he did it. Listen and learn! But don't get despondent if it isn't you telling your tale every day – there can only be one winner each day, and as long as you enjoyed yourself then you were certainly not a loser. Above all, remember that your priority is to have fun!

One other point: safety. You cannot win competitions from a hospital bed! Know your limits and stick to them. If you are not happy about flying on a particular day (perhaps because of the weather), then don't. And when you are flying, make sure that you maintain a really good lookout – competitions inevitably tend to involve a lot of pilots flying in the same bit of the sky.

Chapter 30: The BHPA Pilot Rating Scheme

The Scheme

The BHPA Pilot Rating Scheme is a structured training programme designed to help you to develop your personal flying skills. It also provides a quick and simple means of indicating your proficiency level to others.

There are three ratings: the Club Pilot, the Pilot and the Advanced Pilot. There is also an award – the Elementary Pilot award – which marks the halfway point in your basic training. Each rating involves completing certain flying tests ('tasks') and passing a multiple-choice exam (detailed later). The tasks are set out in The Student Training Record Booklet and The Pilot Task Book, which you will be supplied with at the appropriate stage in your training.

Elementary Pilot award (EP)

This is awarded by your school during your training to mark the successful completion of the introductory phase, and to indicate your suitability to undertake the further school training required to gain your first rating.

Club Pilot (CP)

This is the 'novice' qualification. It marks the end of your formal basic instruction, and qualifies you to leave the school environment and to fly without formal instruction in BHPA member clubs. But you will still be very much in a learning phase, and so should seek advice and guidance from coaches as you perfect your skills and work towards your Pilot rating.

Pilot (P)

Now you can consider yourself qualified: a 'pilot' in the true sense of the word. You will now possess well-rounded skills and abilities, along with enough experience to know how and when to exercise them! You should hold this rating before embarking on cross-country flights.

Advanced Pilot (AP)

This rating is for the above-average pilot who is a total master of his or her aircraft and is enjoying to the full the challenges the sport can offer.

Changing disciplines and craft

Because of the wide diversity of aircraft types and launch methods used within the BHPA –ranging from tow-launched round canopies to hill launched rigid-wing hang gliders – the ratings are specific to the aircraft category and launch method. For example, your rating might be HG: P(H), which means Hang Glider: Pilot (Hill). As you gain ratings, endorsements and licences (explained below), these will be added on your membership card.You are only qualified to undertake the activities shown on your membership card.

Endorsements and licences

If you wish to add an alternative form of launch to your rating, this is done by completing a short **endorsement** course. A hill-endorsement for tow-trained pilots will typically involve a weekend or so with an instructor in a school environment; a tow-endorsement for hill-trained pilots can be undertaken at a tow school or within a tow club.

Licences qualify you to undertake activities where you are to a greater or lesser extent responsible for the safety of others – e.g. dual licence, instructor licence.

Changing glider type

If you wish to qualify with a different aircraft type (e.g. swap from paragliders to hang gliders) then you will need to start from the beginning again.Your instructor will obviously take your experience into account during your training and you won't have to re-sit your exams.

How to pass your exams!

As mentioned earlier, to gain a particular rating you must pass a theory examination in addition to completing the required flying tasks. Like any other task in the Pilot Rating Scheme, exams require some preparation work. This section indicates the level of understanding required for each exam, and should help you decide which areas to swot up on.

The Elementary Pilot exam

You will take this simple exam at your school.The information required will be readily available from your instructors, school lectures and from *Skywings Training Issue* – this handbook goes into far more detail than is required for the EP exam. The exam is in multiple-choice form; it includes questions on the Rules of the Air that you must answer correctly in order to pass.

The Rules of the Air and collision avoidance

You should know what actions are taken by which pilot, and what priorities prevail, to prevent the danger of collision between two aircraft – when approaching each other, when on converging courses, or when one aircraft wishes to overtake or land.

Flight theory

You should:

- be able to define the terms lift, drag and angle of attack
- understand the relationship between pressure and airflow above and beneath the canopy or wing
- understand what causes a wing to stall
- understand what happens to lift and drag when control inputs are applied.

Meteorology

You need to understand:

- wind gradient and its effects
- how ground obstacles can affect local airflow
- what to look for when assessing take-off, flying and landing areas
- the basic principles of wind and airflow over hills
- how turbulence is produced, and its hazards to a pilot.

Airmanship

You must understand the relationship between airspeed, wind-speed and the resultant groundspeed and be able to work given examples. You should also know your responsibilities to other air users, and the law regarding CAA permission for tow-launched operations and its limitations.

The Club Pilot exam

This is more demanding than the Elementary exam, although the areas covered are much the same. The pass mark for the examination is 70 percent, and there is a compulsory section with questions that must be answered correctly to gain a pass, irrespective of the overall mark. Your instructors, school lectures, *Skywings Training Issue* and this handbook will provide the information that you need. You have to arrange with your instructor a time and place to sit the exam.

Club Pilot swotting guide

Air law

You should:

- know the collision-avoidance rules (failure on these questions results in automatic failure of the whole exam!)
- know the low-flying rules
- understand the way airspace in the UK is divided
- know the constraints placed upon tow-launched operations by the CAA
- understand the process for notifying an active site using the CANP (see Chapter 1)
- know the legal definitions of night, sunset and sunrise and the relevant flying restrictions relating to them.

Meteorology

You should be able to:

- link basic cloud types and their associated weather
- recognise key symbols on a synoptic weather chart and understand their meaning
- understand the basics of hill, wave and thermal lift
- know how to obtain a forecast and how to measure the wind on site
- identify deteriorating conditions.

Airmanship and navigation

You should:

- understand the need to keep a logbook
- understand the purpose of the red streamer
- be familiar with the demands of flying in company with your fellow pilots, both on the ridge and when thermalling
- be familiar with aeronautical charts (air maps)
- understand how a hang glider or paraglider is able to gain height
- be able to name the symptoms of an impending stall. In addition,

paraglider pilots should be able to:

- differentiate between symmetric and asymmetric canopy tucks – how they are caused and how to use the controls to effect a recovery
- state what action to take in the event of a towline-release failure
- know how to deal with hazardous (tree/water/obstacle) landings.

Principles of flight (paragliding)

You should:

- be able to define standard terms – stall, lift, centre of pressure, drag (in its various forms), aspect ratio, etc.
- understand the relationship between airspeed, lift and drag, know how lift is created and proportioned between the top and bottom wing-surfaces, and describe the forces acting on a glider in steady flight
- be able to work examples of airspeed/wind-speed/groundspeed and height loss/gain (given minimum-sink rates and airmass ascent rates)
- understand terms such as angle of attack, l/d ratio, glide ratio and wing loading, and be able to assess the effect that pilot weight changes have on paraglider performance
- understand the purpose and effect of trim tabs and the factors affecting canopy stability.

Principles of flight (hang gliding)

You should:

- be able to define standard terms – stall, lift, centre of pressure, drag (in its various forms), aspect ratio, etc.
- understand the relationship between airspeed, lift and drag, know how lift is created and proportioned between the top and bottom wing-surfaces, and describe the forces acting on a glider in steady flight
- be able to work examples of airspeed/wind-speed/groundspeed and height loss/gain (given minimum-sink rates and airmass ascent rates)
- understand terms such as centre of pressure, centre of gravity, washout, reflex, angle of attack, l/d ratio, glide ratio, wing loading, maximum glide and minimum sink

- understand the way various features of hang-glider design play a role in ensuring adequate stability in all three axes.

The Pilot exam

Any keen pilot who devotes a few evenings' study to the matter should have no problems with this exam. Most of the required information is contained in this handbook, although close study of an up-to-date aeronautical chart (especially the legend) is essential. Background reading (see the panel on page 278) is always advisable, and attendance at club lecture evenings is strongly recommended.

The paper has three sections: Air Law and Navigation, Meteorology, and Flight Theory and Instruments. To pass you must achieve at least 70 percent in each section. The papers use the multiple-choice format, although a few questions require you to supply the 'missing word'.

Once you have completed all the flying tasks for the Pilot rating, you will need to arrange a time and place to sit the exam with your club's coaching officer, a coach who has already passed the exam, or a qualified instructor. Clubs often arrange sessions where several candidates can sit their exams at once.

Pilot swotting guide

Air law and navigation

You should:

- be able to name the official documents, sources and promulgation methods of UK aviation law
- understand the law regarding Royal Flights and glider radios
- be able to interpret aeronautical charts (including scales, differences in the level of information depicted, validity periods, and symbols)
- understand the basic structure of Zones, Areas and Airways
- know the dimensions of ATZs and MATZs
- understand the usage of various altimeter settings (QFE, QNH, 1013.2 mb)
- know the Rules of the Air (especially the low-flying rules, the right-hand traffic rule, and the aerial collision avoidance rules)
- be able to define VMC and VFR (minima, rules)

- know the legal definitions of night, sunset and sunrise and the relevant flying restrictions relating to them
- be able to define IMC and IFR (basic differences from VMC rules)
- appreciate the factors affecting compasses (deviation and variation)
- be able to interpret warning signs
- understand commonly used abbreviations and initials
- be able to distinguish between types of airspace that permit glider entry and those that don't (e.g. AIAAs, MATZs, Danger Areas).

Meteorology

You should:

- understand the relationship between wind direction and areas of high and low pressure
- be able to describe in detail a cold front and a warm front (typical clouds, conditions, pressure changes, wind changes)
- be able to identify some common high, medium and low cloud types, and give their approximate heights
- fully understand convection (the birth and development of a thermal, through to plotting the progress of a thermal given the ELR and initial temperature)
- understand, and be able to define and use, meteorological terms such as stability, instability, veer, back, ELR, DALR, SALR, tephigram, anabatic, katabatic
- be able to describe the usual conditions associated with high- and low-pressure weather systems
- understand the causes of: valley winds throughout the day, sea breezes and sea-breeze fronts, wave lift, fog (of various types)
- fully understand and be able to interpret a synoptic chart – to the extent of being able to describe the current weather at selected locations, and to forecast likely changes
- be able to link cloud types to precipitation.

Flight theory and instruments

You should:

- be able to explain in detail how a wing creates lift, including the relevance of venturi tubes and Bernoulli's theorem

- be able to define and use terms such as chord line, angle of attack, aspect ratio, centre of pressure, washout
- be able to describe the aerodynamics of the stall
- be able to simply describe factors affecting stability in pitch, roll and yaw
- understand the relationship between glide ratio and l/d ratio
- understand the effect of ballast
- be able to name the forces on a glider in steady flight and explain their relationship
- be able to name the various types of drag and explain their causes
- be able to describe the relationship between the induced, parasitic and total drag and airspeed using drag curves
- understand and be able to use a polar curve
- understand the basic working principles of altimeters and variometers
- understand terms such as total energy and airmass in connection with variometers.

The Advanced Pilot exam

The Advanced Pilot rating requires a re-examination of air law to Pilot level. All the details above thus apply.

Background reading

Not all the air law governing light aircraft applies to hang gliders and paragliders; similarly, the mechanisms involved in ensuring the pitch stability of conventional aircraft are rather different from those used on tail-less flexwings and paragliders. So you must take care if using books intended for pilots of light aircraft or sailplanes. Fortunately, however, meteorology is meteorology no matter what you fly, so you can safely take advantage of the wealth of weather lore published by and for sailplane pilots over the years.

Chapter 31: Becoming a coach or instructor

Coaching

The coach, operating through a club, takes over from where the school instructor finishes. Their role is to provide encouragement, education and guidance for qualified Club Pilots, especially those fresh from a school.

Good clubs provide new members with a list of their coaches and how to contact them. A newcomer may also find that he or she has been assigned to a specific coach, perhaps living in the same locality. Other clubs have less formal arrangements, relying instead on the probability that at least one coach will be on site on most flyable days.

There are two levels of coach: the **coach** and the **senior coach**: The coach isn't necessarily highly experienced, as it has been found that coaches who are fairly new in the sport often relate best to novice pilots. They are also more likely to be using the same sites. All coaches must have attended a BHPA two-day coaching course, must have at least a Club Pilot rating, and must be recommended as suitable by their club's chief coach. This last point is of prime importance.

Senior coaches are the club's wise men and women, and they normally help to co-ordinate the coaching activities within the club. They will all have passed the BHPA Senior Coach course and will be experienced fliers who are well thought of in their club.

Instructing

The first stage in becoming an instructor is to find a school with a chief flying instructor (CFI) who is prepared to take you on and train you. You need to hold a Pilot rating. If the CFI agrees to train you, you must then register with the BHPA as a trainee instructor.

You will now be taught how to teach all of the training exercises. As you become proficient at each, your CFI will sign it off in your instructor log. He will also ensure that early in the process you attend a BHPA coach course (to learn some basics). As you progress you will also attend a first-aid course, and then a BHPA instructor course. Once you have been signed off as proficient at teaching all the exercises, and have attended all the courses, your CFI will prepare you for your instructor examination. The exam is conducted by an external examiner, and is very thorough. If you pass, you will be awarded your BHPA instructor's licence.

When you have held an instructor's licence for a few years, and have amassed considerable experience, you may want to start working towards the BHPA senior instructor licence. This involves attending and passing a BHPA senior instructor course, and another lengthy external examination. Experienced senior instructors can be appointed as a chief flying instructor, which is the very top of the tree!

APPENDICES

Bibliography

Books

Articles, papers and standards

Glossary

Index

Bibliography

Books

R. H. Barnard and D. R. Philpott, *Aircraft Flight* (Harlow: Longman, 1989)

T. Bradbury, *Meteorology and Flight* (London: A & C Black, 1989)

CAA, *Air Navigation: The Order and the Regulations CAP 393* (CAA, frequent updates)

R. D. Campbell and M. Bagshaw, *Human Performance and Limitations in Aviation*, (Oxford: BSP, 1999)

I. Currer and R. Cruickshank, *Touching Cloudbase* (York: Air Supplies, 1996)

E. S. Gates, *Meteorology and Climatology* (London: Harrap, 1980)

I. Holford, *The Air Pilot's Weather Guide* (Shrewsbury: Airlife, 1988)

A. C. Kermode, *Mechanics of Flight* (Harlow: Longman, 1987)

T. W. Knacke, *Parachute Recovery Systems Design Manual* (Santa Barbara: Para Publishing, 1992)

D. Pagen, *Hang Gliding Training Manual* (Sports Aviation Publications: USA, 1995)

D. Pagen, *Performance Flying* (Sports Aviation Publications: USA, 1993)

D. Piggott, *Understanding Flying Weather* (London: A & C Black, 1988)

D. Poynter, *The Parachute Manual Vols. 1 & 2* (Santa Barbara: Para Publishing, 1991)

M. Simons, *Model Aircraft Aerodynamics* (Hemel Hempstead: Argus Books, 1987)

D. Stinton, *The Design of the Aeroplane* (Oxford: BSP, 1987)

D. Stinton, *The Anatomy of the Aeroplane* (Oxford: BSP, 1998)

C. E. Wallington, *Meteorology for Glider Pilots* (London: John Murray, 1986)

N. Whittall, *Paragliding: The Complete Guide* (Shrewsbury: Airlife, 1997)

Articles, papers and standards

British Equestrian Trade Association (BETA) Standard for Body Protectors for Equestrian Use, 2nd ed., June 1992

J. B. Pedder and N. J. Mills (eds), *Head Protection, The State of the Art*, Symposium at Birmingham University 25 September 1982 (University of Birmingham, 1982)

Dr A. Segal, 'Pilot Safety', *Sailplane and Gliding*, June/July 1986

Dr A. Segal, 'Crashworthiness Test', *Sailplane and Gliding*, June/July 1989

Dr A. Segal, 'Jump or Bump Pt. 1', *Sailplane and Gliding*, Jan 1992

Dr A. Segal, 'Jump or Bump Pt. 2', *Sailplane and Gliding*, Feb/March 1992

Glossary

Cross-references within the glossary are indicated by SMALL CAPITALS.

AAL Above Aerodrome Level.

accuracy competitions Competitive aspect of tow-launched paragliding involving extremely accurate spot-landings.

ACPULS [1] Early French-based paraglider manufacturers' association.
[2] Old airworthiness standard for paragliders, superseded circa 1996.

adiabatic process Change in temperature of a mass of air caused by changes in pressure without any gain or loss of heat from its surroundings.

aerodynamics The study of air in motion.

aerofoil Longitudinal cross-section of a wing, shaped to produce lift efficiently. Also used to describe streamlined hang-glider uprights.

AFNOR [1] French standards organisation – equivalent to the BSI in Britain and the DIN in Germany. **[2]** Colloquial term used to denote certification issued in France after testing in accordance with the French edition of the CEN 'development standard' for paraglider airworthiness.

A-frame (or **control frame**) The triangular frame used to control a hang glider; part of its structure.

AGL Above Ground Level.

AIAA Area of Intense Aerial Activity.

AIP Aeronautical Information Publication.

airspeed Speed of a glider through the air; not necessarily the same as its GROUNDSPEED.

all-up weight Total airborne weight of the aircraft, pilot and all equipment.

alpine launch See FORWARD LAUNCH.

altimeter Electronic or mechanical instrument to measure an aircraft's ALTITUDE.

altitude Vertical distance above mean sea-level (AMSL).

AMSL Above Mean Sea-Level.

anchor person Assistant to a GROUND-HANDLING paraglider pilot.

angle of attack Angle at which the airflow meets the chord line of a wing.

angle of incidence Rigged angle of the wing or parts of the wing relative to some datum.

anhedral Opposite of DIHEDRAL: the tips of the wing are lower than the roots. Promotes roll response on a hang glider by reducing roll stability.

anti-dive rods See TIP-RODS.

ASI Air-Speed Indicator.

aspect ratio Ratio of the wing span to its average chord.

ASR Altimeter Setting Region.

ATC Air Traffic Control.

ATZ Aerodrome Traffic Zone.

B-line stall, B-lining Paraglider rapid-descent technique.

backup [1] The secondary HANG-LOOP on a hang glider, usually slightly longer than the main hang-loop. **[2]** RESERVE parachute.

base-bar (or **control bar**) The horizontal part of a hang-glider A-FRAME.

battens Profiled aluminium or composite shafts in a hang-glider wing used to maintain its section.

best-glide speed Airspeed at which the maximum glide (or l/d ratio) is achieved.

big ears Paraglider rapid-descent technique.

blue thermal Bubble or column of rising air with no attendant cloud.

brakes Colloquial name for paraglider primary controls.

CAA Civil Aviation Authority.

C of A Certificate of Airworthiness. In Britain these are issued by the BHPA to tested and approved types of hang glider and parascending canopies.

camber The curvature of the theoretical centre line of an AEROFOIL section.

canopy The fabric wing of a paraglider, sometimes used loosely to mean the complete paraglider.

Capewell Quick-release connection between harness and risers, used in some tow-launched paragliding.

cell Longitudinal division of a CANOPY, usually open-fronted, which maintains the aerofoil shape when inflated.

CEN European standards organisation which produces standards covering a very wide range of equipment.

chord The distance between the leading and trailing edges of a wing.

chord line Imaginary straight line between the leading and trailing edges of a wing.

clip-in weight Total suspended weight of hang-glider pilot, harness and equipment.

collapse See DEFLATION.

control handles Handles on paraglider CONTROL LINES. Sometimes called 'toggles' when parascending.

control lines Lines which are connected to the trailing edge of the canopy and are manipulated by the pilot so as to control and manoeuvre the paraglider.

convert To trade excess airspeed for height.

CP Club Pilot.

cravat Paraglider wing-tip which has deflated and become trapped in the suspension lines.

cross-bracing Method of paraglider-harness construction, promoting stability.

cross-port vents Holes connecting adjacent canopy CELLS to allow pressure equalisation.

cross-tubes (or **cross-booms**) A pair of large-diameter tubes of a hang glider airframe holding the leading edges out and the sail in tension.

cumulus Small, separate, fluffy cloud which often forms at the top of a thermal.

deep stall (or **parachutal stall**) A stalled state in which a paraglider has no forward airspeed but a very high descent rate.

deflation (or **tuck** or **collapse**) Loss of pressure in a paraglider wing, causing failure to maintain its flying shape; usually caused by an excessively low ANGLE OF ATTACK.

DHV [1] German hang gliding and paragliding association **[2]** Term used to denote German paraglider (and hang glider, harness and parachute) testing and certification standard. Paraglider standard is now LTF.

dihedral Upward angling of an aeroplane wing viewed from in front. Promotes roll stability.

downtubes See UPRIGHTS.

drag Aerodynamic forces resisting the forward motion of a body.

dual (or **tandem**) **flight** Two people flying aboard one glider. A special pilot licence and a dual hang glider or paraglider are needed.

Dyneema Trade name for a type of paraglider line material.

EN 926 Europe-wide paraglider testing and certification standard.

fichet A small peg used to mark the first point of ground-contact in ACCURACY COMPETITIONS.

FIR Flight Information Region.

FL See FLIGHT LEVEL.

flare [1] Action taken to slow or stop a hang glider or paraglider, used to effect a landing. **[2]** A triangular piece of fabric distributing the load from a line to the canopy.

Flight Level (FL) Vertical distance above the 1013.2mb pressure level.

forward launch (or **alpine launch**) Paraglider take-off technique – used in light winds – in which the pilot initially faces away from the canopy.

glide ratio (or **glide angle**) Ratio of height lost to horizontal distance travelled by a glider in still air, and thus a measure of performance. It is equal to the L/D RATIO.

ground effect Enhanced glide performance achieved by a hang glider being flown close to the ground.

ground-handling Controlling the glider on the ground.

groundspeed The speed of an aircraft over the ground, which varies according to wind strength and direction.

gust A sudden increase in wind-speed.

Gütesiegel Old term for German airworthiness tests for paragliders and hang gliders.

hang-loop Loop of webbing connecting a hang-glider pilot's harness to the glider.

height Vertical distance above ground or above aerodrome level (AAL).

HIRTA High-Intensity Radio Transmission Area

ICAO International Civil Aviation Organisation

IFR Instrument Flight Rules

IMC Instrument Meteorological Conditions

instability [1] Lack of stability. **[2]** Departures from normal paragliding flight which demand a rapid and correct response by the pilot to return to safe flight.

ISA International Standard Atmosphere.

karabiner (or **'crab'**) Steel or aluminium closing link used to connect the harness to the risers or hang-loop.

keel Longitudinal member of hang-glider structure.

keeper Metal ring stitched to a paraglider's rear riser to retain the control lines.

Kevlar A strong synthetic fibre used in some paraglider lines, hang-glider sails and helmets.

kingpost Part of hang-glider structure above the wing, supporting the upper rigging.

lapse rate Rate of decrease of air temperature with height.

lark's foot A special knot used for attaching hang-loops, suspension lines, etc. (see Figure 8.6 on page 73).

l/d ratio Ratio of the lift produced by a glider to its drag, and thus a measure of performance. It is equal to the GLIDE RATIO.

leading edge The front part of the wing – and, on a hang glider, the structural member forming this part.

lift [1] Upward aerodynamic force acting perpendicularly to the direction of motion, created by the wing moving through the air. **[2]** Air which is rising faster than the sinking speed of the glider, so enabling the glider to climb.

lines Thin cords of a paraglider's suspension system, connecting the risers to the canopy. A-lines go to the leading edge of the canopy; B-, C- and (sometimes) D-lines are progressively further aft.

lock-out (or **rotation**) Potentially dangerous turning away from the winch or tug on a tow-launch.

lock-up Uncontrolled pitch up under tow.

LTF German paraglider testing and certification standard.

luff-lines Wires or cords between a hang-glider KINGPOST and the trailing edge of the sail, holding reflex into sail.

maillon Small steel link used to connect paraglider lines to risers, and often used to connect risers to the harness.

MATZ Military Aerodrome Traffic Zone

maximum glide (or **max. glide**) The best possible glide ratio of a particular glider and pilot. Also another phrase for best glide speed. minimum-sink rate (or min. sink) A glider's lowest possible rate of descent.

minimum-sink speed The airspeed at which the MINIMUM-SINK RATE occurs.

moment Turning force around a point.

Mylar [1] Stiff plastic material inserted in the leading edge of a hang glider sail or sewn to a paraglider rib to maintain its shape. **[2]** A Mylar laminated sailcloth.

nose person Assistant to a GROUND-HANDLING hang-glider pilot.

NOTAM Notice to airmen.

overdrive See TRIMMER.

pitch Angular movement of an aircraft about its lateral axis, i.e. nose-up and nose-down. See also ROLL, YAW.

PLF Parachute Landing Fall: a technique for breaking a pilot's fall in a heavy landing.

polar curve Graphical representation of sink rate against airspeed, giving an indication of glider performance.

PPL Private Pilot's Licence.

pulled-down apex A design of emergency parachute in which the centre is pulled down to approximately the level of the rim.

pump To use the paraglider's controls repeatedly to re-inflate a collapsed part of the canopy.

QFE Altimeter-setting datum based on the local atmospheric pressure at the level of an aerodrome.

QNH Altimeter-setting datum based on the local atmospheric pressure at sea level.

reflex Upward curve in the trailing edge of special wing-sections, important for hang-glider pitch stability.

reflex rods See TIP-RODS

release **[1]** The mechanism by which the pilot attaches and releases the towline. **[2]** The command used by hang-glider pilots to tell the nose person to let go.

reverse launch Paraglider take-off technique in which the pilot initially faces the canopy while it inflates.

rigging **[1]** Suspension system of paraglider. **[2]** Steel wires supporting the structure of a hang glider.

risers Webbing connecting the paraglider harness to the suspension lines.

roll Angular movement of an aircraft about its longitudinal axis, i.e. increasing or decreasing bank. *See also* PITCH, YAW.

rotation See LOCK-OUT.

rotor Potentially dangerous turbulence downwind of a ground feature or mountain.

SHV **[1]** Swiss hang gliding and paragliding association. **[2]** Colloquial term used to denote certification issued in Switzerland after testing in accordance with the Swiss edition of the CEN 'development standard' for paraglider airworthiness.

sink **[1]** The action of a glider descending. **[2]** An area of descending air.

sink rate Rate of descent of a glider, measured in still air. Usually expressed in ft/min or m/s.

SIV *Simulation d'Incident en Vol* (French). Paraglider instability exercises, conducted over water and under the (radio) supervision of an instructor.

span Total width of glider from wing-tip to wing-tip.

spiral dive Manoeuvre for losing height. It greatly increases the loading on the structure of a hang glider or paraglider.

speed-bar **[1]** Hang glider base-bar with bends to permit pilot to weightshift further forward. **[2]** Paraglider SPEED SYSTEM.

speed system Method of increasing a paraglider's top speed by altering the relationship of the risers, controlled by a foot stirrup.

stability Tendency of an aircraft to return to normal flight after a disturbance.

stall Loss of lift due to increasing the ANGLE OF ATTACK to the point where airflow separation occurs. Usually the result of flying too slowly.

stirrup An old design of hang-gliding harness, useful to beginners. Also part of a paraglider SPEED SYSTEM.

suspension lines The lines which connect the paraglider canopy to the risers. They are referred to by letters from A to D (sometimes more), starting at the leading edge and moving towards the rear or trailing edge.

swages Small sleeves which are crimped onto wire cables to fasten them; usually applied under hydraulic pressure.

sweepback The angle at which the leading edges of a wing sweep backwards from the nose.

tangs Small plates connecting cable eyes with bolts or other fastenings.

TE Total Energy. A facility on a vario enabling it to ignore vertical accelerations caused by a pilot's control inputs.

tensiometer Instrument used in tow-launching to measure towline tension.

tephigram Chart or graph of changes in temperature and humidity with altitude.

thermal A rising bubble or column of air heated by earlier contact with the surface, in which a glider can gain height.

thimbles Reinforcement inserts for cable eyes.

tip-rods (or tip sticks, tip struts, reflex rods, washout rods or anti-dive rods) Part of the structure of a hang glider, angled backwards and upwards at the wing-tips to assist in pitch stability.

TMA Terminal Control Area.

toggles Alternative name for paraglider CONTROL HANDLES.

tow-launch A method of launching using remote mechanical means (boat, tug aircraft, vehicle or winch) and a towline.

trailing edge The rearmost part of the wing.

trigger temperature The critical temperature for the formation of thermals.

trimmer (also **overdrive, VB** or **VG**) System of increasing sail tension on a hang glider to increase performance, usually at the expense of handling.

trim speed Speed at which a paraglider or hang glider flies without pitch-control input.

trim tabs Devices for adjusting the relationship of the risers to alter a paraglider's trim speed. (Also sometimes called **trimmers**.)

tuck [1] Sudden total inversion of a hang glider due to poor pitch stability, pilot input, turbulence or a combination of these factors. **[2]** DEFLATION of a portion of the leading edge of a paraglider canopy.

uprights (USA **downtubes**) The two more nearly vertical components of a hang glider's A-FRAME.

vario Variometer: electronic instrument which detects rates of climb and descent.

VB See TRIMMER.

VB compensator (or **luff-line compensator**) Method of maintaining the correct amount of reflex with VB/trimmer operation.

VFR Visual Flight Rules.

VG See TRIMMER.

VMC Visual Meteorological Conditions.

washout [1] A twist in the wing which reduces the ANGLE OF INCIDENCE towards the wing-tips. Essential on a hang glider for pitch stability. **[2]** (verb) The action of producing such a twist.

washout rods See TIP-RODS.

wave Standing waves generated in an airflow, which can give remarkable height gains but also heavy sink and turbulence.

weak link A short loop of material fitted in the towing line that will break at a known tension, so preventing overload.

weight range [1] (paraglider) The manufacturer's stated maximum and minimum ALL-UP WEIGHT (including the canopy and harness) for a particular canopy. **[2]** (hang glider) The manufacturer's stated maximum and minimum CLIP-IN WEIGHT (including harness, clothing etc. but not the glider).

weightshift Transferring the pilot's body weight to one side: the primary method of controlling a hang glider. Paraglider pilots with a suitable harness can use weightshift to exert a limited amount of roll control.

wind gradient The progressive reduction in wind strength near the surface due to frictional effects.

wind shear Turbulence experienced between wind layers.

wing loading The total weight of the glider (including pilot) divided by the wing area.

wrap To loop the CONTROL LINES one or more times around the hands, effectively to shorten the lines.

XC Cross-country.

yaw Angular movement of an aircraft about its vertical axis (nose to left or right). See also PITCH, ROLL.

Airspace abbreviations

As used in ICAO aeronautical charts and other publications.

AIAA Area of Intense Aerial Activity
AIP Aeronautical Information Publication
ATC Air Traffic Control
ATZ Aerodrome Traffic Zone
CAA Civil Aviation Authority
CTA Control Area
CTR Control Zone
FIR Flight Information Region
FL Flight Level
HIRTA High Intensity Radio Transmission Area
ICAO International Civil Aviation Organisation
IFR Instrument Flight Rules
IMC Instrument Meteorological Conditions
MATZ Military Aerodrome Traffic Zone
NOTAM Notice to Airmen
TMA Terminal Control Area
UIR Upper Flight Information Region
VFR Visual Flight Rules
VMC Visual Meteorological Conditions

Some useful conversion factors

Note that these conversion factors are accurate only to the number of decimal places given.

Weight

1kg = 2.2lb	1lb = 454g

Distance

1in = 25.4mm	1m = 39.4in
1ft = 30cm	1m = 3.3ft
1 mile = 1.6km	1km = 0.62 miles
1 nautical mile = 1.85km	1km = 0.54 nautical miles

Speed

1 knot = 1.15mph	1kph = 0.54 knots
1mph = 1.6kph	1kph = 0.62mph
1 knot = 101ft/min	1m/s = 196.8ft/min
100ft/min = 0.5m/s	1m/s = 2.24mph

Index

Where a keyword is followed by multiple page references, **bold** type indicates a major reference. Illustrations that occur on the same page as the text to which they relate are not indexed separately.